Representing Blackness

Rutgers Depth of Field Series

Charles Affron, Mirella Jona Affron, Robert Lyons, Series Editors

Richard Abel, ed., Silent Film

John Belton, ed., Movies and Mass Culture

Valerie Smith, ed. Representing Blackness: Issues in Film and Video

Janet Staiger, ed., The Studio System

Linda Williams, ed., Viewing Positions: Ways of Seeing Film

Edited with an introduction by
Valerie Smith

Representing
Blackness

Issues in Film
and Video

Rutgers
University
Press
New Brunswick,
New Jersey

Library of Congress Cataloging-in-Pulication Data

Representing Blackness : issues in film and video / edited and with an introduction by
   Valerie Smith.
      p.   cm.—(Rutgers depth of field series)
      Includes bibliographical references and index.
      ISBN 0-8135-2313-3 (cloth : alk. paper). —ISBN 0-8135-2314-1 (pbk.: alk. paper)
      1. Afro-Americans in motion pictures.   2. Afro-Americans in the motion picture
   industry.   I. Smith, Valerie, 1956–   . II. Series.
   PN1995.9.N4R47   1997   96-36075
                                                                                 CIP

British Cataloguing-in-Publication information available.

Manufactured in the United States of America

In memory of
Fred Irving
Susan Irving
Marguerite Rembert
Marlon Riggs
James Snead

Contents

Representing Blackness

Valerie Smith

Introduction

D. W. Griffith's *Birth of a Nation*, considered by many to be the symbolic, although not literal, origin of U.S. cinema, is frequently offered up by film critics and historians as the inaugural moment of African American cinema as well.[1] Based on Thomas Dixon's best-selling novel *The Clansman* and authenticated by Woodrow Wilson's *History of the American People*, *Birth*, the first feature-length studio production, established codes of narrative film practice and circulated as truth a range of black stereotypes for record-breaking audiences.

As Michael Rogin demonstrates, Griffith went to great lengths to persuade his viewers that the vision of history provided in *Birth* was accurate.[2] Moreover, not only was *Birth* constructed as conveying the truth about race relations in nineteenth-century U.S. culture, but it also had a direct impact on contemporaneous race relations. Antiracist individuals and organizations alike believed that *Birth*, released during the height of Jim Crow segregation and lynching, enhanced tolerance of racial, especially Klan, violence.

Thomas Cripps, Manthia Diawara, Ed Guerrero, and others have argued that the images of African Americans found in *Birth* and reproduced throughout the history of U.S. cinema—types that run the gamut from indolent, subservient, buffoonish men and women to vicious black male rapists—have set the terms of black-directed narrative film. Historically, black directors have considered such types to be negative and, by extension, false representations of African Americans that threaten the lives and conditions of "real" black people. As a result, they have struggled to offer up alternative, truer representations of black life. To the extent that it seeks to replace "false" representations with positive, by extension "true" or "authentic" ones, the project of black film might thus be read as the search for an authentic black subject.

This search has taken various forms, but an admittedly cursory overview reveals two dominant trajectories in black cinematic practice, trajectories that recall debates about "Negro Art" that began during the Harlem Renaissance and persist until the present time. The first impulse reads "authentic" as synonymous with "positive" and seeks to supplant representations of black lasciviousness and irresponsibility with "respectable" ones. By this light, the authentic black subject is shown to be at least diligent and morally upright if not also refined and prosperous. These figures may be found throughout the history of African American film, from the early works such as the Colored Players Company's *The Scar of Shame* (1928), Oscar Micheaux's *Girl from Chicago* (1932), *Veiled Aristocrats* (1932), and *God's Stepchildren* (1938), and Bernard B. Ray's *Broken Strings* (1940), to more recent movies such as Gordon Parks' *The Learning Tree* (1968), Sidney Poitier's *A Warm December* (1973), Michael Schulz's *Cooley High* (1975), and Robert Townsend's *The Five Heartbeats* (1991).[3] Additionally, these characters recur in mainstream black-themed motion pictures such as Stanley Kramer's *Home of the Brave*, Louis De Rochemont's *Lost Boundaries*, and Joseph Mankiewicz's *No Way Out* (all 1949), James Clavell's *To Sir, with Love*, Kramer's *Guess Who's Coming to Dinner*, and Norman Jewison's *In the Heat of the Night* (all 1967), or, more recently Richard Attenborough's *Cry Freedom* (1987), Russell Mulcahy's *Ricochet* (1991), and John Sayles' *Passion Fish* (1992).

The second impulse might be understood to respond both to mainstream representations and to the putatively more positive ones. Films in this tradition are unconcerned with demonstrating the extent to which black characters can conform to received, class-coded notions of respectability. Rather, they equate authenticity either with the freedom to seize and reanimate types previously coded as "negative" (most notably, the criminal or the buffoon) or with the presence of cultural practices rooted in black vernacular experience (jazz, gospel, rootworking, religion, and so on). Early examples might include Duke Ellington's *Black and Tan* (1929), or Spencer Williams' *The Blood of Jesus* (1941), *Go Down Death* (1944), and *Dirty Gertie from Harlem USA* (1946). Works such as *Black and Tan* showcased African American vaudeville talent, generally at the expense of the narrative line. *Blood* and *Death* allowed Williams to pay tribute to African American religious practices and institutions. Indeed, one might read *Go Down Death* as an attempt to find a cinematic language appropriate to African American literary and religious practices.[4]

More recently, this conception of the authentic black subject has undergone dramatic transformation in response to the changing demographics of African American communities. While early in the twentieth century the majority of African Americans were located in the rural South, waves of migration to the North and West led to concentrations of blacks in urban communities in these other regions.[5] The subsequent deindustrialization and underdevelopment of urban centers, and the decline in steady, decent-paying jobs for semi- and unskilled laborers thus affected black communities disproportionately. As a result, the idea of the urban has become virtually synonymous with notions of blackness and blight in public discourse; markers of drug and gang culture, rather than those of indigenous or vernacular black culture, have circulated and been read increasingly as signs of racial (and geographic) authenticity. Blaxploitation pictures of the 1970s—*Shaft* (1971), *Super Fly* (1972), *Cleopatra Jones* (1973), and *The Mack* (1973), for instance—established inner cities as context, drug and gang violence as themes, and rhythm and blues as the sound track of black cinema. The new jack pictures of the 1990s—such as *New Jack City* (1991), *Juice* (1992), and *Menace II Society* (1993)—replaced heroin with crack, and rhythm and blues with hip hop, but reinscribed the conventions associated with their 1970s counterparts.

If strategies of African American visual representation have tended to respond to the existence of presumptively negative images, the criticism of black film has been similarly preoccupied. Groundbreaking extended studies of race and cinema were concerned primarily with identifying and critiquing the recurrence of stereotyped representations in Hollywood films. Works such as Edward Mapp's *Blacks in American Films* (1972), Donald Bogle's *Toms, Coons, Mulattoes, Mammies, and Bucks: An Interpretive History of Blacks in American Films* (1973), James P. Murray's *To Find an Image* (1973), Gary Null's *Black Hollywood: The Negro in Motion Pictures* (1975), Daniel Leab's *From Sambo to Superspade: The Black Experience in Motion Pictures* (1975), and Thomas Cripps's *Slow Fade to Black* (1977) inventoried the reproduction of certain types of black characters in visual media.

These texts served an important function in the development of African American film criticism, for they gave voice to impressions and responses shared by generations of African American viewers and heightened awareness of the persistence of these representations. However, they also legitimated a binarism in the discourse around strategies of black representation that has outlived its usefulness. Granted, despite their constructedness, media representations of members of historically disenfranchised communities reflect and, in turn, affect the lived circumstances of real people. But the relationship between media representations and "real life" is nothing if not complex and discontinuous; to posit a one-to-one correspondence between the inescapability of certain images and the uneven distribution of resources within culture is to deny the elaborate ways in which power is maintained and deployed.

Several problems exist with the positive/negative debate as it has been constituted. First, it focuses critical scrutiny on the ways in which African Americans have been represented in Hollywood cinema, often at the expense of analytical, theoretical, or historical work on the history of black-directed cinema.[6] Second, it presupposes consensus about what a positive or negative (or authentic, for that matter) image actually is. To some viewers, images of hardworking, middle-class, heterosexual African Americans are inherently positive and to be celebrated wherever they are found, because they replace models of African

American pathology with signs of the fact that "we are like everyone else" (read mainstream representations of whites). However, the uncritical acceptance of this equation allows the hegemony of mainstream representational strategies to go uninterrogated. Additionally, it denies the significance and impact of works that seek to make visible aspects of African American life that traditionally have remained concealed for the sake of decorum.

Third, such presumptive consensus forestalls nuanced debate. It focuses viewer attention on the existence of certain types and not on the more significant questions around what kind of narrative or ideological work that type is meant to perform. If, for example, all mammy figures are dismissed as inherently negative characters, then how are we to assess the varying uses to which such figures are put?

Fourth, the imprecise nature of the positive/negative distinction has the potential to essentialize racial identity and deny its dynamic relation to constructions of class, gender, sexuality, region, and so on. In certain critical contexts, the term "positive" is synonymous with "middle class" or "heterosexual"; in others, it is invoked to mean "suburban" or "working class." Stuart Hall's critique of essentialized notions of blackness is useful here. The overreliance on the positive/negative discourse, like the uncritical deployment of the term "black," "[mistakes] what is historical and cultural for what is natural, biological and genetic" and "[valorizes] the very ground of the racism we are trying to deconstruct."

Although popular reactions may be influenced excessively by the positive/negative debate or discourses of authenticity, criticism of black visual culture in recent years has moved beyond this preoccupation. To borrow Hall's formulation, increasingly black cultural criticism in general and film criticism in particular have been concerned more with the diversity than with the homogeneity of black experience. As a result, critics such as bell hooks, Michele Wallace, Jacquie Jones, Jacqueline Bobo, and Gloria Gibson-Hudson have deployed black feminist theory in the interpretation of Hollywood and independent cinema; Phillip Brian Harper, Kobena Mercer, and Isaac Julien have explored the usefulness of queer theory to the study of black visual culture; Manthia Diawara has brought insights gleaned from Lacanian psychoanalysis to bear on black media; and Hazel Carby, Clyde Taylor, Wahneema Lubiano, and others have brought cultural studies problematics to complicate the study of visual media.

With the rise of media studies in high school, undergraduate, and graduate programs, the resurgence of black-directed film, a heightened awareness in journalism of the significance of race in representation, and public debates around race and representation,[7] the present moment is ripe for a volume such as this one. This collection seeks to intervene in ongoing debates about black representation in visual media in a variety of ways. To the extent that questions of authenticity and representation have recurred throughout the history of African American film (and televisual) criticism, this volume in part indicates how these debates have been presented and critiqued. It includes instances of the new research that expands the project of black visual studies. And it contains extended discussions of a selected group of black-directed films in order to contribute to the growing body of work in the field.

These types of essays are not neatly separable. Stuart Hall's "What Is This 'Black' in Black Popular Culture?" and Tommy Lott's "A No-Theory Theory of Contemporary Black Cinema" are, strictly speaking, theoretical reflections on racial essentialism in cultural criticism; however, in their contributions, Wahneema Lubiano, Mike Murashige, and David Van Leer bring illuminating analyses of specific films together with sustained critiques of authenticity discourse.

The collection begins with the first chapter of Donald Bogle's *Toms, Coons, Mulattoes, Mammies, and Bucks: An Interpretive History of Blacks in American Film*, entitled "Black Beginnings: From *Uncle Tom's Cabin* to *The Birth of a Nation*." Bogle defines and provides examples of persistent stereotypes of African American behavior: the tom, the coon, the tragic mulatto, the mammy, and the brutal black buck. Bogle's essay historicizes the collection; it exemplifies the seminal work on black images in U.S. cinema that has continued to influence both critical and popular responses to practices of representing African Americans in visual media. Moreover, several subsequent essays engage with the assumptions of Bogle's (and other similar) work.

"Spectatorship and Capture in *King Kong:* The Guilty Look" first appeared in print in the posthumously published collection of James Snead's essays, *White Screens/Black Images: Hollywood from the Dark Side* (1994), although I was privileged to hear him deliver a version of this chapter as a lecture in 1988. This essay provides the landmark critique of familiar discussions of stereotypes that helped usher in a new direction in discussions of race, gender, and representation. Snead is concerned with more than mere identification and enumeration of stereotypes; rather, drawing on semiotic theory, he studies how these representations are constituted in order to perform specific kinds of ideological work. As he writes: "My work on Hollywood film analyzes film stereotypes in terms of *codes* they form, and makes these codes legible, inspecting their inner workings as well as the external historical subjects they would conceal" (p. 25–26).

Snead begins by identifying several devices—mythification, marking, and omission—which have been used to relegate blacks to subordinate positions on screen. He is especially interested in the persistence of metaphysical stasis as a code surrounding cinematic representations of African Americans, for this code has enabled their exclusion from constructions of historical process. The bulk of the essay is given over to a detailed analysis of *King Kong*. Snead tracks the relationship between the surface narrative of the adventure plot and what he calls the political subplots, where cultural anxieties about black cultural interlopers and imperiled white womanhood reside. For a contemporary reader/viewer, Snead's discussion of the links among discourses of race, gender, and imperialism may seem familiar, but for its time, his analysis was illuminating and original and brought renewed excitement to the study of race in Hollywood cinema.

Thomas Cripps' "'Race Movies' as Voices of the Black Bourgeoisie: *The Scar of Shame*" exemplifies some of the best early work on black cinema. In this essay, Cripps situates *The Scar of Shame* (1927) within the context of early-twentieth-century U.S. cultural history. The essay provides a valuable introduction to the genre of race pictures and suggests how they may have functioned for emergent black urban populations in the wake of the first wave of the Great Migration. Cripps offers a condensed yet thorough discussion of the film, and argues that it complicates prevailing constructions of the impact of class on racial identity.

While Cripps explores the ways in which *Scar* participates in ongoing debates about black class politics, Jane Gaines is interested in the applicability of feminist paradigms of spectatorship in melodrama to discussions of black viewers of race pictures. As a result, she contextualizes the film more broadly and reads it more closely. Like Cripps, Gaines places *Scar* in the context of early-twentieth-century U.S. social history. However, she argues that the film both invokes and revises conventions of cinematic melodrama and raises questions about the impact of social change on the position of black spectators. Articulations of gender ideology are crucial to Gaines' analysis; she is therefore careful also to read the protagonist in relation to literary representations of mixed race women. Taken together, the two essays speak to the complexity of *Scar* and suggest the diversity of interpretive approaches to which early black cinema might productively be submitted.

The next three essays address in distinct but related ways the challenge cultural studies has posed to the questions of racial authenticity that have dominated black film criticism. In "A No-Theory Theory of Contemporary Black Cinema," Tommy Lott reflects on the paradoxes inherent in the very category of "black film." His essay presupposes that viewers and critics alike often deploy the notion of "black film" as a biologically determined category that is meant to signify ideologically. In other words, the essentialist criteria by which a "black" film is understood to be one directed by a person of African American descent too frequently allows biological categories to stand in for ideological ones. Conversely, aesthetically grounded definitions of black film risk privileging independent productions uncritically. In the face of these and other contradictions, Lott argues that the assumptions that underlie the notion of Third Cinema might inform the notion of black film as well:

What makes Third Cinema third (i.e., a viable alternative to Western cinema) is not exclusively the racial makeup of a filmmaker, a film's aesthetic character, or a film's intended audience, but rather a film's political orientation within the hegemonic structures of postcolonialism. When a film contributes ideologically to the advancement of black people, within a context of systematic denial, the achievement of this political objective ought to count as a criterion of evaluation on a par with any essentialist criterion. (p. 92)

In "But Compared to What?: Reading Realism, Representation, and Essentialism in *School Daze, Do the Right Thing,* and the Spike Lee Discourse," Wahneema Lubiano reflects on two early Lee films in order to consider some of the difficulties surrounding discussions of African American cultural production. Like Lott, she is concerned about the uncritical way in which ideological categories are used to describe black cultural production in general and Lee's work in particular. She is also troubled by the nature of the truth-claims that are made about his films. By examining Lee's assessments of his own work, others' discussions of his work, the problems raised by his position in the film industry and in discussions of black film, and the films *School Daze* and *Do the Right Thing,* she illuminates the discursive limits and possibilities of exploring black popular culture.

Lubiano uses the discourse around Spike Lee to challenge facile assumptions about the idea of the "real" and the "oppositional." She begins by critiquing the "possibilities of oppositional, resistant, or subversive cultural production as well as the problems of productions that are *considered* oppositional, resistant, or subversive without accompanying analysis sustaining such evaluation" (p. 98). She argues that terms such as "oppositional," "resistant," and "subversive" are often used with insufficient attention to the complex ways in which ideologies get circulated and maintained. Specifically, she questions the nature of the political work Lee's films perform, given their misogyny and homophobia, his appeal to studio money and wide audiences, and the relative invisibility of other African American filmmakers.

Lubiano then offers an extensive consideration of the difficulties surrounding the place of realism, authenticity, and essentialism in black film. She concludes by juxtaposing Lee's two films in order to argue that, contrary to popular opinion, *Do the Right Thing* undermines its own progressive political agenda while *School Daze* more effectively opens up a space for the critique of dominant gender ideological positions.

Stuart Hall's "What Is This 'Black' in Black Popular Culture?" is the culmination of this section; he articulates the theoretical and cultural problematics on which Lubiano and Lott draw. Earlier critics might comfortably have divided up the arena of representation into positive and negative, black and non-black, high and low, resistant and assimilated, authentic and inauthentic, or other such oppositions. But, as Hall argues, the conditions of postmodernity displace such binarisms. Rather, he invites readers to understand culture generally, and black popular culture more specifically, as always contradictory and contested.

For Hall, black popular culture is characterized by three qualities: its style becomes its subject; it is grounded deeply in music; and it uses the body as a "[canvas] of representation" (p. 129). These features do not guarantee its authenticity, however, since cultural forms are inevitably hybrid. As he writes:

> Always these forms are the product of partial synchronization, of engagement across cultural boundaries, of the confluence of more than one cultural tradition, of the negotiations of dominant and subordinate positions, of the subterranean strategies of recoding and transcoding, of critical signification, of signifying. (p. 129)

In place of the impulse to essentialize either the black subject or forms of black popular culture, he invites readers to acknowledge the sites of difference contained within the category of blackness. This kind of recognition marks the interplay of ideologies of sexuality, gender, and class with constructions of race, thereby complicating ideas of race. Second, it avoids the trap of reading black positionality as always inevitably progressive. Third, it prevents the privileging of experience outside the realm of representation: "There is no escape from the politics of representation, and we cannot wield 'how life really is out there' as a kind of test against which the political rightness or wrongness of a particular cultural strategy or text can be measured" (p. 131).

The final four essays focus more specifically on cinematic texts. Only one has been previously published; taken together, they expand the body of available scholarship on key African American directors. In varying degrees they engage as well the critique of the discourse of authenticity that links the previous three.

Nathan Grant's "Innocence and Ambiguity in the Films of Charles Burnett" is the first thorough discussion of most of the films of Charles Burnett.[8] Grant explores how Burnett has responded to changes in the idea of urban African America throughout his career. His analyses display myriad ways in which Burnett maps his exploration of the impact of sweeping cultural changes on constructions both of African American communities and of black masculinity in particular.

David Van Leer's "Visible Silence: Spectatorship in Black Gay and Lesbian Film" offers a comprehensive, insightful discussion of black gay and lesbian film and video practice in the context of an overview of the history of black representations in gay and lesbian film more broadly defined. He focuses in particular on the films and videos of Marlon Riggs; he positions Riggs' gay-themed work in relation to *Ethnic Notions* and

Color Adjustment, both of which address the history of African American images in visual media. Although Van Leer identifies a range of practices by which black gays and lesbians have been excluded or mocked in black heterosexual or white gay film, he does not set up black gay and lesbian film as the locus of "truer" representations. Rather, he describes how various works in this tradition problematize the notion of authenticity altogether.

Mike Murashige's "Haile Gerima and the Political Economy of Cinematic Resistance" centers on an important work by an especially influential contemporary black filmmaker in the United States. A key member of the group of filmmakers Clyde Taylor has designated the L. A. Rebellion,[9] Gerima is perhaps best known for his *Sankofa* (1993). However, the "diasporic consciousness" that characterizes that work is evident in Gerima's earlier films as well, especially in his masterpiece, *Bush Mama,* on which Murashige's essay concentrates. Murashige identifies four levels of critical interrogation necessary to understand Gerima's project in the film: the effects of state terrorism and state control on those who live in impoverished urban centers; the search for an adequate explanation for the crisis-induced contradictions in the protagonist's everyday life; the necessity for multiple narratives that address different aspects of the crisis as preconditions for sustained resistance and for the creation of communities of struggle; and the search for resistant representational practices that overturn the content and form of these classic cinematic narratives. Informed by cultural studies and theoretical geography, Murashige constructs a theoretical and ideological frame that enables a dense and nuanced interpretation of both the content and the form of the film.

The final essay in the collection is my own "Telling Family Secrets: Narrative and Ideology in *Suzanne Suzanne* by Camille Billops and James V. Hatch." This essay focuses on the first work by one of the leading African American directors of experimental documentary, positioning it within the context of black feminist critiques of domestic violence. In addition, it shows how the directors use the genre of documentary film to destabilize ideas of truth and the "real."

Billops and Hatch may perhaps be better known for controversial films such as *Older Women and Love* (1987), *Finding Christa* (released in 1991 and winner of the Grand Jury Award in the documentary category at the 1992 Sundance Film Festival), or *The KKK Boutique Ain't Just Rednecks* (1994), but *Suzanne Suzanne* begins their exploration of the unreliability both of visual records and of family narratives. The essay examines how the juxtaposition of Bell & Howell home movies, still photographs, interviews, and music problematize the authority of the medium itself and sustain the critique both of a particular family and of the myth of the normative, nuclear family. It concludes with a discussion of the significance of a staged conversation between Billops' sister and niece that simultaneously provides the film's emotional peak and challenges the idea of authentic emotion in documentary.

Gang violence and the urban underclass recur as subjects of African American film (and especially of the most financially lucrative black movies), suggesting that for certain audiences, studio executives, and production companies, only this content is "really black." Yet as critiques of racial authenticity surface in and inform African American cultural criticism, public policy debates, and popular culture, they inform cinematic practice and the expectations of viewing audiences as well. The recent wave of black-directed films with a wider range of content, styles, and perspectives indicates a growing desire on the part of directors and viewers alike to expand the conventions by which black life is made visible on screen.

Works such as Wendell B. Harris' *Chameleon Street* (1989), Julie Dash's *Daughters of the Dust* (1991), Leslie Harris' *Just Another Girl on the IRT* (1992), Charles Burnett's *To Sleep with Anger* (1990) and *The Glass Shield* (1995), Carl Franklin's *One False Move* (1991) and *Devil in a Blue Dress* (1995), Bill Duke's *Rage in Harlem* (1991) and *Deep Cover* (1992), Darnell Martin's *I Like It Like That* (1994), Tim Reid's *Once upon a Time When We Were Colored* (1996)—an admittedly partial list— represent the inclination among many black directors to move beyond the conventions of representing inner-city lives and conflicts for mass consumption. Films such as these undertake myriad challenges: revising the assumptions about black lives in earlier historical periods; addressing the complex nexus of issues of race, class, and sexuality; considering problematics of race beyond the overly familiar black–white binarism; examining the impact of place on constructions of race; and exploring how genre conventions are shaped when deployed within an explicitly racialized context.[10]

While all of these works saw only limited theatrical release, and none were commercial successes, many outperformed studio expectations, often because of the word of mouth of enthusiastic fans and the impassioned recommendations of film reviewers. Such challenges to reality and authenticity claims bode well for the future of black cinema; they also open African American films and videos from earlier periods to closer scrutiny, thus raising new questions about how blackness is coded and represented in visual media.

NOTES

1. This assumption informs such works as Ralph Ellison, "The Shadow and the Act," in *Shadow and Act* (New York: Random House, 1972), pp. 273–81; Thomas Cripps,

Black Film as Genre (Bloomington: Indiana University Press, 1978); Ed Guerrero, *Framing Blackness: The African American Image in Film* (Philadelphia: Temple University Press, 1993); and Manthia Diawara, "Black American Cinema: The New Realism," in *Black American Cinema*, ed. Manthia Diawara (New York: Routledge, 1993), pp. 3–55

    2. Michael Rogin, "'The Sword Became a Flashing Vision': D. W. Griffith's *The Birth of a Nation*," in *Ronald Reagan, the Movie, and Other Episodes in Political Demonology* (Berkeley: University of California Press, 1987), pp. 190–235.

    3. According to Thomas Cripps, the list of early black films that sought to correct the representations circulated in *Birth* ought to also include the Lincoln Motion Picture Company's *By Right of Birth* (1921) and the Colored Players Company's *A Prince of His Race* and *Ten Nights in a Bar Room* (1926). See Cripps, *Black Film as Genre*, pp. 15–29. The search for this sort of "positive" as "authentic" representation also informs the discourse around African American televisual representations. Witness the enthusiasm for shows such as "The Cosby Show," "Frank's Place," or "Under One Roof," which provided an alternative to the familiar African American working-class comic or underclass criminal types.

    4. *Go Down Death* is based on the sermon in verse of the same name found in James Weldon Johnson's *God's Trombones* (1927).

    5. As Nicholas Lemann writes, "Between 1910 and 1970, six and a half million black Americans moved from the South to the North; five million of them moved after 1940, during the time of the mechanization of cotton farming. In 1970, when the migration ended, black America was only half Southern, and less than a quarter rural." See *The Promised Land: The Great Black Migration and How It Changed America* (New York: Vintage Books, 1991), p. 6.

    6. A notable, early exception to this generalization is Cripps, *Black Film as Genre*. In recent years, scholars have turned increasingly to the study of black-directed filmmaking. See, for instance, Guerrero, *Framing Blackness*; Mark Reid, *Redefining Black Film* (Berkeley: University of California Press, 1993); Jacqueline Bobo, *Black Women as Cultural Readers* (New York: Columbia University Press, 1995); Gloria Gibson-Hudson, "Aspects of Black Feminist Cultural Ideology in Films by Black Women Independent Artists," in *Multiple Voices in Feminist Film Criticism*, ed. Diane Carson, Linda Dittmar, and Janice R. Welsch (Minneapolis: University of Minnesota Press, 1994), pp. 365–79; and a variety of essays in *Black American Cinema*, ed. Diawara.

    7. As but one example, witness the controversy surrounding the "Black Male" show curated by Thelma Golden when it opened at the Whitney Museum in New York City in the fall of 1994 and at UCLA at the Arm and Hammer Museum in Los Angeles in the spring of 1995.

    8. This essay was submitted for publication before the release of Burnett's most recent film, *The Glass Shield* (1995).

    9. Clyde Taylor, "The L. A. Rebellion: New Spirit in American Film," *Black Film Review* 2 (1986): 11, 29.

    10. Apropos of this last observation, see Manthia Diawara's brilliant reading of *A Rage in Harlem* as film noir. See his *"Noir* by *Noirs:* Towards a New Realism in Black Cinema," *African American Review* 27, no. 4, 525–38.

Donald Bogle

Black Beginnings:
From *Uncle Tom's Cabin*
to *The Birth of a Nation*

In the beginning, there was an Uncle Tom. A former mechanic photographed him in a motion picture that ran no longer than twelve minutes. And a new dimension was added to American movies.

The year was 1903. The mechanic-turned-movie-director was Edwin S. Porter. The twelve-minute motion picture was *Uncle Tom's Cabin.* And the new dimension was Uncle Tom himself. He was the American movies' first black character. The great paradox was that in actuality Tom was not black at all. Instead he was a nameless, slightly overweight white actor made up in blackface. But the use of whites in black roles was then a common practice, a tradition carried over from the stage and maintained during the early days of silent films. Still, the first Negro character had arrived in films, and he had done so at a time when the motion picture industry itself was virtually nonexistent. The movies were without stars or studios or sound. There were no great directors or writers. And the community of Hollywood had not yet come into being.

After the tom's debut, there appeared a variety of black presences bearing the fanciful names of the coon, the tragic mulatto, the mammy, and the brutal black buck. All were character types used for the same effect: to entertain by stressing Negro inferiority. Fun was poked at the American Negro by presenting him as either a nitwit or a childlike lackey. None of the types was meant to do great harm, although at various times individual ones did. All were merely filmic reproductions of black stereotypes that had existed since the days of slavery and were already popularized in American life and arts. The movies, which catered to public tastes, borrowed profusely from all the other popular art forms.

Whenever dealing with black characters, they simply adapted the old familiar stereotypes, often further distorting them.

In the early days when all the black characters were still portrayed by white actors in blackface, there was nothing but the old character types. They sat like square boxes on a shelf. A white actor walked by, selected a box, and used it as a base for a very square, rigidly defined performance. Later, when real black actors played the roles and found themselves wedged into these categories, the history became one of actors battling against the types to create rich, stimulating, diverse characters. At various points the tom, the coon, the tragic mulatto, the mammy, and the brutal black buck were brought to life respectively by Bill "Bojangles" Robinson, Stepin Fetchit, Nina Mae McKinney, Hattie McDaniel, and Walter Long (actually a white actor who portrayed a black villain in *The Birth of a Nation*), and later "modernized" by such performers as Sidney Poitier, Sammy Davis Jr., Dorothy Dandridge, Ethel Waters, and Jim Brown. Later such performers as Richard Pryor, Eddie Murphy, Lonette McKee, Whoopi Goldberg, and Danny Glover also found themselves struggling to turn old stereotypes inside out. Often it seemed as if the mark of the actor was the manner in which he individualized the mythic type or towered above it. The types were to prove deadly for some actors and inconsequential for others. But try as any actor may to forget the typecasting, the familiar types have most always been present in American black movies. The early silent period of motion pictures remains important, not because there were any great black performances—there weren't—but because the five basic types—the boxes sitting on the shelf—that were to dominate black characters for the next half century were first introduced then.

The Tom

Porter's tom was the first in a long line of socially acceptable Good Negro characters. Always as toms are chased, harassed, hounded, flogged, enslaved, and insulted, they keep the faith, n'er turn against their white massas, and remain hearty, submissive, stoic, generous, selfless, and oh-so-very kind. Thus they endear themselves to white audiences and emerge as heroes of sorts.

Two early toms appeared in the shorts *Confederate Spy* (c. 1910) and *For Massa's Sake* (1911). In the former, dear old Uncle Daniel is a Negro spy for the South. He dies before a Northern firing squad, but he is content, happy that he "did it for massa's sake and little massa." In *For Massa's Sake* a former slave is so attached to his erstwhile master that he sells himself back into slavery to help the master through a period of financial difficulties.

During the silent period, there were also remakes of the Harriet Stowe novel in which the tale of the good Christian slave was again made the meat of melodrama. The first remakes in 1909 and 1913 had little in style or treatment to distinguish them. But a fourth version, directed by William Robert Daly in 1914, distinguished itself and the tom tradition by starring the Negro stage actor Sam Lucas in the title role. Lucas became the first black man to play a leading role in a movie. Later, in 1927, when Universal Pictures filmed *Uncle Tom's Cabin,* the handsome Negro actor James B. Lowe was signed for the leading role. Harry Pollard directed the Universal feature. Twelve years earlier, Pollard had filmed a version of the Stowe classic in which he portrayed the Christian slave in blackface. But for this new venture Negro Lowe was selected to fit in with the "realistic" demands of the times. Congratulating itself on its liberalism, Universal sent out press releases about its good colored star:

> James B. Lowe has made history. A history that reflects only credit to the Negro race, not only because he has given the "Uncle Tom" character a new slant, but because of his exemplary conduct with the Universal company. They look upon Lowe at the Universal Studio as a living black god. . . . Of the directors, critics, artists, and actors who have seen James Lowe work at the studio there are none who will not say he is the most suited of all men for the part of "Tom." Those who are religious say that a heavenly power brought him to Universal and all predict a most marvelous future and worldwide reputation for James B. Lowe.

Although a "heavenly power" may have been with actor Lowe, it had little effect on his interpretation of the role. Tom still came off as a genial darky, furnished with new color but no new sentiments. Yet to Lowe's credit, he did his tomming with such an arresting effectiveness that he was sent to England on a promotional tour to ballyhoo the picture, thus becoming the first black actor to be publicized by his studio. The film also introduced the massive baptism scene, which later became a Hollywood favorite. Curiously, in 1958 this version of *Uncle Tom's Cabin,* although silent, was reissued with an added prologue by Raymond Massey. Because it arrived just when the sit-ins were erupting in the South, many wondered if by reissuing this film Universal Studios hoped to remind the restless black masses of an earlier, less turbulent period, when obeying one's master was the answer to every black man's problems.

The Coon

Although tom was to outdistance every other type and dominate American hearth and home, he had serious competition from a group of coons.

They appeared in a series of black films presenting the Negro as amusement object and black buffoon. They lacked the single-mindedness of tom. There were the pure coon and two variants of his type: the pickaninny and the uncle remus.

The pickaninny was the first of the coon types to make its screen debut. It gave the Negro child actor his place in the black pantheon. Generally, he was a harmless little screwball creation whose eyes popped, whose hair stood on end with the least excitement, and whose antics were pleasant and diverting. Thomas Alva Edison proved to be a pioneer in the exploitation and exploration of this type when he presented *Ten Pickaninnies* in 1904, a forerunner of the Hal Roach *Our Gang* series. During his camera experiments in 1893, Edison had photographed some blacks as "interesting side effects." In *Ten Pickaninnies*, the side effects moved to the forefront of the action as a group of nameless Negro children romped and ran about while being referred to as snowballs, cherubs, coons, bad chillun, inky kids, smoky kids, black lambs, cute ebonies, and chubbie ebonies. In due time, the pickaninnies were to be called by other names. In the 1920s and the 1930s, such child actors as Sunshine Sammy, Farina, Stymie, and Buckwheat picked up the pickaninny mantle and carried it to new summits. In all the versions of *Uncle Tom's Cabin,* the slave child Topsy was presented as a lively pickaninny, used solely for comic relief. When the 1927 version of *Uncle Tom's Cabin* opened, the character was singled out by one critic who wrote: "Topsy is played by Mona Ray, a wonderfully bright youngster who seems to have the comedy of her part in extraordinary fashion. . . . her eyes roll back and forth in alarm. She also evinces no liking for her plight when she is found by Miss Ophelia while dabbing powder on her ebony countenance." In her day, the character Topsy was clownish and droll and became such a film favorite that she starred in *Topsy and Eva* (1927), in which her far-fetched meanderings and her pickaninnying won mass audience approval.

Shortly after Edison introduced the pickaninny in 1904, the pure coon made its way onto the screen in *Wooing and Wedding of a Coon* (1905). This short depicted a honeymooning black couple as stumbling and stuttering idiots. Later the coon appeared in *The Masher* (1907), which was about a self-styled white ladies' man who is rebuffed by all the women he pursues. When he meets a mysterious veiled woman who responds to his passes, the hero thinks he has arrived at his blue heaven. And so finding success, he removes the veil only to discover that his mystery lady love is *colored!* Without further ado, he takes off. He may have been looking for a blue heaven, but he certainly did not want a black one.

Before its death, the coon developed into the most blatantly degrading of all black stereotypes. The pure coons emerged as no-account niggers, those unreliable, crazy, lazy, subhuman creatures good for nothing more than eating watermelons, stealing chickens, shooting crap, or butchering the English language. A character named Rastus was just such a figure.

How Rastus Got His Turkey (1910) was the first of a series of slapstick comedies centering on the antics of a Negro called Rastus. Here Rastus tries to steal a turkey for his Thanksgiving dinner. Next came *Rastus in Zululand*, about a darky who dreams of going to Zululand in the heart of Africa. There he wins the affections of the chief's daughter. He is willing to flirt with the girl, but when asked to marry her, in true unreliable, no-account nigger fashion, he refuses, expressing a wish for death rather than matrimony. The savage chief (from the beginning, all Africans are savages) nearly grants that wish, too. *Rastus and Chicken*, *Pickaninnies and Watermelon*, and *Chicken Thief* were other shorts in the series, all appearing during 1910 and 1911. In some respects, this series and its central character simply paved the way for the greatest coon of all time, Stepin Fetchit.

The final member of the coon triumvirate is the uncle remus. Harmless and congenial, he is a first cousin to the tom, yet he distinguishes himself by his quaint, naïve, and comic philosophizing. During the silent period he was only hinted at. He did not come into full flower until the 1930s and 1940s with films such as *The Green Pastures* (1936) and *Song of the South* (1946). Remus's mirth, like tom's contentment and the coon's antics, has always been used to indicate the black man's satisfaction with the system and his place in it.

The Tragic Mulatto

The third figure of the black pantheon and the one that proved itself a moviemaker's darling is the tragic mulatto. One of the type's earliest appearances was in *The Debt* (1912), a two-reeler about the Old South. A white man's wife and his black mistress bear him children at the same time. Growing up together, the white son and the mulatto daughter fall in love and decide to marry, only to have their relationship revealed to them at the crucial moment. Their lives are thus ruined not only because they are brother and sister but also—and here was the catch—because the girl has a drop of black blood!

In Humanity's Cause, In Slavery Days, and *The Octoroon*, all made around 1913, explored plights of a fair-skinned mulatto attempting to pass for white. Usually the mulatto is made likable, even sympathetic (because of her white blood, no doubt), and the audience believes that the girl's life could have been productive and happy had she not been a "victim of divided racial inheritance."

The Mammy

Mammy, the fourth black type, is so closely related to the comic coons that she is usually relegated to their ranks. Mammy is distinguished, however, by her sex and her fierce independence. She is usually big, fat, and cantankerous. She made her debut around 1914, when audiences were treated to a blackface version of *Lysistrata*. The comedy, titled *Coon Town Suffragettes*, dealt with a group of bossy mammy washerwomen who organize a militant movement to keep their good-for-nothing husbands at home. Aristophanes would no doubt have risen from his grave with righteous indignation. But the militancy of the washerwomen served as a primer for the mammy roles Hattie McDaniel was to perfect in the 1930s.

Mammy's offshoot is the aunt jemima, sometimes derogatorily referred to as a "handkerchief head." Often aunt jemimas are toms blessed with religion or mammies who wedge themselves into the dominant white culture. Generally they are sweet, jolly, and good-tempered—a bit more polite than mammy and certainly never as headstrong. The maids in the Mae West films of the 1930s fit snugly into this category.

The Brutal Black Buck and *The Birth of a Nation*

D. W. Griffith's *The Birth of a Nation* (1915) was the motion picture that introduced the final mythic type, the brutal black buck. This extraordinary multidimensional movie was also the first feature film to deal with a black theme and at the same time to articulate fully the entire pantheon of black gods and goddesses. Griffith presented all the types with such force and power that his film touched off a wave of controversy and was denounced as the most slanderous anti-Negro movie ever released.

In almost every way, *The Birth of a Nation* was a stupendous undertaking, unlike any film that had preceded it. Up until then American movies had been two- or three-reel affairs, shorts running no longer than ten or fifteen minutes, crudely and casually filmed. But *The Birth of a Nation* was rehearsed for six weeks, filmed in nine, later edited in three months, and finally released as a record-breaking hundred-thousand-dollar spectacle, twelve reels in length and over three hours in running time. It altered the entire course and concept of American moviemaking, developing the close-up, crosscutting, rapid-fire editing, the iris, the split-screen shot, and realistic and impressionistic lighting. Creating sequences and images yet to be surpassed, the film's magnitude and epic grandeur swept audiences off their feet. At a private White House screening President Woodrow Wilson exclaimed, "It's like writing history with lightning!" *The Birth of a Nation,* however, not only vividly re-created history, but revealed its director's philosophical concept of the universe and his personal racial bigotry. For D. W. Griffith there was a moral order at work in the universe. If that order were ever thrown out of whack, he believed chaos would ensue. Griffith's thesis was sound, relatively exciting, and even classic in a purely Shakespearean sense. But in articulating his thesis, Griffith seemed to be saying that things were in order only when whites were in control and when the American Negro was kept in his place. In the end, Griffith's "lofty" statement—and the film's subject matter—transformed *The Birth of a Nation* into a hotly debated and bitterly cursed motion picture.

It told the story of the Old South, the Civil War, the Reconstruction period, and the emergence of the Ku Klux Klan. Basing his film on Thomas Dixon's novel *The Clansman* (also the original title of the film), Griffith focused on a good, decent "little" family, the Camerons of Piedmont, South Carolina. Before the war, the family lives in an idyllic "quaintly way that is to be no more." Dr. Cameron and his sons are gentle, benevolent "fathers" to their childlike servants. The slaves themselves could be no happier. In the fields they contentedly pick cotton. In their quarters they dance and sing for their master. In the Big House Mammy joyously goes about her chores. All is in order. Everyone knows his place. Then the Civil War breaks out, and the old order cracks.

The war years take their toll. In Piedmont, the Cameron family is terrorized by a troop of Negro raiders, and all the South undergoes "ruin, devastation, rapine, and pillage." Then comes Reconstruction. Carpetbaggers and uppity niggers from the North move into Piedmont, exploiting and corrupting the former slaves, unleashing the sadism and bestiality innate in the Negro, turning the once congenial darkies into renegades, and using them to "crush the white South under the heel of the black South." "Lawlessness runs riot!" says one title card. The old slaves have quit work to dance. They roam the streets, shoving whites off sidewalks. They take over the political polls and disenfranchise the whites. A black political victory culminates in an orgiastic street celebration. Blacks dance, sing, drink, rejoice. Later they conduct a black congressional session, itself a mockery of Old South ideals, in which the freed Negro legislators are depicted as lustful, arrogant, and idiotic. They bite on chicken legs and drink whiskey from bottles while sprawling with bare feet on their desks. During the congressional meeting, the stench created by the barefoot congressmen becomes so great that they pass as their first act a ruling that every member must keep his shoes on during legislative meetings! Matters in *The Birth of a Nation* reach a heady climax later when the renegade black Gus sets out to rape the younger Cameron daughter. Rather than submit, the Pet Sister flees from him and throws herself from a cliff—into the "opal gates of death." Then the mulatto Silas Lynch attempts to force the white Elsie Stoneman to marry him. Finally, when all looks hopelessly lost, there emerges a group of good, upright Southern white men, members of an "invisible empire," who, while wearing white sheets and hoods, battle the blacks in a direct confrontation. Led by Ben Cameron in a rousing stampede, they magnificently defeat the black rebels! Defenders of white womanhood, white honor, and white glory, they restore to the South everything it has lost, including its white supremacy. Thus we have the birth of a nation—and the birth of the Ku Klux Klan.

The plot machinations of the Griffith epic may today resound with melodramatic absurdities, but the action, the actors, and the direction did not. The final ride of the Klan was an impressive piece of film propaganda, superbly lit and brilliantly edited. Indeed it was so stirring that audiences screamed in delight, cheering for the white heroes and booing, hissing, and cursing the black militants. *The Birth of a Nation* remains significant not only because of its artistry but also because of its wide-ranging influence. One can detect in this single film the trends and sentiments that were to run through almost every black film made for a long time afterward. Later filmmakers were to pick up Griffith's ideas—his very images—but were to keep them "nicely" toned down in order not to offend audiences.

Griffith used three varieties of blacks. The first were the "faithful souls," a mammy and an uncle tom, who remain with the Cameron family throughout and staunchly defend them from the rebels. By means of these characters, as well as the pickaninny slaves seen dancing, singing, and clowning in their quarters, director Griffith propagated the myth of slave contentment and made it appear as if slavery had elevated the Negro from his bestial instincts. At heart, Griffith's "faithful souls" were shamelessly naïve representations of the Negro as Child or the Negro as Watered-Down Noble Savage. But these characters were to make their way through scores of other Civil War epics, and they were to leave their mark on the characterizations of Clarence Muse in *Huckleberry Finn* (1931) and *Broadway Bill* (1934) and of Bill Robinson in *The Little Colonel* (1935) and *The Littlest Rebel* (1935).

Griffith's second variety were the brutal black bucks. Just as the coon stereotype could be broken into subgroups, the brutal black-buck type could likewise be divided into two categories: the black brutes and the black bucks. Differences between the two were minimal. The black brute was a barbaric black out to raise havoc. Audiences could assume that his physical violence served as an outlet for a man who was sexually repressed. In *The Birth of a Nation*, the black brutes, subhuman and feral, are the nameless characters setting out on a rampage full of black rage. They flog the Camerons' faithful servant. They shove and assault white men of the town. They flaunt placards demanding "equal marriage." These characters figured prominently in the Black Congress sequence, and their film descendants were to appear years later as the rebellious slaves of *So Red the Rose* (1935), as the revolutionaries of *Uptight* (1969), and as the militants of *Putney Swope* (1969).

But it was the pure black bucks that were Griffith's really great archetypal figures. Bucks are always big, baadddd niggers, oversexed and savage, violent and frenzied as they lust for white flesh. No greater sin hath any black man. Both Lynch, the mulatto, and Gus, the renegade, fall into this category. Among other things, these two characters revealed the tie between sex and racism in America. Griffith played on the myth of the Negro's high-powered sexuality, then articulated the great white fear that every black man longs for a white woman. Underlying the fear was the assumption that the white woman was the ultimate in female desirability, herself a symbol of white pride, power, and beauty. Consequently, when Lillian Gish, the frailest, purest of all screen heroines, was attacked by the character Lynch—when he put his big black arms around this pale blond beauty—audiences literally panicked. Here was the classic battle of good and evil, innocence and corruption. It was a master stroke and a brilliant use of contrast, one that drew its audience into the film emotionally.* But in uncovering the attraction of black to white, Griffith failed to reveal the political implications. Traditionally, certain black males have been drawn to white women because these women are power symbols, an ideal of the oppressor. But Griffith attributed the attraction to an animalism innate in the Negro male. Thus the black bucks of the film are psychopaths, one always panting and salivating, the other forever stiffening his body as if the mere presence of a white woman in the same room could bring him to a sexual climax. Griffith played hard on the bestiality of his black villainous bucks and used it to arouse hatred.

Closely aligned to the bucks and brutes of *The Birth of a Nation* is the mulatto character Lydia. She is presented as the mistress of the white abolitionist carpetbagger, Senator Stoneman. Through Lydia, Griffith explored the possibilities of the dark, sinister half-breed as a tragic leading lady. Although merely a supporting character, Lydia is the only black role to suggest even remotely genuine mental anguish. She hates whites. She refuses to be treated as an inferior. She wants power. Throughout, she anguishes over her predicament as a black woman in a hostile white world.

Lydia is also the film's only passionate female. Griffith was the first important movie director to divide his black women into categories based on their individual colors. Both Lydia and Mammy are played by

---

*Lillian Gish's comments in the January 1937, issue of *Stage* verify the fact that Griffith was well aware of this contrast and that he used it to arouse his audience. Said Gish: "At first I was not cast to play in *The Clansman*. My sister and I had been the last to join the company and we naturally supposed . . . that the main assignments would go to the older members. But one day while we were rehearsing the scene where the colored man picks up the Northern girl gorilla-fashion, my hair, which was very blond, fell far below my waist and Griffith, seeing the contrast in the two figures, assigned me to play Elsie Stoneman (who was to have been Mae Marsh)."

white actresses in blackface. But Mammy is darker. She is representative of the all-black woman, overweight, middle-aged, and so dark, so thoroughly black, that it is preposterous even to suggest that she be a sex object. Instead she was desexed. This tradition of the desexed, overweight, dowdy *dark* black woman was continued in films throughout the 1930s and 1940s. Vestiges of it popped up as late as the 1960s with Claudia McNeil in *A Raisin in the Sun* (1961) and Beah Richards in *Hurry Sundown* (1967). A dark black actress was considered for no role but that of a mammy or an aunt jemima. On the other hand, the part-black woman—the light-skinned Negress—was given a chance at lead parts and was graced with a modicum of sex appeal. Every sexy black woman who appeared afterward in movies was to be a "cinnamon-colored gal" with Caucasian features. The mulatto came closest to the white ideal. Whether conscious or not, Griffith's division of the black woman into color categories survived in movies the way many set values continue long after they are discredited. In fact, it was said in 1958 and 1970 that one reason why such actresses as Eartha Kitt in *Anna Lucasta* and Lola Falana in *The Liberation of L. B. Jones* failed to emerge as important screen love goddesses was that they were too dark.

Influential and detrimental as the Griffith blacks were to be for later generations, they were not meekly accepted in 1915. *The Birth of a Nation*'s blackfaced baddies aroused a rash of hostilities. At the film's New York premiere, the NAACP picketed the theater, calling the movie racist propaganda. Later the Chicago and Boston branches of the NAACP led massive demonstrations against its presentation. Other civil rights and religious organizations were quick to protest. Race riots broke out in a number of cities. Newspaper editorials and speeches censured the film. Black critics such as Laurence Reddick said it glorified the Ku Klux Klan, and Reddick added that the film's immense success was at least one factor contributing to the great and growing popularity the organization enjoyed during this period. In the South, the film was often advertised as calculated to "work audiences into a frenzy . . . it will make you hate." In some regions, the ad campaign may have been effective, for in 1915 lynchings in the United States reached their highest peak since 1908. Ultimately, *The Birth of a Nation* was banned in five states and nineteen cities.

The anger and fury did not die in 1915 either. The film was reissued at regular intervals in later years. At each reopening, outraged moviegoers, both black and white, vehemently opposed its showing. In 1921, *The Birth of a Nation* was attacked as a part of a "Southern campaign to stimulate the Ku Klux Klan"—which it had already done. The Museum of Modern Art temporarily shelved the picture in 1946. Because of "the potency of its anti-Negro bias," read the Museum's press announcement, "exhibiting it at this time of heightened social tensions cannot be justified." The 1947 revival of the movie by the Dixie Film Exchange was blasted by the Civil Rights Congress, and the NAACP picketed New York's Republic Theatre where it was to be shown. "It brings race hatred to New York City," said NAACP Secretary Walter White, "and we don't want it here." The Progressive Labor Party led demonstrations against the film during the following year. In 1950, there were renewed outcries when word leaked out that a Hollywood company was to remake the movie in sound. The remake plans were quickly aborted, as were the 1959 proposals to present it on television.

Throughout the years, D. W. Griffith defended himself as a mere filmmaker with no political or ideological view in mind. Surprised and apparently genuinely hurt when called a racist, Griffith made speeches across the country, wrote letters to the press, accused the NAACP and its supporters of trying to bring about screen censorship, and even went so far as to issue a pamphlet entitled "The Rise and Fall of Free Speech in America," all in an effort to squelch the controversy. As late as 1947, one year before his death and some thirty-two years after the movie's release, D. W. Griffith still maintained that this film was not an attack on the American Negro.

The Birth of a Nation has become one of the highest grossing movies of all time. (The amount it has earned has never been fully tabulated.) Eyeing its profits, a number of Hollywood producers undertook projects with similar anti-Negro themes. *Broken Chains* (c. 1916) and *Free and Equal* (filmed in 1915, but not released until 1925) were prominent imitations. The former failed miserably. The latter's release was held up for some ten years while the producer waited for the furor to cool down. For one thing was certain after *The Birth of a Nation:* never again could the Negro be depicted in the guise of an out-and-out villain. This treatment was too touchy and too controversial. Griffith's film had succeeded because of its director's artistry and technical virtuosity, but no studio dared risk it again. Consequently, blacks in Hollywood films were cast almost exclusively in comic roles. And thus even the great comic tradition of the Negro in the American film has its roots in the Griffith spectacle. Finally, many of Hollywood's hang-ups and hesitations in presenting sensual black men on screen resulted, in part, from the reactions to the Griffith spectacle. So strong was his presentation, and so controversial its reception, that movie companies ignored and avoided such a type of black character for fear of raising new hostilities. Not until more than a half century later, when Melvin Van Peebles' *Sweet Sweetback's Baadasssss Song* (1971) appeared, did sexually assertive black males make their way back to the screen. Afterward, when the box office success of that film indicated that audiences could at long last accept such a type, the screen was bombarded with an array of buck heroes in such films as *Shaft* (1971), *Super Fly* (1972), *Slaughter* (1972), and *Melinda* (1972).

With *The Birth of a Nation* in 1915, all the major black screen types had been introduced. Literal and unimaginative as some types might now appear, the naïve and cinematically untutored audiences of the early century responded to the character types as if they were the real thing.

As far as the audiences were concerned, the toms, the coons, the mulattos, the mammies, and the bucks embodied all the aspects and facets of the black experience itself. The audience's deep-set prejudice against any "foreigners" accounts for the typing of all minorities in all American films. But no minority was so relentlessly or fiercely typed as the black man. Audiences rejected even subtle modifications of the black caricatures. When Jack Johnson became the first black heavy-weight champion of the world in 1908, filmed sequences of him knocking out white Tommy Burns so disturbed the "racial pride" of white America that the films were banned for fear of race riots. Thereafter, black boxers in films were invariably defeated by their white opponents. Similarly, when the first film versions of *Uncle Tom's Cabin* were released in the South, advertisements announced that the black characters were portrayed by white actors. Even at this stage, the evolving film industry feared offending its dominant white audience.

Once the basic mythic types were introduced, a number of things occurred. Specific black themes soon emerged. (The Old South theme proved to be a great favorite.) And the basic types came and went in various guises. Guises long confused many movie viewers. They were (and remain) deceptive, and they have traditionally been used by the film industry to camouflage the familiar types. If a black appeared as a butler, audiences thought of him as merely a servant. What they failed to note was the variety of servants. There were tom servants (faithful and submissive), coon servants (lazy and unreliable), and mammy servants, to name just a few. What has to be remembered is that the servant's uniform was the guise certain types wore during a given period. That way Hollywood could give its audience the same product (the types themselves) but with new packaging (the guise).

With the Griffith spectacle, audiences saw the first of the guises. The brutes, the bucks, and the tragic mulattoes all wore the guise of villains. Afterward, during the 1920s, audiences saw their toms and coons dressed in the guise of plantation jesters. In the 1930s, all the types were dressed in servants' uniforms. In the early 1940s, they sported entertainers' costumes. In the late 1940s and the 1950s, they donned the gear of troubled problem people. In the 1960s, they appeared as angry militants. Because the guises were always changing, audiences were sometimes tricked into believing the depictions of the American Negro were altered too. But at heart beneath the various guises, there lurked the familiar types.

James A. Snead

Spectatorship and Capture in *King Kong:* The Guilty Look

In the mid-1970s, film studies witnessed an increased awareness of the place of blacks in the history of American films. A rich and generally informative series of books appeared around the overall subject of "the black image in films." Among these were Edward Mapp's *Blacks in American Films* (1972), Donald Bogle's *Toms, Coons, Mulattoes, Mammies, and Bucks: An Interpretive History of Blacks in American Films* (1973), James P. Murray's *To Find an Image* (1973), Gary Null's *Black Hollywood: The Negro in Motion Pictures* (1975), Daniel Leab's *From Sambo to Superspade: The Black Experience in Motion Pictures* (1975), and Thomas Cripps's *Slow Fade to Black* (1977). These studies all, in various ways, stressed the need for more positive roles, types, and portrayals, while pointing out the intractable presence of "negative stereotypes" in the film industry's depiction of blacks. While the thoroughness of such books was welcome, their clustered appearance contributed to an unfortunate homogeneity. For the mid-1970s were also the period of a most productive ferment in film theory, one that the above-mentioned books on blacks in film either uniformly ignored or were unaware of. Invaluable semiotic, poststructuralist, feminist, and psychoanalytic tools were neglected, and still have not been adequately applied to the large body of Hollywood films in which blacks appear. The "black Hollywood" books of the 1970s took a binary approach, sociological in its position, hunting down either "negative" or "positive" images. Such a method could not grasp what closer rhetorical and discursive analysis of racial imagery can. Few of these books investigate the filmic text or its implied audience. When black images and spectatorship are the issues, then such an approach seems indispensable.

I submit that this is part of a larger project, one that understands film (in the words of Jean-Luc Comolli and Jean Narboni) as "ideology presenting itself to itself, talking to itself, learning about itself."[1] My work on Hollywood film analyzes film stereotypes in terms of *codes*

From *White Screens, Black Images: Hollywood from the Dark Side* (New York: Routledge, 1994). Used by permission of George Snead and the Estate of James Snead.

they form, and makes these codes legible, inspecting their inner workings as well as the external historical subjects they would conceal. My term "code" is informed by the usage developed by Umberto Eco in *A Theory of Semiotics*: roughly, a set of conventions defining perception in limited and predictable ways within any given culture. Roland Barthes, particularly in his *S/Z*, conceives of an allied concept of codes, one related to the social and artistic conventions and rituals of everyday life. There are, according to Barthes, three major categories of narrative codes: codes that involve conventions of plot content (code of enigma and action); codes that involve the structure of the plot (symbolic codes); and codes that the text borrows from outside sources (cultural or semic codes), or what we might call "stereotypes."

I shall outline a general conceptual framework and then move to a discussion of a well-known Hollywood film, *King Kong*.

My work on Hollywood films has to do with broad issues of power, domination, and subordination as represented in visual media, but I concentrate here mainly on Hollywood's perceptions of blacks. In other words, much of what I say here might apply to other non-white groups that filmmakers have depicted in their stories: American Indians, Spanish Americans, Asians, and so on. But I agree with W. E. B. Du Bois, when he said that the "Negro" is the metaphor of the twentieth century, the major figure in which these power relationships of master/slave, civilized/primitive, enlightened/backward, good/evil, have been embodied in the American subconscious.

From the very first films, black skin on screen became a complex code for various things, depending on the social self-conception and positioning of the viewer; it could as easily connote white superiority and self-regard as black inferiority. The message of black inferiority, however, was addressed to viewers who desired a sense of clearcut dominance within the often confusing uncertainties of American history. Historical ambiguity requires some sense of transhistorical certainty, and so blacks were as if ready-made for the task. On screen and off, the history that Western culture has made typically denies blacks and black skin historical reference, except as former slaves or savages.

One of the prime codes surrounding blacks on screen, then—one much at variance with the narrative codes that mandate potential mobility for other screen characters—is an almost metaphysical stasis. The black, particularly the black woman, is seen as eternal, unchanging, unchangeable. (Recall Faulkner's appendix to *The Sound and the Fury*: "They endured.") The code of stasis arises in order to justify blacks' continuing economic disadvantage. Throughout the history of Hollywood cinema, in films from King Vidor's 1929 *Hallelujah!* through Steven Spielberg's 1985 *The Color Purple*, blacks' character is sealed off from the history into which whites have trapped them. The notorious "Africa" films have as their main function the reinforcement of the code of the "eternal" or "static" black. From *Tarzan, the Ape Man* (1932) right through such recent efforts as *The Jewel of the Nile* (1985), blacks in Africa are seen to behave with the same ineptitude and shiftlessness, even before the three hundred years of slavery and oppression, which they exhibited, according to Hollywood films, years later in America. The only explanation can be an enduring "black nature" that no historical tragedy or intervention has ever or could ever have been responsible for.

In such examples and others, one may formulate the history of black film stereotypes as the history of the denial of history in favor of an artificially constructed mythology about unchanging black "character" or "nature." The problem is that, especially in film, stereotypes and codes insulate themselves from historical change, or actual counterexamples in the real world. Caricatures breed more caricatures, or metamorphose into others, but remain in place.

Although films are not necessarily myths, as is sometimes asserted, certain films have managed to remain repeatedly compelling and thus to assume a permanent, quasi-mythic status in a society's consciousness. The tireless popularity of such films might be related to Claude Lévi-Strauss's notion of myths as narratives that endure because they resolve—by venting latent social contractions—conflicts that otherwise would remain troublesome.[2]

Yet poststructuralism has somewhat revised Lévi-Strauss's contention, and the difference is crucial for understanding Hollywood stereotyping of blacks. For whereas Lévi-Strauss sees myths as *unifying* communities by giving concentrated and vicarious forms to contradictions that plague them, I would suggest that modern myths precisely illustrate social *divisions,* exposing audience fantasies that are anything but communally shared. In a pluralistic society, myths—especially where they rely on the subordination of particular groups in society—are inevitably political and cannot enforce or sustain a uniform scheme of mythic reconciliation.

The three most frequent devices whereby blacks have been consigned to minor significance on screen include what I refer to as mythification, marking, and omission.

Mythification involves the realization that filmic codes describe an *interrelationship* between images. American films do not merely feature this or that debased black image or this or that glorified white hero in isolation, but rather they correlate these images in a larger scheme of semiotic valuation. For the viewer, the pleasure of recognizing this ranking displaces the necessity of verifying its moral or actual validity.

Mythification is the replacement of history with a surrogate ideology of elevation or demotion along a scale of human value. Mythification also implies identification, and requires a pool of spectators ready to accept and identify themselves with film's tailor-made versions of reality. This device engages audiences on the level of their racial allegiance, social background, and self-image. Film translates the personal into the communal so quickly that elevation of the dominant and degradation of the subordinate are simultaneous and corporate. When we consider *The Birth of a Nation* or *Gone with the Wind*, for example, the mechanisms of racial mythification are clear—the dominant "I" needs the coded "other" to function: white female stars (themselves coded as subordinate to white males) employ black maids to make them seem more authoritatively womanly; white male stars need black butlers or sidekicks to make them seem more authoritatively manly. Soon, by mythification and repetition, white and black filmed images become large-scale models, positive or negative, for behavior, describing (in the manner of myth in non-Western societies) structures, limits, and an overall repertoire from which both white and black viewers in the real world select possibilities of action and thought.

The second tactic is *marking*. As if the blackness of black skin itself were not enough, we seem to find the color black repeatedly overdetermined, marked redundantly, almost as if to force the viewer to register the image's difference from white images. Marking makes it visually clear that black skin is a "natural" condition turned into a "man-made" sign. Initially because of the shortcomings of early lenses and film stocks, but later due purely to the needs of image-making rhetoric, black skin has been overmarked in order to eliminate ambiguity. (In his article for the Fall 1985 edition of *Daedalus*, Brian Winston argues that from Edison through the present day, film stocks were designed to show off white skin to greatest advantage, but have never conveyed other skin tones with any degree of verisimilitude or subtlety.)

Marking is necessary because the *reality* of blackness or of being "colored" cannot always, either in films or in real life, be determined. The racial terms "black" and "white" refer to a wide range of hues that cannot be positively described—by being this or that—but only by negative contrast: black is not "white" (where "white" itself is a term difficult to fix). In early films, white actors used blackface, but even when black actors and actresses played black roles, studios required them to darken their skins (Bert Williams, Lena Horne, Nina Mae McKinney, and Fredi Washington are only a few examples of black stars who had to be so marked). The Hollywood black had to be made either very black or very light. In the movies *Pinky* (1949), and the second version of *Imitation of Life* (1959), the roles of mulatto black women passing for white are actually played by white actresses, to make sure that a visual ambiguity does not compound an already difficult conceptual leap.

Film is a medium of contrasts in light, and so the shades of skin color between black and white often must be suppressed, so that binary visual opposites might serve cinematographic as well as political purposes. Chauffeurs, domestics, porters, jazz musicians, and other blacks are marked by the black/white codings in the contrast between their skins and white articles of clothing. Aprons, gloves, dresses, scarves, headbands, and even white teeth and eyes are all signifiers of a certain coding of race in Hollywood films that audiences soon came to recognize. This is not to say that whites on film would not bulge out eyes, or wear servants' clothes; only that (1) blacks seemed to do it exclusively; and (2) these signifiers have a different coding when whites are associated with them—indeed, this is what makes looking at them so interesting. White gloves, for instance, on a white butler spell "reserve, efficiency, and service," whereas on a black butler, they might contribute to an overall connotation of "racial inferiority." A white with an apron on might mean: "poor/lazy/unfortunate person—could end up either on the high or the low end of society, depending on the outcome of the film (role *not* connected to color)." A black with an apron on might mean: "they're so good with food/children/animals—will remain in that position forever (role indistinguishable from color)." Other common markings include "Negro dialect" (early title cards in silent films even felt constrained to write dialect when blacks were seen to speak!); elevation/lowness; motion/stasis; cleanliness/dirtiness; distinction/groupmass. All these semes, or smallest units of meaning, combine to form larger codes, like letters combining into words.

The third device is *omission*, or exclusion by reversal, distortion, or some other form of censorship. Omission and exclusion are perhaps the most widespread tactics of racial stereotyping but are also the most difficult to prove because their manifestation is precisely absence itself. The repetition of black absence from locations of autonomy and importance creates the presence of the idea that blacks belong in positions of obscurity and dependence. From the earliest days of film, omission was the method of choice in designing mass images of blacks. For example, the film of Jack Johnson's victory over his white opponent Tommy Burns (1908) was banned because of feared inflammatory effects. Typically in the 1930s and 1940s, filmmakers would relegate their black stars to optional numbers that were edited out for southern distribution. In general, filmscripts edited out the reality of blacks as lawyers, teachers, and doctors, in favor of far more arcane and restrictive black stereotypes. Even within the individual frame, we often (though not always) find the black excluded, peripheral, distant from the source and focal point of action. But since "framing," "editing," and "cutting out" are indeed the exigencies of filmic and aesthetic practice, it was possible to hide ideologically motivated distortions under the masks of artistic economy or exigency.

Against this general background, then, I would like to move on to a discussion of a film most of you know, *King Kong*. *King Kong* provides an especially telling example of the use of the devices of mythification, marking, and omission because of its blatant linkage of the idea of the black with that of the monster. "Monstrousness" is a complex dimension of Hollywood film, and for our purposes I mention here the work of only one of the more incisive critics to have written about it,

Robin Wood. Basing his insights on Herbert Marcuse's notion of surplus repression, Wood has argued that contemporary society, repressing sexual desires that would otherwise threaten its stability, vents these desires through the figure of the monster.[3] The Hollywood monster film allows, among other things, a safe outlet of such sexual desires in a surrogate form and a vicarious experience—pleasurable and horrific—of the chaos that such a release would bring about in reality. More specifically, Wood states that society represses: (1) "sexual energy itself"; (2) "bisexuality" (which he defines as the arbitrary nature of social norms surrounding masculinity and femininity); and (3) "female sexuality/creativity." A too strictly practiced internal repression may end in external oppression—a generalized hostility directed against a societal "other," especially the "other" as women or non-Western peoples. Applying Wood's paradigm to *King Kong*—a monster movie about blackness that stretches all boundaries, temporal, spatial, and natural—we see that repression and oppression are inescapably bound one to the other. For while surplus repression is primarily sexual, we must remember that the oppression it spawns is largely political. (Indeed, it has been variously argued that some whites oppress blacks on the outside in order to repress elements of "blackness" inside.)[4]

In *all* Hollywood film portrayals of blacks, I am arguing here, the political is never far from the sexual, for it is both as a political and as a sexual threat that the black skin appears on screen. And nowhere is this more plainly to be seen than in *King Kong*. There are very few instances in the history of Hollywood cinema in which the color black has been writ so large and intruded so powerfully into the social plane of white normality. Blackness in motion is typically sensed as a threat on screen, and so black movement in film is usually restricted to highly bracketed and containable activities, such as sports or entertainment. *King Kong* is an exception to this rule: the attempt to contain Kong fails, and he makes off with not just any woman, but with a white woman. *King Kong*, then, as a noteworthy, though perhaps surprising, instance of "the coded black"—in this case, the carrier of blackness is not a human being, but an ape, but we shall see that the difference can easily be bridged.

In their August 1970 analysis of "John Ford's *Young Mr. Lincoln*," the editors of *Cahiers du cinéma* say that films often contain "constituent lacks" or "*structuring absences* . . . the unsaid included in the said and necessary to its constitution." These absences "have some connection with the sexual other scene, and that 'other scene' which is politics."[5] My reading of *King Kong* will attempt to supply some of these constitutive omissions. Through a reading of the subplots in *King Kong*, we can see that the film's political aspects are hidden by the emotive nature of the sexual plot's covert buildup and ambiguous release. *King Kong* is able to cloak and leave unresolved a potentially explosive allegory of racial and sexual exploitation by manipulating the codes whereby films typically portray romantic conflict and resolution.

Unraveling the relationship between the sexual and political plots in the film means tracing the surface plot, the political subplot, and the transformations of audience perspective implied by each. Few products of the American cinema have made such a rapid and indelible impression as *King Kong*. From its first release in 1933, the film was immensely popular, and it helped RKO at least temporarily survive bankruptcy. In *King Kong's* wake, the director/producer team of Ernest B. Schoedsack and Merian C. Cooper made two sequels, *Son of Kong* (1933) and *Mighty Joe Young* (1949), and others have followed these. Kong, the center of attention, has joined that group of cultural reference points and large-scale metaphors that includes Frankenstein, Moby-Dick, Santa Claus, and Sherlock Holmes—neither kin nor foreign, neither completely real nor completely fictitious. One can buy postcards of Kong scaling the Empire State Building (recently, an inflated facsimile of Kong was temporarily hung there), or buy bumper stickers stating that "King Kong died for your sins."

Kong has become a classic in large part because of his very "humanness." As we shall see, the ape's "humanness" engages, but also conceals, the underlying political point the film illustrates. Early on in the production, there was some debate over just how human Kong should appear. The chief technician and animator, Willis O'Brien, wanted a sympathetic, anthropomorphic Kong, and won out over Cooper's more "monstrous" conception. In the end, O'Brien's artistic virtuosity helped "humanize" Kong, giving an eighteen-inch clay model familiar and often endearing gestures and expressions. The humanness of King Kong, the key to *King Kong's* success, also tips us off to the various ways in which the film appeals to its spectators.

Plot Summary

The plot of *King Kong* is, as its makers continually stressed in interviews, absurd, very much like that of any typical adventure yarn. If we compare it with the plot of Melville's *Moby-Dick*, for instance, we find both similarities and differences: a somewhat obsessive leader and his crew journey into unknown seas without their full knowledge of his intentions. The group encounters a terrifying, murderous creature of fantastic dimensions. Yet here Carl Denham returns to New York with King Kong and even lives to make an oration over his corpse, while neither Ahab nor his men (except for Ishmael) returns from the encounter with the whale. Another variation is the presence of Ann Darrow (her name almost certainly alludes to Clarence Darrow, defense lawyer in the 1925 Scopes "monkey" trial), usually referred to simply as "the girl"—in most cases, such seafaring adventure tales are womanless. These two peculiarities—the importation of the monster into civilized society and the addition of a woman to the adventure model—are quite pertinent. The film has four main divisions: (1) New York and the discovery of the girl; (2) the voyage; (3) encounter with natives and Kong in the primeval jungle; (4) New York and the death of Kong.

The first shots of the film place us in New York Harbor, seen from Hoboken, and the various docks, ships, and cargoes suggest "trade," "commerce," and "transportation." As in *Moby-Dick*, we hear about the expedition's leader before we see him. Carl Denham (Robert Armstrong) is a theatrical producer, ruthless in his pursuit of "pictures," even under the most dangerous circumstances. He has chartered a ship called the *Venture* and its hold, curiously, is full of explosives and gas bombs. Denham wants to get underway, but he has not found what he needs most for his film: "The public, bless 'em, must have a pretty face to look at." The aggressive Denham searches Depression breadlines for the right woman. In the Bowery he sees Ann Darrow (Fay Wray) reaching for an apple from a fruitstand. The proprietor berates her, but Denham "rescues" her by paying for the fruit. The girl is well bred, and has some acting experience, so Denham promises her "the thrill of a lifetime" if she will come with him, and assures her that he has no improper interest in her. Haltingly, she agrees to sail with crew.

The second part takes place as the ship is underway. Ann seems to be enjoying the trip more than the first mate, Jack Driscoll (Bruce Cabot), who is openly hostile to women. In their first encounter, he slaps her accidentally. He apologizes to her, but insists that she does not belong on such a dangerous mission: "Women just can't help being a bother." As time goes by, however, their relationship warms. Meanwhile, Denham has told Driscoll and Captain Engelhorn (Frank Reicher) about an island west of Sumatra, in uncharted waters, where he has heard there is a huge wall, "built so long ago the people who live there now have slipped back, forgotten the higher civilization that built it." The wall is there to keep something out, "something neither beast nor man . . . monstrous, all-powerful, still living, still holding that island in a grip of deadly fear. . . . I tell you there's something on that island that no white man has ever seen. . . . If it's there, you bet I'll photograph it." He gives Ann Darrow a screen test on the shipdeck, coaching her to react in fear to an invisible assailant.

In part 3, the ship reaches what they now call "Skull Island." Through the dense fog, the crew hears the sound of drums. At daybreak, a party lands on the island, and sees the wall: "it might almost be Egyptian. . . . Who do you suppose could have built it?" Denham exclaims: "What a chance! What a picture!" Soon, they see a group of blacks dancing in a rite that seems to center around a young girl with garlands around her neck. Denham shouts out: "Holy mackerel! What a show!" Ann shouts, "I want to see," and pushes forward from the protective men around her. Denham says "If I could only get a picture of that before they see us." Soon the chief (Noble Johnson) stops the dancing. The witchdoctor (Steve Clemento) has complained that the Americans' presence has spoiled the ceremony. The captain, who by chance knows their dialect, tries to placate the chief, who is now demanding Ann as the sacrificial object, to be exchanged for six black women. To this offer, Denham says "Yeah, blondes are pretty scarce around here," and signals a slow retreat to the boats.

Ann and Jack declare their love for each other that night: "I'm scared for you"—Jack says—"I sort of guess I'm scared of you, too." Reluctantly, they kiss. Soon afterwards, two blacks abduct Ann from the ship. Jack, discovering her absence, organizes a rescue party armed with guns. Meanwhile, the blacks have substituted Ann for the girl in the rite. Now decked with garlands, Ann has been strapped to a high altar beyond the wall and abandoned there. Watching from the wall's ramparts and gates, the chief hits a giant gong, invoking Kong, who approaches the stone columns to which Ann has been tied. She screams, in earnest now, as Kong takes her into the primeval jungle.

The rescue party forces its way past the gates into a realm of prehistoric creatures. Denham says: "If I could only bring back one of these alive." Some of his men are eaten by a plesiosaurus, others fall into a deep ravine as Kong shakes them off of a tree trunk they have been using as a bridge. Soon Kong is taking Ann up to his cliffside lair. Jack follows him there, arranging that Denham should return to the ship for help.

Jack, by lucky timing, rescues Ann from Kong's dwelling. They swim back to the beach, pursued by Kong, who devastates the village in his wake. Denham shouts, "We came here to get a moving picture, and we've found something worth more than all the movies in the world . . . if we can capture him alive." Finally, Denham is able to immobilize the ape with gas bombs. He stands over the fallen ape's hulk and says, "Why the whole world will pay to see this. . . . We'll give him more than chains. He's always been king of his world, but we'll teach him fear. . . . We're millionaires, boys."

In the fourth part, Denham is seen backstage at a Broadway theater with Ann and Jack, telling reporters about the "eighth wonder of the world" he is about to unveil. He tells the first-night audience: "I'm going to show you the greatest thing your eyes have ever beheld. He was king and a god in the world he knew. But now he comes to civilization, merely a captive, a show, to gratify your curiosity." The curtain rises, and the terrified crowd sees Kong standing on a huge platform, restrained by a halter around his neck and chained to steel crossbars by the wrists.

Denham tells the photographers to take the first pictures of Kong in captivity, but as the flashbulbs go off, Kong stirs, thinking they are harming Ann. He breaks free and searches New York for Ann, causing death and havoc. He finds her in an upper-story hotel room and takes her from Jack while he is still unconscious. Perhaps mistaking it for a tree, he climbs the Empire State Building with Ann in his hand. Jack suggests that the police try to shoot him down. Kong, now at the top of the building, puts Ann on a ledge and fights off the planes, but in vain. Six fighters attack him repeatedly with machine guns; he falls off the building and dies. Jack climbs to embrace Ann while Denham stands over the fallen ape's corpse delivering the final lines: "It wasn't the airplanes. It was beauty killed the beast."

Supplying the Omitted Plots

One of the more interesting aspects of this synopsis is that it betrays immediately the contradictions and instabilities of the presumably "happy" ending. Whose story is it? Certainly for Ann Darrow the narrative ends happily: she has gone from a solitary Bowery existence to her lover's arms atop the Empire State Building, and has achieved no small degree of fame in the process. Similarly, the lure of beauty has taken Jack from the sea and promised him a blissful domesticity. But in the end, the relationship between Ann and Jack survives only at the cost of an execution. The narrative pleasure of seeing the (white) male–female bond reestablished at the end tends to screen out the full meaning of the final shot: the accidental (black) intruder lies bloody and dead on the ground, his epitaph given glibly by the very person who has trapped him. Kong's plot has the least happy ending of all. As we shall see in D. W. Griffith's *The Birth of a Nation* (1915), a desired political end (the erasure of the black/savage from white/civilized society) has been represented in a plot that gives it a justification that seems necessary for narrative reasons (the reconciliation of the white marriage unit). For whose sins, then, did King Kong die?

The story of King Kong becomes comprehensible only if we replace what has been left unsaid, and refuse to be diverted by the familiar mechanics of the "love plot." It is no accident that Denham is the keenest proponent of the "love angle" on the events he has brought about. From the beginning, he has explained Ann's presence by the need for there to be a "beauty" if there is to be a "beast," and at every juncture until Kong's death, he underlines the "beauty and the beast" notion. His interpretation is supported by the opening titles, with their relation of "an Arab proverb" that claims that once the beast disarms himself in the face of beauty, he is as good as dead. The opening moments of the film, then, predispose the spectator to accept Denham's platitudinous reading of the film. But, as we learn during the film, Denham is anything but a reliable and disinterested commentator. An alternative reading would suggest that the film is not about Jack and Ann, or about Kong's actions, but really more about the motives and effects of Carl Denham's deeds—

all the more so, since he is the only character who remains unchanged from beginning to end, and is throughout the tale the driving force behind the plot's events. What, then, is the deeper nature of his "venture"?

On a purely film historical level, we could call *King Kong* an autobiographical, self-referential film, and not be too far from the mark. Cooper and Schoedsack met under trying circumstances in a foreign country, and seemed bent on repeating that initial experience on film. Their early film careers took them on dangerous expeditions to bring back, not animal skins or precious artifacts, but pictures of exotic subjects. Their joint ventures *Grass* (1925) and *Chang* (1927), filmed respectively in Iran and Thailand, still count as milestones in the ethnographic film tradition. While *Grass,* almost in spite of its makers' efforts, ended up as a more or less straight ethnographical document, in *Chang,* Cooper and Schoedsack manage to integrate a preconceived plot with location shooting (to the detriment of the film's ethnographic value).[6] While on another expedition in Africa, they came up with the idea of a film involving many of the elements of *King Kong,* although their first idea was—incredibly—to make the film in Africa without the use of any special photography. Many incidents in the film, including the "discovery" of Ann Darrow in the Bowery, were based on actual events. According to one source, Cooper told the scriptwriter, Ruth Schoedsack (his collaborator's wife): "Put *us* in it. . . . Give it the spirit of a real Cooper–Schoedsack expedition."[7] Moreover, Cooper and Schoedsack used the same secrecy and tantalizing advertising about *King Kong* the film that the fictional Denham uses to promote King Kong, "the eighth wonder of the world," and the creature also makes a rather striking debut on the stage of a large Broadway theater. In fact, one of Cooper's publicity gambits involved placing large cannons at the entrances to the theaters where *King Kong* was showing, with placards reading "this theater is armed to defy King Kong." Possibly, then, Denham's coup fulfills the imaginary desire of the Cooper–Schoedsack type of moviemaker, and also the imaginary fear of the horror movie audience: instead of bringing back pictures, Denham brings back the real thing.

Plot One: Blackness Captured

On a more deeply historical level, we discern the first stage of what I called earlier "the political plot." Let us rewrite the plot in the form of a question: what happens when an entrepreneur engages on a "venture" to capture certain views of what he calls a "lower" civilization? Denham's adventure resembles any one of a number of forays to Europeans to non-European nations in search of animals, minerals, artifacts, photographs— and even human beings. The moral of the tale might concern what happens when "savages" are brought back into "civilization" for profit. Recall that although at the beginning of the film, Denham's explicit purpose is only to take pictures, it is not long until he begins to think of taking things, and soon after, he gets what he wants, as a merely natural continuation of visual forms of capture. A sort of *optical colonization* precedes and prepares for an actual one. *King Kong* cleverly distorts the metaphorical connection between Denham's journey and the European-American trade in African slaves by setting the story in the Pacific, "west of Sumatra," and yet portraying the islands not as Malays, but as "Oceanic Negroids."[8] As an allegory of the slave trade, then, and of various other forms of exploitation and despoilment, Denham's journey might be expected to resemble what we already know about Europe's encounters with traditional (and, in this case, African) peoples.

The ambitions of the *Venture*'s crew and leader evoke ideals at the heart of the West's economic success and psychological self-esteem. The ship, as we learn in the first few minutes, is leaving with dangerous "cargo" (dynamite, guns, and bombs), and will likely return with tamed "cargo" (in the event, black cargo). This transaction is the very definition of "trade," and no less of the slave trade. Hence, Denham's expedition, eccentric on the surface, is intimately linked (as in the establishing shots of New York Harbor) with the centers of world trade, and the very authority of American commerce and enterprise. He has an inherent right to go to other cultures and interfere in their affairs, as long as his plans work out. He is just trying to make an honest return on his backers' venture capital.

The assumption about the white male's "other"—other races, women—is that they will remain passive means to Denham's ends. The venturers make a clear separation between "lower cultures" and "higher cultures," and jump to the racist conclusion that the island's great wall could not possibly have been built by "the [black] people who live there." Despite their sense of separateness from the "native" population, the *Venture*'s crew enlists its aid when it is expedient (when, for example, Kong storms the walls looking for Ann): "Good work!" Captain Englehorn shouts at the blacks. Yet the arrogance of the crew toward these "ethnics" is more than just a reprehensible attitude. Historically (in slavery and colonialism) as in this film, such attitudes culminate in the often successful attempt to humble, humiliate, or even annihilate the victim. Recall Denham's words just after Kong has succumbed to the gas grenades: "He's always been the king of his world, but we'll teach him fear." Reading Kong as a captive, Denham's pleasure in showing Kong off on a stage platform (in every sense, an "auction block") takes on a certain historical pungency.

Women, similarly to blacks, appear not as people or potential partners, but as objects of others' stares, a sort of visual capital. Remember that, despite Ann's early fears, Carl Denham's interest in her is not even remotely sexual. In fact, his contempt for women in the film is only matched by Jack Driscoll's. The nonsexual, homocentric impulses of the leading men, left unchecked, will eventually destroy the fabric of society as certainly as King Kong would destroy its exterior. Carl is obsessed with money, orally aggressive, and visually avaricious (greedy for things to see and photograph); Jack mistrusts women and desires solitude or, at best, all-male companionship. Carl's interest in Ann is purely economic, not personal—her blonde hair, blue eyes, and fair skin qualify her for his preconceived "beauty and the beast" scenario. Soon, one sees that the misogyny of the males (Jack and Carl) threatens the continuance of a potential white marital bond more surely than King Kong's infatuation with Ann.

The visual design of the film itself encourages a strict separation and hierarchy of blacks and whites: the black "natives" receive the kind of cinematic *marking* of "jungle blacks" that we have seen elsewhere, and which films like *King Kong* and *Tarzan, the Ape Man* (made the year before) helped canonize. We already know what can be expected from the Skull Islanders, as they are coded in advance for their later demise. Blacks' function here is literally that of "props" (derived from "stage properties"): figuratively owned by the whites' appropriating "look"; soon to be literally owned through various modes of exploitation. They are well "directed" in the film, and provide the "jungle film"—no less than the grass huts or the wall or the palm trees—with its indispensable and unchanging background. The first marking is an auditory one: drums. Since the *Venture's* crew arrives at the island in fog, they actually *hear* the island and its blacks before they *see* it. *King Kong's* score (composed by Max Steiner) is a virtual handbook for aural coding, managing to convey in Wagnerian-style leitmotifs the semantics of particular scenes. Cooper was not exaggerating when he claimed that as much as a quarter of the film's overall effectiveness came from Steiner's music. The creature's horrific growlings and the orchestral climaxes vie with each other in trying to convey in sound the extreme transgressions of normality on the screen. Steiner's coding of blackness by "the drum" founds (in the relatively youthful art of synchronized movie sound) a longstanding cinematic device—though it was seldom used as subtly as it is here.

Later, we see the blacks in their ritual dance. For a 1933 screen audience, black skin was a code for limited narrative range. Blackness in such a context could not but mean "the primitive," "the elemental," as well as "the marginal," the "unproductive." So the blackness of the South Pacific islanders serves a semiotic function, introducing us, as it were, to the most primitive human beings before we later encounter the most primitive flora and fauna (foremost of these fauna, Kong himself!). The islanders' facial paint, shields, spears, headdresses, and lack of clothing are physical markings that restrict their potential for narrative action: we suspect that, like Kong, they are futureless: they will either disappear and perish or be forced to serve or entertain those who have "rescued" them.

The filmic marking of the islanders as small-scale surrogates for Kong—whose mass seems to have absorbed the conglomerate blackness of his worshipers—becomes even clearer when one notes that some of the blacks in the ritual have made themselves up in Kong-like skins. In Western culture, the literary and historical tendency to identify blacks with ape-like creatures is quite clear and has been well documented. A willed misreading of Linnaean classification and Darwinian evolution helped buttress an older European conception (tracing from as early as the sixteenth century) that blacks and apes, kindred denizens of the "jungle," are phylogenetically closer and sexually more compatible than blacks and whites: "the Negro-ape connection served as a sufficiently indirect means by which the white man could express his dim awareness of the sexual animal within himself."[9] Merian Cooper's actual words to Fay Wray take on new meaning against this background. She asked him for some information about who her leading man in his new project (Cooper was being much like Carl Denham, quite secretive) would be. Cooper could only promise her that she would be playing opposite "the tallest, darkest leading man in Hollywood."[10] Indeed, in the film, Carl Denham's description of Kong as "neither beast nor man" might serve as a racist's description of the black person.

In light of the issues discussed above, one might read *King Kong* as a way of dealing with the question: what is the worst that can happen, now that the monster-savage has come into civilization? America, in the midst of the Great Depression in the early 1930s, was already undergoing profound traumas, and several have suggested that King Kong's rampage through the streets of Manhattan "served to release the pent-up anger and frustration and fear of the millions who had been pitched headlong into the Great Depression. . . . A rampaging gorilla . . . scales [the] bastion of capitalism, the Empire State Building."[11] There were racial as well as economic tensions in the North, however. Black migration from the South to the North doubled between 1920 and 1930 as compared to the previous decade. The race riots of the early 1920s (many of them in the North) still hovered in the collective memory, their recurrence an ever-present possibility. In divergent but equally insistent ways, the Harlem Renaissance and the first Scottsboro trial (1931) kept the unsolved question of race at the forefront of white attention, even as whites often attempted to ignore the presence of the black. So for audiences in 1933, and presumably ever since, the image of an amorous black ape running amok in New York City with a white woman he has abducted must indeed have addressed on some profound level the question of how to deal with the "cargo" that the twin imperatives of trade and greed have caused to be imported from the non-Western world.

Plot Two: Endangered Women

A second and related political plot involves the use of the figure of the woman as a justification for various kinds of subterfuge and violence. As we have seen, *King Kong* diverges from typical adventure plots both by including a woman on the voyage and by bringing the monster back. Both variations allow related ideological propositions to be advanced. Ann Darrow ("the girl") has more in common with King Kong than it seems at first. If Kong is objectified blackness ("beastliness" in the white aesthetic), then the girl is objectified beauty—both are "freed" from a lowly state, but must then "serve" Denham's design. They only exist to satisfy the male viewer's active and erotic look. Denham's wish to see what "no white man has ever seen" testifies to a peculiar sort of cross-racial voyeurism, ostensibly shared by the spectator he serves, particularly given the way in which he plans to excite the black ape by teasing his appetites with the "bait" of the grid (the film's German title of the film, *King Kong und die weisse Frau*, "King Kong and the White Woman," conveys what is at stake with greater explicitness than the English). Just as Kong and the natives are coded for their blackness ("primitiveness," "earthiness"), the woman is "coded for strong visual impact so that [she] can be said to connect *to-be-looked-at-ness*."[12] For Denham, the value of the beast and the girl lies only in their juxtaposition, a combination based on preexisting sexual and visual conventions in Western iconography—a positioning that for most of the film threatens to destroy the girl, and that does (as the opening titles already reveal) finally annihilate Kong.

But the coding of Ann's body goes even further. She is not just "beauty," but also "endangered beauty." Freud might locate a certain sadomasochistic nucleus in Denham's desire to see the "girl" molested or at least scared out of her wits by a black ape representing remorseless phallic potency. But these drives are not confined to Denham's case: instances of the endangered woman pervade the history of Hollywood film. The agents threatening the woman are often, if not always, black, then coded as representatives of darkness. If the covert result of endangered beauty is to furnish the spectator with a certain illicit titillation, the overt result, as here, is to elicit the attention—and usually, the violent retribution—of the white male. Only a violent abduction of the girl by two blacks (small-scale surrogates for Kong, who later abducts her himself) can shock Jack out of his male-centered fancies and into an active concern for the heterosexual bond.

The girl has several other functions on this particular voyage. As we have seen, the film uses her as the center of erotic energy, thereby diverting both visual and intellectual attention from the purposes of Denham's trip. For the audience at least, she offers a secondary rationalization for Denham's theft of Kong. The reasoning would be: the blacks (and later, Kong) have stolen the girl, and therefore Denham is justified in stealing Kong (and anything else he wants to take) in return. True to form, Denham does not even use this justification, because he sees the removal of Kong not as theft, but as a good business proposition. In any case, the viewer's attention focuses on the danger that the girl seems to be in, while overlooking the actual dangers to which Kong (blacks) is being exposed. As opposed to the graphic display of the blacks' acts of theft, the film's discourse completely ignores the "removal" of Kong to New York. The film leaves out, as it were, the entire slave trade, the voyage, and the two hundred years of slavery in the New World. It goes straight from the African "discovery" to the American "insurrection."

The silencing of the plots sketched out above takes place on the level of filmic diegesis. One simply refuses to notice these concerns, swept along by the techniques of smooth closure and suture at which film practice had, by 1933, become very adept.[13]

Plot Transformations: Spreading the Guilt

I would like to outline three ways in which the political plots are transformed, and suggest why these transformations are so effective. The first transformation, as we have seen, subsumes all sense of political reality beneath the "love plot." The second engages the spectator in a series of fantasized visual exchanges that loosens the initially heavily coded oppositions of black/white, female/male, savage/civilized, beast/human. This temporary suspension of racial and sexual fixity only makes them seem even more necessary once the viewer returns to more ordinary reality. The third transformation makes the narrative of Denham's conquests into a story about *seeing,* and thereby draws us into a necessary complicity with its imperatives.

The rhetorical problem of the monster film is to elicit the spectator's guilty participation in a number of normally repressed fantasies, and to project the viewer's sense of guilt onto the otherness that the monster represents. The manipulation of the spectator occurs through the usage of the coding measures outlined above, but as key moments, film also manipulates point of view as a way of suggesting identifications that will have an ideological effect later. Part of the pleasure of the cinema, after all, is the sense it gives us of spatial ubiquity and authority (a sense that Lacan, at least, would term "imaginary"). At times, as in a novel, the spectator is placed in the film by an omniscient point of view, at times by a character, at times by both, and at times steps completely out of the filmic point of view (the spectator then realizes he or she is in a theater, watching a film). The spectator's place "is a construction of the text which is ultimately the product of the narrator's disposition towards the tale."[14] It is not true that we identify only with those in a film whose race or sex we share. Rather, the filmic space is subversive in allowing an almost polymorphically perverse oscillation between possible roles, creating a radically broadened freedom of identification. But this freedom only increases the guilt that comes from looking at that which should remain hidden.

For the white male viewer, the forceful and successful Carl Denham and perhaps even the "love interest" Jack Driscoll are obvious locations of identification. Black male viewers might identify in an alienated way with Denham's authority, experiencing their identification with that authority almost as a compensation for their submission in real life to similar authorities. Women viewers might not find Ann as "ideal" a "model" as Denham does. Her sniffling timidity and incessant screaming grate on one's sensibilities, yet they are only extreme versions of behavioral codes that here and elsewhere connote female weakness. The weakness of the female, as we have seen, provides the chance for males to test and confirm the range of their strength.

Ann's terror, if not her reactions to her terror, is believable enough. Through her, white male and female viewers experience fear and passivity vicariously, although for a black spectator, her position—being terrorized by blackness—could only be shared with the greatest psychic conflict.

If Robin Wood's paradigm is correct, then the figure of King Kong would allow the white male to vent a variety of repressed sexual fantasies: the hidden desire of seeing himself as an omnipotent, phallic black male; the desire to abduct the white woman; or the combined fantasy: to abduct a white woman in the disguise of a phallic black male. Barthes suggests that bourgeois society's initial response to otherness is either to ignore it, to deny it, or to assimilate its privileges and trappings, albeit at a safe distance.[15] But that assimilation of otherness, particularly if it releases repressed desires, is brief, and comes at the cost of increased guilt, a guilt that is often discharged in the oppression of the other. Kong's ultimate punishment (public execution by firing squad) seems an expression of this dynamic. The ending, then, would have different effects on different viewers. A white male viewer might sense in Kong's death a cleansing of his previous identification with the beast. A black viewer might not only reject the price Kong pays for his own "guilt," but also would wonder why there is no price to be paid by Kong's explorers.

As we have seen, there is a tenderness about the ape, which would imply that it has absorbed all aspects of otherness: not only the black male, but also the female. The black spectator, while free to assume any position in the film, would need to contain temporarily a wrenching ambivalence about its white-centered discourse—one that connects exclusionary or debasing signifieds to the black's chief signifier of skin color—since it is from this discourse that the narrative pleasures of the film derive. Identifying with Kong would bring similar pleasures to black audiences as to white viewers, but it would be less easy for a black viewer, in most cases, to shrug off Kong's demise and death and to replace it with the image of the happily unified white couple.

The camera's visual rhetoric facilitates an almost promiscuous violation of social roles and limits: monster/human; woman/male; savage/civilized; black/white. By various exchanges of glances, looks, and camera angles, a space of mixed identity soon arises, exchanging and connecting our (here, the camera's) "look" with the viewpoints of normally discrete subjects. For example, the film tends to pose threats to the girl from the left-hand side of the frame, with the girl on the right. And the film's (as well as the publicity posters') basic black–white confrontations involve blackness threatening whites from the left: the first landing; Ann's kidnapping from the boat; King Kong's first approach to her on the sacrificial altar. Yet during the screen test on the boat, whites threaten Ann in the same way: Denham, on the left, photographs Ann, on the right. The series of shots that follow (close-up of Denham; Ann sends a mock scream in the direction of Denham's camera, and us) exactly anticipates the sequence that occurs when Kong later approaches her (close-up of Kong; Ann sends a real scream in Kong's direction). Rather than providing us in both cases with a distanced spectatorial setup, the camera shuttles us between subjective points of view, even those of the monster: Denham's and Kong's. The ubiquitous camera has no scruples, it seems, about class, race, or even species: the *need to see* is more important, as the film progresses, than the *need to separate* or the *need to repress.*

There is one telling exception to this rule: the camera never assumes the subjective point of view of the blacks on the island (although a "third-person" view reports certain events that the white crew cannot have witnessed). Given their absurd behavior and witless manner, identification with them would require an emotional generosity that most white spectators simply could not muster (perhaps a few black spectators would be able to separate the actual black actors from the degraded roles they assume).

Perhaps the most difficult transformation to resist is our gradual implication in Denham's optical colonialism. Even a viewer repulsed by Denham's many negative qualities would have difficulty escaping the pull of his powerful voyeurism, or the way in which his obsessive need to look at spectacles—to see things immobilized on stage or on screen—imposes on its objects not a neutral mechanical process, but a deleterious form of framing. The "capture," applicable to photography as well as the hunt, well expresses the dual aspect of framing otherness. The political ideology of the film soon becomes inextricable from the pleasure we take in the very act of seeing. The power of staging a "show" (watching a "girl" scream or "natives" dancing) is no longer Denham's alone. *King Kong*, by a rather devious movement, makes us cheer him on. Indeed, Denham frequently justifies his most ruthless wants by calling them ours: "the public, bless 'em, must have a pretty face to look at."

The ideology that the public represents would only be able to use blacks and women as something singing, dancing, or otherwise "to be looked at." We never question Denham's right to "pick up" the girl, or to interrupt and photograph the island rite, or to abduct Kong, because it is precisely the act of photographing that defines his (and our) feeling of mastery over what we see. And only through photography have we been able to satisfy our own "need-to-see." Yet it becomes clear that for Denham, the line between importing a "show" and importing a "captive" has blurred. Recall that he introduces Kong to the New York audience as "merely a captive, a show, to gratify your curiosity." His usage of the same word, "show," for his first sight of the blacks' ritual recalls the slavery plot again: "Holy mackrel, what a show!" Black captivity is not far away.

Denham not only transforms the political plot into a plot of seeing, but he also continually changes his own definition of what seeing entails. At the beginning, he claims that he only needs a picture of "beauty," but in fact he does not photograph Ann but takes her (as he later takes Kong) into his physical possession. In a sense he has already reached his stated goal at the start of the plot: he can have both the picture of "beauty" and the real thing (Ann) herself without even leaving New York. But what he really wants (although he does not say this) is the girl's *meaning* as an ideological *code*. His picture must show her *in danger*, thus eliciting a display of "manly" protectiveness and supporting the connection between "female weakness" and "male strength." So Denham needs a photograph of the girl being threatened by King Kong. In this sense, Kong is both a part of his goal and a potential pitfall for his design.

In the event, Kong not only threatens Ann, but abducts her as well, seeming to undermine the quest for the perfect film, but in fact hastening its production. For Kong's actual abduction of the girl incites the male response better than a mere picture could. It also brings the threat itself into Denham's physical possession: now he has not only got his pictures, but he has at least two subjects—the girl and Kong—that others will pay to see and photograph, especially as a pair. Denham's obsession with seeing licenses unlimited ventures, but it can never be satiated, particularly in its specific form as the wish to see (and later possess) what "no white man has ever seen."

The momentum of the plot transforms the viewer's question "what will Carl Denham's venture exploit or destroy next?" into the question "what will I see next?"—a question that seems more harmless than the first one until one considers the close linkage among seeing, capturing, and killing that Denham's actions and the film establish. The photographers that Denham invites to Kong's "showing" threaten to restart the "seeing–capturing" cycle, and so it is no accident that at this point, Kong intervenes to stop the vicious visual cycles.

"An ethnographic film may be regarded as any film which seeks to reveal one society to another," but *King Kong*, however unflatteringly, is an ethnographic film that reveals one society to itself, or perhaps more exactly, reveals to its spectators the diversity and ambivalence of spectatorship.[16] *King Kong* teaches us that the viewer's need for spectacle and vicarious enjoyment may issue from deeper needs, ones that many people are willing to pay, steal, and even kill in order to satisfy. Denham, although his obsession is particular, would stage fantasies about generally repressed sexual, political, and historical violations. Hence, King Kong dies for everyone's sins, not just for Denham's. The general guilt inheres in the general gaze.

NOTES

1. Jean-Luc Comolli and Jean Narboni.

2. See Claude Lévi-Strauss, "The Structural Study of Myth," in *Structural Anthropology* (New York: Anchor, 1967), pp. 202–28.

3. See Robin Wood, "An Introduction to the American Horror Film," in *The American Nightmare: Essays on the Horror Film* (Toronto: Festival of Festivals, 1979).

4. See, for instance, the argument of Calvin C. Hernton's *Sex and Racism in America* (New York: Grove Press, 1966) or Joel Kovel's *White Racism: A Psychohistory* (New York: Random House, 1971), or the chapter entitled "First Impressions: Initial English Confrontations with Africans," in Winthrop D. Jordan, *White over Black: American Attitudes Towards the Negro, 1550–1812* (New York: Norton, 1968).

5. Editors of *Cahiers du cinéma*, "John Ford's *Young Mr. Lincoln*," in *Movies and Methods*, vol. 1, ed. Bill Nichols (Berkeley: University of California Press, 1976), p. 496.

6. See David MacDougall's article, "Beyond Observational Cinema," in *Principles of Visual Anthropology*, ed. Paul Hockings (The Hague: Mouton, 1975).

7. Orville Goldner and George E. Turner, *The Making of King Kong: The Story Behind a Film Classic* (New York: A. S. Barnes, 1975), p. 78.

8. Ibid., p. 38.

9. Jordan, *White over Black*, p. 491.

10. Goldner and Turner, *The Making of King Kong*, p. 68.

11. Robert Walker, "*King Kong* (1933)," *Cinema Texas: Program Notes* 7, no. 7 (September 12, 1974): 2.

12. Laura Mulvey, "Visual Pleasure and the Narrative Cinema," *Screen* 16, no. 3 (Autumn 1975).

13. Daniel Dayan, "The Tutor-Code of Classical Cinema," in Nichols, *Movies and Methods*, vol. 1, pp. 449–51.

14. Nick Browne, "The Spectator-in-the-Text: The Rhetoric of *Stagecoach,*" *Film Quarterly* 34, no. 2 (Winter 1975–76).

15. Roland Barthes, *Mythologies,* trans. Annette Lavers (New York: Hill and Wang, 1972), pp. 151–52.

16. David MacDougall, "Prospects of the Ethnographic Film," *Film Quarterly* 23, no. 2 (Winter 1969–70).

Thomas Cripps

"Race Movies" as Voices of the Black Bourgeoisie: *The Scar of Shame*

The depiction of African Americans in Hollywood movies is so well known as to be overstated. One observer of the phenomenon described it in the title of his book: *Toms, Coons, Mulattoes, Mammies, and Bucks.* Unfortunately, in their eagerness to cast blacks as the victims of Hollywood cupidity, some critics present them as passive lambs in an abattoir.

Throughout the history of American movies, blacks with uneven success pressed moviemakers to alter their conceptions of the black characters who appeared on the screen. One of the tactics that persisted throughout the period between the World Wars was the production of "race movies" for the consumption of black Americans.[1] Oftentimes these movies were the products of interracial and even white companies with a good ear and eye for the social and aesthetic concerns of blacks.

Because these movies were tailor-made for a specific audience, they often precisely reflected an authentic black morality, social ethic, and point of view. *The Scar of Shame* (1927), a product of a white-owned Philadelphia studio shrewdly named the Colored Players, provides one of the best examples of a movie intended to convey black middle-class social values to a black urban audience.

Race movies grew to maturity simultaneously with the growth of northern black urban ghettos. The coincidence of visual medium of expression and growing audience contributed to the development of race movies into a distinct genre. Almost every race movie, in spite of its surface melodrama, presented black audiences with sharply etched messages of advocacy, aspiration, group unity, and slogans against racism. *The Scar of Shame* not only stated the messages, but also laid the blame for black misfortune at the door of poor environment.

Thus *The Scar of Shame* provides the historian not only with a work of popular art but also with a document through which to study

From *American History/American Film*, ed. John E. O'Connor and Martin A. Jackson (New York: Ungar, 1979). Used by permission of the author.

the social thrust of a cohesive group who shared a common core of values. In order to appraise the significance of such artifacts they must be seen as tiles in a mosaic—that is, as coherent message units set in larger contexts that impart more sophisticated layers of meaning.

The Scar of Shame, and for that matter, all race movies, appeared at the end of a quarter of a century of a black diaspora that spread outward from southern farms to northern cities. Indeed, it could be said that race movies signaled the maturing of the consciousness of this black northern audience, at once more urbane and wealthier than southern blacks, and more important, heavily concentrated in a mass capable of supporting a small film industry. The resulting movies were made for a black audience that had grown in both size and self-consciousness. Therefore the films often depicted half-hidden internal social forces at work within black society. It is through this interaction between moviemaker and presumed audience that the messages are created through which the historian may view group values such as those that permeate *The Scar of Shame*.

In the especially violent decade of the 1890s the black urban migration began in earnest. The white South had seemed to grow more race-conscious than ever. The Mississippi and South Carolina constitutions of 1890 and 1895 provided models for disfranchising southern black voters while at the same time the growing incidence of racial violence moved beyond individual lynchings toward proto-military actions such as the Wilmington race riot of 1898. The press and the pulpit joined in proclaiming a revival of southern white aggression against blacks.[2]

Between 1900 and 1920, black flight from the South became a social protest movement against this racial savagery. Pushed out by southern pressures and pulled northward by northern labor agents, by invitations from such black newspapers as the *Chicago Defender*, and by the promise of higher wages in industrial cities, southern blacks moved to northern cities. In those twenty years black Chicago alone grew more than threefold, from thirty thousand to over one hundred thousand. Similar figures marked the growth of Darktowns, Bronzevilles, and Harlems in ten other northern cities.[3]

Blacks were transformed by the experience from a southern peasantry into a northern proletariat. The pyramid of black class structure grew into a broad, flat profile founded on a vast pool of unskilled, underemployed, recent migrants from southern farms wracked by sharecropping, boll weevils, and dustbowls. Crowded into noisome, newly formed ghettos beset by crime, violence, and squalor were the disaffiliated, dislocated, untutored, unadaptable southerners who threatened the status of "the old settlers," whose skills had allowed them to eke out stable, if petty, bourgeois lives founded on jobs in proximity to white centers of power and authority. In order to restore the old order the old settlers would have to teach the newcomers "respectable" ways.[4]

This is not to say that sociologists studied or even took note of this cultural basis of social class. On the contrary, as late as the 1950s, most scholars gave undue attention only to skin color as an index of stratification. For example, the distinguished student of African American social class, E. Franklin Frazier of Howard University, was a careful scholar who once broke the constraints of objectivity in a little book so intemperate in its treatment of black social class in Washington that it proved awkward to publish in America. His *Black Bourgeoisie* (1955, 1957) owed at least some of its feisty reputation to its insistence on skin color and descent from the antebellum servant class as the most telling determinants of black social class rather than more eclectic criteria such as antiquity of residence and lineage, stable employment, professional achievement, academic success, West Indian kinship, closeness to whites as in government posts or clinging to a respectable lifestyle in the face of surrounding trends toward urban decay. Frazier's tour de force diverted historians from seeing a broader basis for determining social class.[5]

Race moviemakers, the authors of movies like *The Scar of Shame*, took a broader view of class and tried to pass on their values to their audiences. The literati of the Harlem Renaissance probably included the respectables in their audiences, but certainly not the newly arrived southerners. Indeed, many black poets and novelists owed their prominence to white patrons and readers with a taste for Negro art. Poor blacks shared little of the literary ferment because of their illiteracy, resistance to urban ways, and isolation from such old-line black institutions as the church. Even black newspapers offered little to the new folk other than advertisements for seers and numerological "dreambooks" that promised "hits" in the daily illegal lottery. The columns ran to heavy fare by the intellectuals, W. E. B. Du Bois, Carter Woodson, and Kelly Miller. Only J. A. Rogers' history in cartoon form reached for a popular audience. Clearly, if the old respectables were to reach the newcomers with a usable set of urban values, movies would be the vehicle, much as visually graphic vaudeville had once spoken to illiterate new immigrants from Europe.[6]

Parallel to the northward migration, blacks developed a new racial consciousness based on a loss of faith in the goals of Reconstruction, the consequent belief that ghettos were permanent fixtures, and the realization that ambition was possible only within a segregated black world. In this social system, the unchurched, untutored, and unaffiliated could expect little, and rewards accrued to those who learned a skill, cultivated a talent, or provided a service in exchange for a steady, but modest, return. The urban bourgeoisie saw deviations from norms of rectitude as temptations that, if heeded, would cast them into the pit of failure, crime, and improvidence where they would live off women and the public dole. In short, the black bourgeoisie feared becoming lower class, while those on the bottom felt contempt for the middle class's apparent emulation of white social values. Ethel Waters remembered that after her mother became a live-in domestic servant, "she stopped living colored" and despaired of her children who "knew nothing and cared nothing about the better side of life" she had seen as a servant to whites.[7]

By the mid-1920s, those at the top of the middle class became race leaders and self-conscious tutors of—as Booker T. Washington had indirectly described him—"the man farthest down." Alain Locke, a black Harvardian and Rhodes Scholar, described this new leader in his brilliantly edited volume, *The New Negro,* which had grown from the famous "Harlem number" (March 1925) of *Survey Graphic* magazine. If this new Negro had a proximate enemy, it was not white racism but Marcus Garvey, the West Indian whose charismatic Universal Negro Improvement Association threatened to win the black proletariat away from the tutelage of race leaders. Most race moviemakers shared the concern for the uplift of the black lower class and hoped to blunt the threat of Garveyism. Indeed, at the end of the silent era two race movies, *Marcus Garland* and *The Black King* (1932), parodied Garvey as a mountebank who exploited the weakness of the black lower class.[8]

The Scar of Shame and every other race movie of the 1920s retailed a black bourgeois success myth, a manual for those on the make, and a caution to the weak-willed who might be diverted from success by urban temptations. Like a typical Horatio Alger hero, the black hero discovered success rather than plodded toward it. Perhaps because the southern blacks who were the prospective audiences expected little from the puritanical work ethic and its promise of success, the quick score seemed a more plausible myth. This black myth included tales of discoveries of bonanzas, sports triumphs, the virtues of rural life, and good–bad kids who are redeemed by the benefits of a healthful environment. In only a few cases is credulity strained by having blacks succeed after working hard. In a racist society, luck always seemed to matter more than pluck.

Among the sports legends was *As the World Rolls On* (Andlauer, 1921) in which boxer Jack Johnson teaches a plucky boy both boxing and baseball so that in the last reel he may pitch a game for the all-black Kansas City Monarchs. A year later Johnson himself played a resourceful lad who learns to box in order to win money to pay restitution for his brother's crime in *For His Mother's Sake* (Blackburn Velde, 1922). Boxers Sam Langford and Tiger Flowers also used the fight game as a vehicle for success myths, while black cowboy Bill Pickett starred in *The Bull-Dogger* (Norman, 1923) as a demonstration that "the black cowboy is capable of doing anything the white cowboy does." In at least three more race movies of the 1920s athletic prowess contributed to heroic attainment.[9]

Bonanzas taken from high-risk extractive industries provided another fanciful alternative to conventional success stories. Romances of prospecting, mining, and wildcatting for oil were the most often used. In

Absent (Rosebud, 1928) a miner and his daughter help a shell-shocked veteran begin a new life. The hero of *The Realization of a Negro's Ambition* (Lincoln, 1916) is a graduate engineer from Tuskegee who strikes oil on his father's farm after losing a job with an oil company because of his race, a denouement similar to that of *The Symbol of the Unconquered* (Micheaux, 1920). The heroes of Oscar Micheaux's *The Dungeon* (1922) and *Smiling Hate* (Superior, 1924) both strike gold in Alaska.

The next best prize was a farm; it provided a source of wealth and symbolized the deep roots that were proof against the demoralization of urban life. In *The Law of Nature* (Lincoln, 1917), for example, the heroine deserts her rancher-husband and child for the high life back East, only to learn in the last reel to prefer the richness of life on the farm. Micheaux's first movie, *The Homesteader* (1919), extolled life on the prairie; *The Colored American Winning His Suit* (Douglass, 1919) used land as the source of tuition for children to attend Spelman and Howard; the hero of *The Virgin and the Seminole* (Micheaux, 1922) uses his reward earned as a Canadian Mountie to buy a ranch; and Micheaux's *The Millionaire* (1927) grows rich ranching on the Argentine Pampas. A treasure map substituted for bonanzas and ranches in at least one movie, Norman's *Regeneration* (1923).[10]

The black hero rarely took up a career that demanded rigorous training; in real life the odds against such black accomplishment were too long. While it is true that characters in *Birthright* (Micheaux, 1924) went to Harvard, in *The Colored American Winning His Suit* to Howard and Spelman, in *The Realization of a Negro's Ambition* to Tuskegee, and the heroes of *Within Our Gates* (Micheaux, 1920), *The Burden of Race* (Reol, 1921), *By Right of Birth* (Lincoln, 1921), and *A Giant of His Race* (North State, 1921) benefited from professional training, eventual fulfillment came not from practicing their craft but from a lucky stroke or a single event like a gusher. *The Trooper of Troop K* (Lincoln, 1916) bumbles through life until he becomes a hero at the battle of Carrizal. Lawyers make it by winning a single case, as in *The Colored American Winning His Suit* and *A Shot in the Night* (North State, 1922).

Occasionally a race movie, such as *Secret Sorrow* (Reol, 1923), contrasted the lives of a good kid and a bad kid as a means of demonstrating that environment, and not race, predicted success. One son, raised in squalor by his poor mother, turned wrong, while the other, adopted by a prosperous doctor, became a New York assistant district attorney.[11]

Artists and scientists also achieved single triumphs. The hero of *A Giant of His Race,* a doctor—the child of slaves who has struggled through medical school driven by an urge "to uplift his people"—strikes a bonanza when "yellow plague" visits his village, forcing him to spend days in his lab affecting a cure that brings him a $100,000 prize. In *The Schemers* (Reol, 1922), a "struggling young chemist" attains wealth when he discovers a substitute for gasoline, a story paralleled in the serial, *Zircon* (Norman, 1923). In black movies novelists, filmmakers, bidders for mail contracts, dealers in Brazilian coffee, preachers, detectives, song-and-dance men, and musicians all succeeded not through accrual of achievements but through the luck and pluck of Alger's *Jed the Poorhouse Boy* (1899).[12]

The race moviemakers' urge to raise up race pride gave character to their work and distinguished it from white films. Sometimes therefore, plots turned on the plight of light-skinned people whose black identities seethed below a lifelong camouflage of white skin—a condition that inspired themes of racial pride that grew out of dramatic last-reel revelations. Many of Oscar Micheaux's films were tangled in such dual identities. In *The Homesteader* (1919), the first film of Micheaux's prolific, quarter-of-a-century career, Baptiste, the hero, wins the heart of a "Scottish" girl only to learn in the last reel that she is a Negro. The same plot twist recurred in his 1920s films *Symbol of the Unconquered, Birthright, The House Behind the Cedars,* and *Thirty Years Later,* always with the result that the hero "becomes proud of his race." Micheaux's rivals took up the issue with equal vigor. In *Loyal Hearts* (Democracy, 1919), the heroes with patronizing tolerance learn to "accept their own people," a denouement shared by *In the Depths of Our Hearts* (Royal Garden, 1920) and *The Call of His People* (Reol, 1922), which ends with hero and heroine together and he "now proud to be one of her people."[13]

But if success and pride were the gospels of the "new Negro," what litanies and epiphanies could black missionaries sing in order to bring the theology to the black masses? Who was to be the black Emile Coué or Bruce Barton, the white acolytes of the success myth in the 1920s? Pivotal in the strategy was the need for a rhetoric that reached the lower class, for the respectable mercantile and meritocratic middle class had little need for more sermons on the theme of ambition, nor did their established churches encourage moviegoing. Thus if race movies were to succeed in the ghetto, their intended audience was necessarily the demoralized poor black on the block. Of all the silent race movies, *The Scar of Shame* most reflected the ambitions of these black respectables.

As early as 1916 black leaders had taken up the issue. Emmett J. Scott, private secretary to Booker T. Washington, attempted to produce a movie version of Washington's autobiography, *Up from Slavery,* as a counterforce to *The Birth of a Nation* (1915) and a celebration "not only of Dr. Washington's personal strivings, but also the strivings of the race climbing up from the tragic period represented by slavery." Like later black filmmakers, he tried to enlist the support of the respectables by appealing to the National Negro Business League. At the same time the Lincoln Motion Picture Company of Los Angeles, led by George P. and Noble Johnson, set out "to picture the Negro as . . . a human being with human inclination, and one of talent and intellect." By the 1920s a host of rivals joined the game, each claiming "to show the better side of Negro life" or "to inspire in the Negro a desire to 'climb higher.'" The black press cheered on the moviemakers, urging readers, in the words of Kennard Williams of the *Afro-American,* to give "sensible support of Negro producers like Micheaux." Lincoln all but formalized this union of moviemen and journalists by using newspapermen as promoters. "Moving pictures," said Robert I. Vann's Pittsburgh *Competitor,* one of Lincoln's hoped-for allies, "have become one of the greatest vitalizing forces in race adjustment, and we are just beginning."[14]

This is not to say race movies enjoyed universal support from black critics. The *Amsterdam News,* for example, charged white theater owners with "a mistaken idea [that] . . . they should exhibit in a colored community [without regard for] the worth of the pictures. With an opportunity of viewing the best things along picture lines, it is hard to expect colored people to accept these Micheaux pictures here in Greater New York." Reviewers insisted on uplift and on "the possibility of individual endeavor and reward of a character of the Negro race," and they took sharp issue when "the story was not elevating." One critic admonished Micheaux: "Society wants a real story of high moral aim that can appeal to the upbuilding of your race." For their part, the moviemakers did their best, but they also believed that audiences preferred "stirring melodrama," "thrilling and realistic" yarns, and lots of "action."[15]

The aesthetic guerrilla war that broke out between the respectables who demanded "uplift" and the unsophisticated moviegoers who demanded "action," may be seen in Micheaux's films of Charles Waddell Chesnutt's *The House Behind the Cedars.* Chesnutt, a staunch black Republican, a civil rights activist, and a widely praised novelist who earned a respectable living as a court stenographer, opened negotiations with Micheaux in 1920. At first Micheaux, an incredibly primitive writer, merely carped at Chesnutt's writing, which "could not very well be filmed" except as "two reel comedies." Poor Chesnutt. "They want to chop it up," he wrote, "and probably change the emphasis of certain characters." He could "only hope that it will be done with reasonable taste."[16]

Micheaux knew his audience. He wished to plunge straightaway into the story, delete expository passages in favor of visual incident, change the hero from bumpkin into a "more intelligent" figure so "the girl could have more than passing respect for him," and tack on an uplifting ending designed for the "colored people whom we must depend upon as a bulwark for our business." The result, predicted Micheaux,

> would, I am sure, in so far as our people are concerned send them out of the theater with this story lingering in their minds, with a feeling that all good must triumph in the end, and with the words "Oh! want that just wonderful [*sic*]!" instead of a gloomy muttering.

Micheaux was so satisfied with is pastiches of upbeat, affirmative ending, "action, thrills, and suspense," and a plot that hinged on concealed racial identity, that he released it in 1924 and again in 1932 as a sound film entitled *Veiled Aristocrats.* Chesnutt, on the other hand, learned that race movies were like Soviet art that served social rather than aesthetic goals. As his daughter reported: "it was not artistic like the story" and "your beautiful English and the soul of the tale were lacking."[17]

The Scar of Shame sprang from no such distinguished literary source, but its social goals sounded a familiar note. Like so many race movies, *The Scar of Shame* was interracial in origin yet took up black social concerns. Its parent firm, the Colored Players Company of Philadelphia, owed its birth to a fairly common alliance of moviemen: black ideamen and performers, white technicians and crews, and white, often Jewish, entrepreneurs.

Sherman H. "Uncle Dud" Dudley, a black veteran of vaudeville and race movies, first conceived an idea for a black Hollywood outside Washington, D.C. He had learned of films by working on *The Simp* (Reol, 1921) with black stars Edna Morton and Percy Verwayen, and "angel" Robert Levy who later backed Harlem's Lafayette Players. White Philadelphian David Starkman, owner of a black theater, dismayed observer of demeaning racial roles in Hollywood movies, and a visionary who shared Dudley's dream, assumed responsibility for operations, management, and raising capital in white Philadelphia. White journeymen Frank Perugini and Al Liguori directed and shot the film. The actors who came from race movies and black stock or commuted from chorus lines in New York included Harry Henderson, Lucia Lynn Moses, Pearl McCormick, Lawrence Chenault, and Ann Kennedy.

Gradually Starkman, a self-educated immigrant from Austria and a "little Napoleon," took over. He sold his theater, converted his wife's inheritance to cash, browbeat capital from South Philadelphia lawyers and hardware merchants, wrote scripts, and, finally, carried release prints to out-of-town play dates and counted the house in person.

The company had tested its skills with *A Prince of His Race* (1926), a social drama now lost, and with a black version of Timothy Shay Arthur's *Ten Nights in a Bar Room* (1926) starring Charles Gilpin, the original *Emperor James* in 1920. As *The Scar of Shame* went into production in 1927, Starkman became demonic, contributing his car, his sister's rooming house as a location, and even his own furniture with which he dressed the set. The effort eventually shattered him. The film opened coincidentally with the debut of sound film, an event that ruined race moviemakers burdened with inventories of silent films, stables of untrained actors, and unwired theaters. The shock changed Starkman from a little engine of ambition into a debt-ridden hanger-on who died of cancer in 1947, his marriage broken and his home foreclosed.[18]

Like many low-budget silent films, *The Scar of Shame* was probably shot without benefit of a fully developed script, which may account for the authentic tone of black social ambience. Even though the star, Lucia Lynn Moses, remembered that "I never took any directions from anybody colored; it was always the two white fellahs," she knew the life of the black respectables and wove it into her role.[19]

The Scar of Shame, as one of the few survivors of the silent era, provides us with an aspect of the new urban black class system neglected by Frazier's social anatomy, *Black Bourgeoisie* (1955, 1957). Frazier's polemic described the outward appearance but not the engine and driveshaft of the system—aspiration for education and achievement. The need to achieve inspired the broad center of black respectables who earned livelihoods in civil service, proprietorship, preaching, teaching, and social work. Not one title card in *The Scar of Shame* mentioned skin color as an index of status, citing instead a need for "the finer things, higher hopes, and higher aims" as middle-class motivations.

The burden of the message was not always evident, but clearly it never included a sermon against color caste. The heroes yearned to be hard-driving and successful black Babbitts, while the heavies compromised this ideal, sold it out for a bottle of booze, or made war on it to satisfy a criminal ambition. Dark skin and light skin were scattered throughout the ranks of the good and the evil, with, perhaps, a light-skinned bias toward the good guys merely because such a skewing reflected the ways white bias inevitably affected the realities of African American life.[20]

In 1927, blacks struggled to rise above poverty into middle-class respectability. *The Scar of Shame* affirmed and dramatized this new Negro ideal—the grasping after "the finer things, the higher hopes, and higher aims." Throughout the film, visual images symbolize this point: success symbols are good; poverty symbols are bad. Life in the parlor is good; on the street corner, bad. The message is so strong that the hero's success at the expense of his suicidal woman is seen as a tolerable price to pay for a victory over shabbiness and poverty.

From the opening in a Philadelphia ghetto, the hero, Alvin Hillyard, an ambitious black composer, is viewed by the landlady of his "select boarding house" as the eventual "greatest composer of our race." The heavy lives in the same house. Snubbed by the genteel boarders, Eddie is brash, cigar-smoking, and dressed in a loudly checked suit. He is as light-skinned as Hillyard, but his manner, style, and saloon-keeping establish him as the heavy.

The drunken Spike lives in the alley, where violence and exploitation are the rule. Louise, his daughter, who marries Hillyard in order to escape her father's brutality, is a heroine as long as she struggles to rise above the ghetto. She must choose among the three men: her dangerous and brutal father, who is broken by alcohol; Eddie, who wants to drag her into a career as a saloon singer; and Hillyard, whose ambition can pull her above the burden of poverty. She is sympathetic as long as she is the victim saved by marriage to Hillyard; she is the heavy once she accepts the compromise with success held out by Eddie's promises. Hillyard's mother symbolizes the prize in the contest. She lives in the suburbs, attended by a butler, reachable only in Hillyard's sporty roadster, as though to tell us that only through the car—the fruit of Hillyard's aspiration—can Louise reach the safe haven of suburbia. Without Hillyard she must rot in the ghetto, exploited by Eddie and beaten by her father.

The stage on which this drama is resolved is the boarding house and its windows looking out on the shabby alley. These symbolic opposites provide the setting for the cluttered plot. Hillyard saves Louise from a backyard beating at the hands of her father; marries her as insurance against future violence; and loses her to Eddie, who contrives to win her with the promise of a career on the stage. Hillyard confronts them and in the ensuing affray Louise is shot and marked by her "scar of shame." Hillyard goes to jail, escapes, and takes up the life of a piano teacher in his predestined upper-class niche. He has won the game of life by wanting it badly; Louise has lost because she sold herself cheaply. Desperately, Louise tries to blackmail Hillyard into returning to her, and when he refuses to give up his hard-won life, she poisons herself. One of her rakish lovers reads her suicide note and explains her death to the audience: "Our people," he says, "have much to learn." If only she had aspired to "the finer things" and been raised in a good "environment."

The notion that African American class consciousness was based on color will not entirely fade. Rhetorically, for example, the title cards refer frequently to "caste" when they must mean "class." Visually, when Louise chooses the saloon, she accidentally crushes her brown-skinned doll and mourns it as "a victim of caste." But these symbols only throw the viewer off the trail. By far the imagery of class conflict predominates, and "environment," not color, is seen as the determinant of social status. Low life and respectable life are seen as opposites: the boarding house versus the saloon; Hillyard's cool manners versus Eddie's oafishness; Louise's drab room versus Hillyard's with its portrait of the black Republican Frederick Douglass on the wall. Eddie sneers at Hillyard, not as a "valler" snob, but as "that dicty sap"—the slang term for *any* pretentious social climber or poseur in black circles. Finally, in the last sequence, Hillyard's musical accomplishments are positively contrasted with Louise's taking up with one of the riffraff who "hit the numbers today." In other words, Hillyard's solid accomplishment is set against Louise's settling for the fleeting thrill of a cheap score in the daily lottery. Skin color is never a matter of rhetorical debate or consistent symbolic contrast.[21] As Lucia Lynn Moses remembered her stage directions, she was thrust into her role and asked to improvise. Perugini would call her onto the set and describe the situation. "This man—you're not in the same category with him—you're not in the same league," he would say. "You take it from there."[22] That is, she was asked to play a part in a class, not a color, conflict, in which Negroes of any color were free to contend for success.

No one knows how widely or clearly *The Scar of Shame* spread its message. We have only a bit of advertising copy, some evidence that it played as far south as Virginia, and a few reviews. Apparently it was sold and portrayed as an elegant expression of the need to pursue the best of American culture without regard for race, perhaps as a spreading of the aspirations of the respectables outward to the black proletariat. The advertising claimed that "Race Film is Classic." And an *Amsterdam News* reviewer praised it as a work that "sets a new standard of excellence." Both sentiments were expressions of an assertive, optimistic, middle class speaking to the moviegoer in need of uplift.[23]

All things considered, *The Scar of Shame* exemplified the highest hopes of the black generation of the 1920s who placed faith in individual aspiration as the path to group emancipation. Unfortunately for blacks, history caught up with the modest boom that had given gloss to the ghettos of the 1920s. The Great Crash of 1929 extended into the white world an economic depression that had already tarnished black well-being. Race movies in the 1930s grew more collectivist in keeping with the New Deal mood, advocated community organization, and called for race unity. Among the best were *Am I Guilty?* (1940), which featured Ralph Cooper as a doctor who must choose between healing gangsters and opening a free clinic; *Moon over Harlem* (1939), which advocated education and cleaning up of Harlem's rackets; *Murder on Lenox Avenue* (1941), which depicted the struggle to form a "business league" on which to base a "prosperous Harlem"; and *Broken Strings* (1940), which ended with a collective effort to raise money to heal the broken hands of a black violinist.[24]

The Scar of Shame, then, remains a parametric expression of the high point of the self-conscious, individualistic, black bourgeoisie of the 1920s. That its message rang hollow testified to the unyielding forces opposed to black aspiration rather than to the inefficiency of the strategy. For historians the film is a lesson in the need to seek out evidence in every medium of expression of group spirit, and not merely to rely on the traditional media of literature and art.

NOTES

1. The handiest compendia of 1920s movie titles are Henry T. Sampson, *Blacks in Black and White: A Source Book on Black Films* (Metuchen, N.J., 1977); Kenneth W. Mundin, exec. ed., *The American Film Institute Catalog of Motion Pictures Produced in the United States,* vol. F2 (New York, 1970); Thomas Cripps, *Slow Fade to Black: The*

Negro in American Film, 1900–1942 (New York: 1977), VII, and the George P. Johnson Collection, Research Library, UCLA (available on microfilm).

2. A useful bibliography on this period is in Jack Temple Kirby, *Darkness at the Dawning: Race and Reform in the Progressive South* (Philadelphia, 1972).

3. Documents and a brief bibliography are in Richard B. Sherman, ed., *The Negro and the City* (Englewood Cliffs, N.J., 1970) and Hollis Lynch, *The Black Urban Condition* (New York, 1973).

4. This social division is carefully defined in David Gordon Nielson, *Black Ethos: Northern Urban Negro Life and Thought, 1890–1930*, "Contributions in Afro-American and African Studies, No. 29," Hollis R. Lynch, ed. (Westport, Conn., 1977), III. He finds the "respectables" constituted "80 or 90 percent" of the urban population (p. 52) that rested on a base of "undisciplined, unchurched, uneducated riff-raff" (p. 60).

5. Frazier denied that he "had written a book attacking 'upper-class, light-skinned' Negroes"; nevertheless he admitted that there were "working-class Negroes who shook my hand for having performed this long overdue service." His intention had been to show that a social system without a true upper-class imitated exogenous white norms. E. Franklin Frazier, *Black Bourgeoisie* (New York, 1957), p. 8, quoted in Nielson, *Black Ethos*, p. 176.

6. The intellectuals may be read in, for example, a survey of the *Amsterdam News.* The connection among art, the respectables, and uplift may be seen in David L. Lewis, *When Harlem Was in Vogue* (New York: Alfred A. Knopf, 1981). On literati, see Nathan Irvin Huggins, *Harlem Renaissance* (New York, 1971).

7. Ethel Waters and Charles Samuels, *His Eye Is on the Sparrow* (Garden City, N.Y., 1951), pp. 8–9, quoted in Nielson, *Black Ethos*, p. 182.

8. Alain Locke, ed., *The New Negro: An Interpretation* (New York, 1925). No print of Oscar Micheaux's *Marcus Garland* survives. See Mundin, *AFI Catalog*, p. 492, and Cripps, *Slow Fade to Black*, p. 191. Sampson, *Blacks in Black and White*, p. 137, finds *The Black King* a product of white racists although black musician Donald Heywood received credit for it. See Cripps, *Slow Fade to Black*, pp. 325–26. *The Black King* is an uneven film but the Garvey figure is brilliantly acted as a charismatic leader by A. B. Comathiere. A print is in the film collection of the University of Illinois, Urbana, Illinois.

9. Cripps, *Slow Fade to Black*, VII. Synopses appear in Mundin, *AFI Catalog*, pp. 27–28, 97, 263; Sampson, *Blacks in Black and White*, pp. 99, 115–16, 112–14.

10. Cripps, *Slow Fade to Black*, VII. Synopses and credits in Sampson, *Blacks in Black and White*, pp. 130–32, 95–96, 111–12, 91–94, 127, 90–91, 117–18, 123, 97–98, 115; Mundin, *AFI Catalog*, pp. 2, 207, 514, 643, 782.

11. Cripps, *Slow Fade to Black*, VII. Synopses and credits in Sampson, *Blacks in Black and White*, pp. 150–51, 100–2, 104–5, 118, 92–93, 98; Mundin, *AFI Catalog*, pp. 61, 98, 102, 288, 693, 711.

12. Cripps, *Slow Fade to Black*, VII; Sampson, *Blacks in Black and White*, p. 114; Mundin, *AFI Catalog*, pp. 687–88.

13. Cripps, *Slow Fade to Black*, VII; Mundin, *AFI Catalog*, 104; Sampson, *Blacks in Black and White*, pp. 132–33, 97, 108–11.

14. Emmett J. Scott to Edwin L. Barker, October 18, 1915; November 6, 1915; contract dated December 20, 1915, in Scott MSS, Morgan State University, Baltimore, Maryland; *California Eagle*, July 31, 1915; Tony Langston to George P. Johnson, October 10, 1916, in G. P. Johnson Collection, UCLA, Los Angeles, California; G. P. Johnson holograph memoir, "A Million Dollar Negro Film Deal Fell Through," in Johnson Collection; copies of the *Competitor* are in the Johnson Collection. See Cripps, *Slow Fade to Black*, pp. 180ff, for the sources of the quoted blurbs.

15. *Amsterdam News* (New York), December 23, 1925; *Chicago Defender*, April 2, 1921; "The Symbol of the Unconquered, New Play," *Competitor*, January–February, 1921, p. 61.

16. George C. Anderson to Charles Waddell Chesnutt, July 27, 1920; Oscar Micheaux to Chesnutt, January 18, 1921; March 24, 1921; Swan F. Micheaux to Chesnutt, correspondence, September 19, 1921–October 26, 1921; in Chesnutt Papers, Fisk University, Nashville, Tennessee.

17. Oscar Micheaux to Chesnutt, January 18, 1921; Ethel Chesnutt to Charles Waddell Chesnutt, April 25, 1932; in Chesnutt Papers, Fisk University.

18. Cripps, *Slow Fade to Black*, pp. 195–98; Ronald Goldwyn, "The Scar of Shame," *Discover: The Sunday Bulletin* (Philadelphia), November 17, 1974, pp. 14ff.; Ronald Goldwyn to Thomas Cripps, n.d.; William Felker, head, General Information Department, the Free Library of Philadelphia, to Thomas Cripps, July 15, 1974; typescript file under "Scar" in Johnson Collection, UCLA; interview between Lucia Lynn Moses and Cripps, Spring 1973, New York; soundtrack, *Black Shadows on a Silver Screen* (Post-Newsweek TV, 1975); print of *Ten Nights in a Bar Room* (Colored Players, 1926) is in the Library of Congress; *Pittsburgh Courier*, January 2, 1926.

19. Moses's anecdotes recur in two interviews, one with Cripps, Spring 1973, another with Stephan Henriquez, two years later, confirming both her exclusion from the script-writing stage and their urging her to improvise. In addition, she implied that the caste system observed in her day was based at least as much on differences in education as on skin color—which she described with only an oblique assertion that "black wasn't beautiful then."

20. A print of *The Scar of Shame* was viewed several times at the Enoch Pratt Free Library of Baltimore through the courtesy of audiovisual director Helen Cyr.

21. For other samples of evidence against the argument from skin color, see *Body and Soul* (Micheaux, 1924) in which the heavy is "Yellow Curly Hines" and the hero is dark brown Paul Robeson as a preacher (print in George Eastman House Museum, Rochester, New York); and *The Girl from Chicago* (Micheaux, 1932), a fragment of which appears in *Black Shadows on a Silver Screen*, in which "the girl" expresses her contempt for low-class people who play the numbers.

22. Moses interviews, 1973 and 1975.

23. *Philadelphia Tribune*, April 16, 1927; Tony Langston to G. P. Johnson, January 15, 1927, in Johnson Collection; *Variety*, August 31, 1927, p. 18; *Amsterdam News* (New York), June 5 and 12, 1927; *Pittsburgh Courier*, June 25, 1927; April 20 and 27, 1929.

24. Cripps, *Slow Fade to Black*, pp. 332ff.

Jane Gaines

The Scar of Shame:
Skin Color and Caste
in Black Silent Melodrama

When blacks began to finance and direct their own films in the teens and early 1920s, they consistently produced domestic melodramas. Some of these early productions have racial themes that reorganize the world in such a way that black heritage is rewarded over white paternity; they are schematic renunciations of the prevailing order of things in white American society where, historically, the discovery of black blood meant sudden reversal of fortune, social exclusion, or banishment.[1] Feminist studies of literary, cinematic, and theatrical melodrama have suggested that the melodramatic worldview favors the weak over the strong as it adheres to a moral order that privileges the lesser and handicaps the greater. Since these new theories have shown that there is something genuinely affirming for women readers in narratives that organize the world around the female character and her domestic haven in the home, I wondered if domestic melodrama had ever produced an analogous position for black viewers or "readers," female or male.[2] What I found surprised me. Although the black viewer is not exactly "affirmed" in the silent film text, this viewer is implicated in it in a way that is still pertinent to the whole project of understanding the subversive potential of domestic melodrama. At the outset I did not expect that it would be necessary to reconstruct the black viewer in history. Nor did I expect to find that cinema aesthetics and the aesthetics of racial distinction could be so closely linked. In fact, as I will argue, they are one and the same.

My reading of *The Scar of Shame* (1927), one of the few silent melodramas with an all-black cast available for rental in the United States, is also an attempt to see how theories of literary and cinematic melodrama can be applied to African American culture. Since, with a few exceptions, this heritage has not been submitted to any systematic analysis as mass culture, I offer this approach as an example of how we

Originally appeared in *Cinema Journal* 26, no. 4: 3–21. Reprinted by permission of the author and the University of Texas Press.

might deal with cultural products that are politically offensive to later generations of black American viewers.[3] The advantage of this approach is that since it does not measure mass culture against high culture, the people who enjoy popular entertainment are not condemned by association with it. In order to consider the black viewer in 1927, whom we will never exactly "know," and about whom we can always ask more, I will take up the problems of melodramatic mode of address, the use of the mulatta type, the subversive aspects of style, and the reception of the "happy ending." An attempt to reconstruct the spectator in history seems especially pressing with this film, even though it will probably baffle the contemporary viewer who might see *The Scar of Shame* screened for the first time in the context of a black film history retrospective. This viewer will undoubtedly note that the narrative represents the tragedy in the film as the consequence of a social class division within the black community. What, then, is meant by the intertitles that lay the blame on a caste system? Why the use of a term that denotes a social ranking scheme that is even more rigid than a class-based system?[4]

Immediately, *The Scar of Shame* raises issues regarding the race and class constitution of the audience that bear on its mode of address. To begin with, the history of black motion picture production and exhibition shows that "race movies," or those films produced specifically for all-black audiences, were created by the black bourgeoisie, often in collaboration with whites, for the entertainment and edification of the group below them. In the 1920s, this class difference would have been further emphasized by the northern urban versus southern rural distinction as the increased migration of southern blacks created a new proletariat that became the audience for the black theatrical product. Two other factors suggest that black entrepreneurs addressed a group of social unequals who would have been finding diversion at the movies. First, "respectable" blacks, who could claim this distinction merely by virtue of having lived longer in the North, held themselves above popular entertainments that were not sanctioned by their churches. Second, literacy levels suggest that motion pictures and records more than printed material provided entertainment for the new arrivals from the South.[5]

Some clarification about the class structure of urban black society in the United States in the 1920s is essential here since the configuration has been historically misunderstood and systematically ignored by blacks as well as whites. Briefly, toward the end of the nineteenth century, black society was characterized by a small group of aristocrats at the top and a small group of social outcasts at the bottom. The group between, made up of 80 to 90 percent of the black population, is difficult to compare with the white middle class in the same period. Although income level and occupation would place individuals in this group below those in the white structural middle, persons in this group had a claim to respectability within the black community. The rearrangement of this center was under way by the 1920s, as the black structure came to resemble the upper-, middle-, and lower-class breakdown of the dominant society.[6]

The Scar of Shame gropes for a target audience in this social shuffle. Thus, the film creates a phantom social hierarchy in which black society struggles to make its own illusory "middle" while economic conditions having to do with the black migration North are enlarging the lower group. My argument depends on seeing race films as part of bourgeois ideology, but at the same time as playing to a race and class consciousness even upper-class blacks would have by virtue of their antagonistic relationship to capital. I will be less interested in making direct connections between political positions espoused in the film and the race and class positions of the producers, although later I will fill out the production history of the film in these terms. The melodramatic text is not, after all, the place where such positions are set out clearly as in a debate; rather, it is the place where they encounter trouble.

British work on film melodrama as bourgeois form helps explain the coexistence within the same film of the "bootstraps" philosophy informing so many of the race movie narratives from this period, and the melodramatic worldview. As a literary form that has thrived in the bourgeois epoch, melodrama carries bourgeois assumptions about power—it presumes that everyone has a little.[7] This assumption that "something can be done" is carried by the bourgeois voice of responsibility—the intertitles that assign fault to the top and bottom classes (e.g., "Our people have much to learn"). This portrait of a self-contained black society makes no reference to the white outer world, but I would argue that the willing self-critical tone of the intertitles betrays a judgmental presence. *The Scar of Shame* is haunted by white society. If the intertitles carry the self-confident bourgeois assumptions about power, the narrative carries a vision of a world in which the strings are pulled somewhere else. The marks of a melodramatic narrative construction—the use of coincidence and ironic twists of fate—create a sense that control is always out of one's hands, confirming the point of view of the disenfranchised. Martha Vicinus, among other critics, distinguishes melodrama from tragedy on the basis of the power position it confirms: "Tragedy appeals to those who feel, however erroneously, that they have some control over lives ruined by personal decision and error; melodrama to those who feel that their lives are without order and that events they cannot control can destroy or save them."[8] The "racial uplift" pitch is attached to a film that speaks defeat in its downward narrative spiral. Melodrama has no trouble with such contradictions, but actually camouflages social inconsistencies by focusing on their traumatic consequences—victimization, despondency, and pathos, although, as theories of melodrama have shown, these inconsistencies are not so easy to disguise in the last moment when the form calls for resolution.

Melodrama reenacts a moral pattern that coincides with the value system in operation within a community at a particular point in history. In the parallel world constructed by melodrama, it is safe to raise emotionally volatile issues and test traumatic outcomes. Because the moral pattern, the distribution of reward and punishment in melodrama, is always tailor-made to fit local assumptions and prevailing theses, it stirs an audience in its time but may never strike a chord for another generation. An extremely malleable and susceptible genre, melodrama accommodates the social problems of every new decade, translating them into hypothetical scenarios.[9] Melodrama, then, may accommodate both the address that assumes some power and the order of events that counsels resignation. Thus it combines a sense of the way things have come down historically in the black community with the bourgeois uplift strategy, saying in effect: "Because we haven't helped ourselves enough, we are all still subject to discrimination, disaster, and degradation." Racial uplift stories lend themselves to melodramatic treatment because the uplift philosophy, like melodrama, is built on a basic paradox. Explaining the peaceful coexistence of oppositional values and traditional norms within the same genre, Vicinus identifies the paradox of melodrama. As she puts it, "while defending an ideal against a vengeful society, in the name of a higher moral order, in actuality this moral order is a reflection of the current values of the very society presumably being attacked."[10] What was problematic about the black bourgeois uplift philosophy was that the better society it proposed was not significantly different from the one that held all blacks down.

The history of the tragic mulatta type in black-authored literature calls our attention to another aspect of the uplift strategy constituting one of the conventional battlefields of melodrama—woman's virtue. I refer here to the type that was first used in the abolitionist melodramas such as *Clotel* (1853) and *Iola Leroy* (1895) and was carried over into such 1920s Harlem Renaissance novels as *Quicksand* (1928), *Passing* (1929), *Plum Bun* (1928), and *There Is Confusion* (1924).[11] This character, which finds its prototype in Clotel, Iola Leroy, and even Eliza Harris, is intelligent, refined, educated, virginal, and exquisitely beautiful according to Caucasian standards. She is like the white romance novel heroine in every way—except that her legal status as slave places her in degrading and compromising situations, designed to play on the guilt of the white reader, who would be appalled by the defilement of a genteel lady. The black abolitionist novelist's use of this character as an ideal certainly indicates the hegemony of white physical standards of beauty, but we might also suppose that giving white readers something other than what they thought they were getting—their own idealized heroine who was *not* white—was a canny trick. This character, who of course did not appear at all in the white antebellum literature, was, in the use black authors made of her, an eloquent statement against several generations of southern male sexual license.[12]

From a contemporary point of view, this type is offensive to blacks, but the portrait of the mulatta as talented and beautiful because of her white paternity might have been flattering to light-skinned read-ers before 1930. The portrayal of the type as tragic and pitiable would later be insulting to blacks as it was used to argue that the mulatta was miserable because she had been denied her rightful place in a society that excluded others of the same race because they were darker.[13] Seen in a historical perspective, the type has more to say about white supremacist ideology than about actual black persons, although the condition of real historical black women can be inferred obliquely from the construction. As Barbara Christian has analyzed the ideological function of the refined mulatta, her "qualities"—traditional femininity and moral purity—were arguments necessary to proving that she was even a woman.[14] If she was a woman, then her honor had to be defended, and she could certainly not be the cause of white male sexual transgression.[15] The type is thus like a several-sided cube that can be made to face in one direction while an-other side is concealed. In the earlier versions, the mulatta heroine could be used as a ruse to turn the tables on whites, or as a political strategy, or even as a utopian vision of security and transcendence.

Louise Howard, the mulatta heroine in *The Scar of Shame*, re-hearses some of the disputes over the territory of the black woman's body raised by her literary predecessors. In the negative sense, she fulfills the prophecy of the poor (black) rather than the fine (white) ingredient in her paternity. Further, since in the 1920s lightness had come to stand for opportunity rather than rightful heritage, following this uplift interpreta-tion she dies because she does not use the advantage her whiteness af-fords her; her tragedy of lost possibility is a setback for the entire race. As she combines exquisite white features and lower-class background, Louise is like those young women within the black community who once earned the snide reference, "a waste of color."[16] The meaning of the tragic mulatta character is not settled once and for all within this film, but she surfaces again as a recurring problem—that of racial respectabil-ity as it has been historically bound up with the virtue that black women were not supposed to have.[17] *The Scar of Shame* explores and exhausts all of the possible explanations for Louise's victimization as it thrashes around looking for culprits within the black community, even resurrect-ing the old nightmare of the loose mulatta.[18]

The Scar of Shame

In 1969, a 35mm original print of *The Scar of Shame* (1927) was discov-ered among other nitrate films in a trash can in the basement of an empty theater in Detroit, Michigan.[19] Now restored and in 16mm dis-tribution, this silent feature with an all-black cast has become one of the most frequently exhibited examples of the black cinema heritage, and has become source material for new black independent film- and videomaking, as evidenced in the reference to it in Kathy Collins' *Losing Ground* (1982).[20] One of at least three films produced by the Colored Players of Philadelphia, *The Scar of Shame* represents a typical division of labor between black and white artists producing race movies in that period.[21] Produced specifically for black motion picture audiences, *The Scar of Shame* was directed and photographed by white professionals and improvised by black actors from a story written by the white producer, David Starkman.[22] Although the Philadelphia production group was really run by Starkman, the idea for the Colored Players originally came from black vaudeville comedian Sherman H. Dudley Jr., who started a theatrical group with the same name in Washington, D.C. Dudley and Starkman, owner of a black theater in Philadelphia, organized the new company in 1926, and the black comedian, listed in the credits as producer of *The Scar of Shame,* also served as company president.[23]

The central victim of the story, Louise Howard (Lucia Lynn Moses), is molested by her "ne'er do well" father Spike, and rescued by Alvin Hillyard, an aspiring composer and pianist (Henry Henderson). Hillyard marries Louise to protect her from the father who continues to assault her, thus lifting her out of the lower class. After their marriage, the father's gambler friend Eddie Blake conspires with him to kidnap Louise and put her to work as a "lure" in a speakeasy. Caught in pistol crossfire between Eddie and Alvin, who tries to prevent the abduction, Louise is wounded in the neck, "her beauty marred for life," according to the newspaper report. Alvin goes to jail for the crime, and Louise takes up a life of prostitution and gambling. When Alvin escapes from jail and the two meet again, he has become engaged to the daughter of the powerful black lawyer Hathaway who frequents Eddie's speakeasy and becomes Louise's lover. Louise tries to win Alvin back, and when she fails, she takes poison. Louise's suicide note, which confesses that she had been wounded by Eddie's gun and not Alvin's, symbolically frees Alvin to marry Alice Hathaway, his social equal.

The opening titles, almost a short lecture on social Darwinism, direct the viewer to interpret the film in terms of social class distinctions:

> Environment—Surroundings, childhood training . . . shapes our destinies and guides our ambitions. If no loving hand lights the lamp of knowledge . . . through lack of love will come sorrow and SHAME!

The social class moral is reiterated in the final titles as the lawyer Hathaway speaks, bestowing his blessing on his daughter and Alvin Hillyard: "A child of environment! If she had been taught higher hopes, finer things in life, she would not be lying cold in death! Our people have much to learn."[24] Social Darwinism would have provided one of the more progressive challenges to theories of genetic determinism, and certainly would have been complementary to the philosophy and goals of

Negro improvement and advancement. The titles proclaim that environment, rather than any person, is the villain, but the urban social condition provides its own anthropomorphic villainous agents in the scum it breeds—Eddie and Spike.[25] What is important to note here is that in blaming the environment, *The Scar of Shame* sidesteps the more devastating color critique, the criticism of black social stratification based on skin color gradations, which would later become a harsh indictment in E. Franklin Fraser's *Black Bourgeoisie*.[26] There would be advantages to the black bourgeois social program in shifting the emphasis from the skin color distinction, about which an individual could do nothing, to education, employment, and income—relatively attainable indicators of status. Understandably, black history and sociology would support a shift of emphasis from the "pettiness" of physiological distinctions that characterized earlier periods, to other signs of differentiation.[27]

In retrospect, we can appreciate the strategy, but, in the determination of social rank, we cannot easily extricate one sign of difference from another, and in American society, race seems to encompass a multitude of distinctions. My emphasis on skin color here is an attempt to fill out the larger picture that *The Scar of Shame* refers to in its silence, to look harder at the visible/invisible dialectic of "racial difference," which, like the signified "breeding," has not always required a signifier in highly stratified societies.

In the preferred version of social conflict in *The Scar of Shame*, however, the highest and lowest classes in black society are responsible for the reputation of the lower orders and especially for the degradation and mistreatment of black women. The black dual responsibility interpretation encourages the discovery of a second victim—Alvin (who his landlady, Mrs. Lucretia Green, expects will become "the leading composer of our race"). Alvin is imprisoned as the direct consequence of the downward pull of the more disreputable Negro element—Eddie, Spike, and Louise (as she works in league with them). Louise's confession reveals not only that it was the shot from Eddie's gun that injured her, but that Eddie and Spike prevented her from telling the truth at the time of the trial. Is the most compelling victim in the film also a villainess? The film seems to hesitate here, at least long enough for one critic to interpret Louise as "wicked."[28] Louise is, after all, no longer the pure mulatta heroine. I would argue, however, that Louise's villainy is effectively canceled since she is so sympathetically and lovingly coded as tragic heroine. Treated to a good deal of soft focus attention in close-up against a dark background, Louise is featured in the same photographic style used on D. W. Griffith's haloed innocents. This sympathetic visual interpretation of Louise is part of my case for seeing an oppositional discourse in the codes of lighting and framing that I discuss in a later section. Following the preferred reading, Louise and Alvin, in competition as victims, contribute to the portrait of black self-victimization on which the "if only" and the "what might have been" appeals are based. Because their fates are linked, Louise's act of sacrifice is pitiable but not glorious, and the union of Alice and Alvin is proper rather than happy. Although one "hope of the race" is rescued and his reputation restored, the resolution is ragged, and, like the often discomforting melodramatic closure, which I will discuss in the conclusion, it leaves the viewer with a bitter taste.

The structure of *The Scar of Shame* further supports the case for the culpability of the upper and lower classes. Plotting to separate Alvin and Louise by sending a fake telegram to Alvin that states that his mother is seriously ill, Eddie and Spike pull Louise back to the gutter. The aristocratic class contributes to the desecration of the black woman in another way. The arrival of the fake telegram occasions Alvin's confession to Louise that his mother does not know that they have married. (Title: "Caste is one of the things mother is very determined about. You don't belong to our set.") The Negro aristocracy and the lower orders then act in league with one another. This characterization of the two classes at the extreme ends of the social spectrum corresponds with a kind of scapegoating seen in the black community during this period. While the lower classes were viewed as dragging others down, the higher were seen as holding up impossible hurdles for other blacks while clamoring upward on their backs.[29]

This joint villainy of the lower and the upper classes is elaborately coordinated in the abduction scene as it is crosscut between Eddie and Spike outside the boarding house, Alvin driving to the suburbs and returning, and Louise alone in her bedroom. Here Louise is the vehicle for elaborating the toll these conflicts take on families—expressed in terms of emotional turmoil and represented by shots of her discovery of the letter from Alvin's mother (shown earlier). The mother's letter states that she hopes her son will marry Helen Smith, who plays the piano and is "very lovely, a lady, and one of our set." Inserts of the letter are alternated with shots of Alvin driving away, and the directionality of these shots suggests his allegiance to his mother and her social position. The mother, although not present in the film, is powerfully evoked by the letter as well as by the uniformed black butler who receives Alvin at the suburban home. After Louise finds the letter in Alvin's dresser drawer and reads it, she slowly rips the paper into fine pieces. The following shot, from her point of view, is an insert of her wedding certificate. Here, the decorous quaintness of this icon is incongruous with the moment. As Louise starts to tear the stiff parchment decorated with garlands of orchids and embossed with the words "Holy Matrimony," the film cuts to Alvin racing to his mother. From here, the film cuts back to the slow vertical movement of Louise ripping up the sacred document. As Alvin leaves his mother's house and drops his door key, the film cuts to close-ups of Louise's hand as she twists off her wedding band. The crosscutting pattern, then, establishes a cause-and-effect relationship between the elitism of the aristocracy and the breakup of black families.

Melodrama, as contemporary critics have asserted, translates ideological dilemmas into private predicaments.[30] The family context serves to intensify these struggles—cruelty and brutality "carry an additional emotional force because they occur between family members."[31] The social injustice of the Negro upper class is here represented in terms of Louise's torn heart. In this emotional whirlpool, Louise's distress is made to seem the cause of the breakup rather than the effect of political conditions beyond her control. Thus, as Alvin is racing back to Louise, his marriage is being destroyed *by her hand.* By the time Eddie arrives to try to abduct Louise, the damage is done; the remnants of respectability lie shredded on the lace doily on top of a chest of drawers.

I have already noted the debt *The Scar of Shame* owes to African American literature and theatrical melodrama. However, aesthetically the film owes all to D. W. Griffith. *The Scar of Shame* seems constructed out of memorable moments from *Intolerance* (1916) and *Broken Blossoms* (1919). Louise's struggles with her father refer to Lucy's beatings in *Broken Blossoms;* the scene in which Spike breaks into his daughter's room makes ugly homage to the elongated rape and murder scene for the earlier film.[32] The shooting scene is likewise almost lifted intact out of the modern story from *Intolerance.* Like the scene in which The Boy is set up for the killing of The Musketeer, it is organized around the fire escape. Alvin is forced to enter up the fire escape because he has lost his key, and he surprises Eddie and Louise as he comes through the window. As in the scene from *Intolerance,* the innocent person is framed because of the disappearance of the guilty one.[33] In addition to these direct references, the intricate crosscutting of the rescue scene reminds us of all the last-minute interventions in silent cinema to save the virtue of a woman. Critics have linked the convention as Griffith used it with his championing of the American home and family. Nick Browne describes the fantasy behind this use of parallel editing: "This scenario of rescue is essentially a chivalrous project couched in a kind of medieval and allegorical idiom that has as its end the stabilization of the place and integrity of the bourgeois family against the threat of abandonment, dismemberment, homelessness, or worse."[34] Ironically, the structure D. W. Griffith used in *Birth of a Nation* (1915) to signify the black threat to white womanhood and the glorious rush to save it, is recruited here to rally around the protection of black womanhood. The double movement in this scene, suggesting Alvin's divided allegiance, shows that this marriage cannot be saved. For Alvin Hillyard, thrust into the heroic position within the crosscutting structure, the rescue of his wife and the maintenance of his family is an impossibility; he walks into a trap. The conflicted black hero cannot protect and will not triumph.

After Louise destroys her marriage certificate, the film shifts premises, as though it, too, must continue even without the benefit of marriage, and it offers a justification for the symbolic annulment of the union between the characters. Although Alvin has acted to protect his rightful marriage, the film represents the cross-caste marriage as wrong from the start. The wrongness of Alvin's marriage is borne out in one clear way—by the kind of evidence pointed to by old wives tales throughout the ages. The sad story is told here by the intertitle that separates Alvin's impassioned proposal to Louise from the first shot representing their married life. From the intertitle "Three months later," the film cuts to a close-up of a dark baby doll in white christening gown and bonnet. In the second shot, the only one with the family intact, Louise cradles the doll, which is remarkably darker than either parent. The faked motherhood tells the tale of Louise's fondest hopes and worst expectations—the marriage is infertile. Later, in the desertion scene, when Alvin tells Louise that she cannot go with him to his mother's home because she doesn't know they have been married, the toy plays another role. The surrogate baby becomes a third victim in the film—and its fate is the most heart-wrenching. As Alvin picks up his suitcase to leave, the doll is accidentally knocked to the floor, and on his way out the door, unknowingly, he steps on its head.[35] Two exterior shots follow, one locating Spike lurking in the street and another showing Alvin getting into his convertible. Then, the film cuts back to the interior showing the doll in close-up without its head. The title carries Louise's exclamation: "Poor little thing! A victim of caste." The disaster of this marriage is told in Louise's tender attention to the headless doll, which she first clasps to her and then throws into the corner and in this gesture we recognize a familiar argument against marriages that go against social convention—children neglected and abused.

Caste and Class

But is the child a victim of caste as the title says, or of class prejudice? This usage, as I have noted, is one of the more curious aspects of the film encountered by the contemporary viewer, and the issues with which the film is dealing are easily missed by the white viewer with no background in African American history. To black audiences in 1927, class and caste would have had resounding significance. The upper or aristocratic class held to an elaborate rationale for maintaining their distinctness from the lower levels, and this engendered certain hostility. Hortense Powdermaker describes how the rest of black society participated in this deference by default as they begrudgingly adhered to the values that reinforced the hierarchy: "The Negro upper class acts out for its race the denial that Negroes are inferior; it demonstrates that they too can be educated, moral, industrious, thrifty. This class also reaps a fair share of resentment from other members of its race, but here resentment is far less keen and less conscious, and is offset by substantial advantages, among which is to be numbered a very gratifying prestige."[36] Philadelphia, the home of the Colored Players, had a very old aristocratic society of Negroes as well as a rich literary tradition that paralleled the Harlem Renaissance.[37] The justification for separateness offered by those who considered themselves superior was that by example they would inspire the lower orders to improve themselves. The author of *Sketches of Colored Society* (1841), writes: "If the virtuous and exemplary members of society should not keep aloof from the vicious and worthless, they would furnish no example to the latter to strive to make them selves reputable, and of like consideration. By associating with such persons we not only thereby give countenance to their doings, but we degrade ourselves to their level, and are adjudged accordingly."[38] Thus their strategy was that full acceptance depended on proving that blacks could be equal to whites in their cultured tastes and their achievements, hence the tight circle dedicated so fiercely to pursing "finer things." Although sensitive about being mistaken for the serving class, some elite families saw nothing inconsistent in employing other blacks as servants. In his turn-of-the-century study of Philadelphia, W. E. B. Du Bois found that in the 277 upper-class families he studied, fifty-two kept servants. It was Du Bois' conviction that the upper classes should help the lower to rise, but he found that this group was too economically unstable and strategically self-protective to do so. As Du Bois explains it, "the class which should lead refuses to head any race movement on the plea that thus they draw the very color line against which they protest."[39] Or, to take a position against racial discrimination would be to distinguish themselves even further from whites, and thus cut themselves off from the small, and possibly imagined, advantage they enjoyed. This group of blacks, then, as John Dollard describes them, "stood beating at the caste barrier, competent and disciplined in the sense desired by our society but categorically debarred from full status." In the sociological literature on race in the period of Reconstruction through the 1940s, caste designates the fixed line between the races one technically could never cross. In the South, the caste division essentially replaced slavery.[40] Theoretically, caste defines a more rigid separation than class, which allows for some fluidity. In the United States, then, there would be social classes within caste, and within the black caste, the class system would operate at particular periods in difference to the whole, according to the rules of caste.[41]

The history of miscegenation and the phenomenon of crossing over or passing in American society have a bearing on *The Scar of Shame* as it fills out our knowledge about the black spectator. Pertinent here is the white society's vacillation regarding the meaning and the value of racial mixing. Originally, during the period of slavery, the established scale of valuation gave a social advantage to Negroes with white blood and an economic advantage to the masters who could claim a higher sale price for slave property with white features. Later, the house slave versus field slave distinctions established by percentage of white blood became the basis of the earliest "blue vein" societies in the northern cities. As black society observed preferential treatment and absorbed white cultural biases, it came to embrace the same physiological ideals. This connection between light skin and economic success was borne out again during Reconstruction, when the first profits in black economic ventures were handed to those who bore the greatest likeness to whites.[42]

Abruptly, white society withdrew the favors offered to the relatively lighter few, taking the position that no fraction of Negro blood was acceptable. Some lighter blacks adjusted to this by passing, but this was a phenomenon more mythic than real, and, especially in the 1920s, racial pride may have kept a check on the practice.[43] Whereas white ancestry had once been a sign of esteem, by the 1940s it would be a sign of disgrace in many communities.[44] The black aristocratic class was slow to respond to the loss of their edge of privilege and continued to insist on it, holding over the tribute to and convenient defense of white supremacy.[45] Also held over were the stubborn tastes and preferences for light skin, Caucasian facial features, and white hair-form. In 1927, there would be deference to a skin color hierarchy in the black community at the same time that there would be antagonism toward it.

The Political Aesthetics of Skin Color

My sense of *The Scar of Shame* is that it accommodates both the deference and the antagonism. However, it seems to me that the way in which it is open to the antagonism is a way that forces us to reconsider theories of the subversive potential of domestic melodrama, particularly the British Marxist work on cinema produced in the early 1970s. The model proposed and refined by the British critics finds a subversive space in melodrama that is not there in other American genres. This space is found in the difference between narrative and mis-en-scène, which are understood as having a kind of contrapuntal relationship.[46] In this two-tiered textual arrangement, the stylistic level below can comment on, and even criticize, the surface level that carries the plotline, characterized as carrying the bourgeois worldview.

This theory of subversive stylistics developed out of an interest in the flamboyant 1950s melodramas of Ophuls, Minnelli, and Sirk. Thus theories of stylistic contradiction in silent melodrama have so far been developed in relation to an exceptional moment in the 1950s. In

Thomas Elsaesser's formation, for instance, there is a line of development from silent film stylists (which evolved as a cinema language to compensate for the lost expressivity of speech) and the aesthetics made possible in the 1950s by technical innovation such as Technicolor, power zooms, and dolly shots. The 1950s auteurs, in this account, stand for the fullest realization of melodramatic expressivity in cinema history.[47] Immediately, there are several problems with adapting this theory to the black audience melodrama. First, there are different degrees of "stylistic comment" in both silent and 1950s melodrama. Most expressivity in silent cinema could not be considered as parodic as, for instance, the Sirkian use of the slow-motion cut-glass baubles in the opening credits of *Imitation of Life* (1959), which offer the famous "through a glass darkly" vision of bourgeois family life.[48] Second, this theory of stylistic orchestration really calls for the hand of the auteur who can be credited with making the text reveal its contradictions. Third, the space that opens up the possibilities for resistance is an empty one. A space in and of itself cannot split a gaping text. What is required is a critic or a reader who is either politically primed or slightly jaundiced.[49] Finally, I would mention the psychoanalytic aspect of this theory, which hypothesizes a cause-and-effect relationship between the stylistic expressivity or excess and the impossibility of closure. The mark of style, like an hysterical symptom, manifests itself before the ending, and the film, like the psychoanalytic patient, must repress the tabooed, which returns in another guise as the formal symptom. I will return momentarily to the issue of closure and the politics of the hysterical text, but first I want to take up the question of the reader-viewer's space.

In *The Scar of Shame*, the stylistic discourse carrying the melos is connected to the aesthetics of skin tone and hair texture played out in light, shadow, and shade. This color scheme or code would be known in its finer gradations and variations only to black audiences—to the group that would read a wealth of significance in the difference between processed and unprocessed coiffure, and would be sensitive to all kinds of hair-splitting along caste lines.

At the end of the film this color scheme becomes stylistically highlighted in the crosscutting between Alice and Louise. Here the empathetic effects clearly favor the latter. Where Alice is filmed in silhouette, backlit against black drapery, Louise is framed full-face in long, languid, glowing close-ups. While the accomplished Alice is playing the piano (unaware that she may be providing the diegetic source for the melos that evokes sympathy for her rival), Louise is dying. Visual style elaborates the contrast between the two worlds—an elegant candelabra provides the illumination behind Alice, while Louise's life is snuffed out as a single candle burns down. The full-bodied suffering woman is preferred over the ethereal but still adolescent piano pupil, and in Alice, with her shiny long dark curls and thin delicate nose, there is an intimation that the sheltered Negro class, living out lives of deference and imitation, is finally anemic.

The mise-en-scène here provides commentary, but can the signifiers in and of themselves cause much trouble in the text? (We are also handicapped in our analysis of those silent films, which do not have original orchestral, organ, or piano scores. This music might have functioned as ironic comment much as Elsaesser's calliope or organ grinder, particularly if a black pianist were simultaneously responding to the audience and interpreting the screen action in an all-black theater.)[50] What is really required to resist, split, or rupture a text is the skeptical audience member who notes that the text is saying more than one thing at once, as texts will do. But we also have to consider that historically situated viewers accommodate contradictions and multiple meanings in much the same way that texts combine levels of signification. Would the text necessarily "rupture" if the black viewer accommodated its split by means of a double consciousness developed as an ingenious adjustment to living in two societies at once?

I find two stories in *The Scar of Shame.* In an earlier part of this essay I discussed the story about an interracially divided community, the story the intertitles hold to and the narrative structure supports. In contrapuntal opposition, in the mise-en-scène, I find the ghost of a second story about life in a racist society, and I would maintain that this other story has not been orchestrated in the authorial sense. But neither is it exactly the doing of the text. "Criticism," says Terry Eagleton, "is not a passage from text to reader; its task is not to redouble the text's self-understanding, to collude with its object in a conspiracy of eloquence. Its task is to show the text as it cannot know itself, to manifest those conditions of its making (inscribed in its very letter) about which it is necessarily silent."[51] *The Scar of Shame* is not able to speak about its own subtle racism or about the racism in the black film industry in the 1920s. On the screen the actors playing Louise, Alvin, Alice, and the baser element, Eddie, appear exactly the same degree of light brown. The actor playing Spike, Louise's father, seems darker than the other actors (with the exception of the inhabitants of the local bar). Since this darkness might be connoted by the stubble on his face, the father's crude behavior could be motivated by either environmental factors (the slovenly habits of the underclass) or by genetic factors (race). Since we are presented with a basically monochromatic cast, it would seem that "on the face of it," *The Scar of Shame* is about the rift within black society and not about color caste distinctions based on the white model at all. Let us assume that the film means what the titles insist it means for a moment— if that is possible—and consider something else.

Could a film that was frankly about color caste within black society have been made at all in 1927, considering the discriminating color caste system operating within the black film industry? At that time, the color bar in Hollywood worked in reverse of the ban in the white world. That is, light-skinned blacks could not find work in white motion pictures. Black and white film stock registered too much truth—on the screen racially mixed actors looked white. Conversely, the dark-skinned blacks preferred by white producers were unacceptable in star roles in race films. They were not idealized (i.e., white) enough.[52] In 1927, it would have been impossible to have made a popular vehicle about an exquisitely beautiful black woman who was cut out of elite blue vein society because she was too dark. A black production company could not have cast such a film.[53]

While the monochrome appearance of the actors guarantees that *The Scar of Shame* is about intraracial strife, the casting qualifies this message. Realism, that unacknowledged attempt to make the screen world correspond with popular notions about the real world so that audiences are not confused, betrays the assumptions that inform the ghost film. Louise and Alice may be the same skin shade, but of the two, on a scale of physical characteristics that also matches hair texture and facial features, Alice, the upper-class woman, is more white. Or, *The Scar of Shame argues* that environmental factors determine social standing, but *represents* a society divided in terms of racial characteristics socially read as percentage of white blood; it pleads for community unity, but warns about the consequences of crossing racial as well as class lines.

Conclusion

"The tendency of melodrama to culminate in a happy end is not unopposed. The happy end is often impossible, and, what is more, the audience knows it is impossible," Nowell-Smith says in the context of his discussion of 1950s melodrama.[54] Further, he says, melodramatic stylistics, the hysterical "symptoms" referred to earlier, are a by-product of commitment to the "realistic" portrayal of a social problem. Here, the analogy between the text and the unconscious does not help the cause of race and class struggle. What kind of political strategy can be forged if racial antagonism is located in the depths of the unconscious?[55] The stylistics of *The Scar of Shame* speaks that which is unspeakable, but the aesthetic excess lavished in the comparison of Louise and Alice tells most as it declares itself socially rather than psychoanalytically symptomatic. If an adherence to representing the situation "the way things are" cannot be consistently maintained through to a happy outcome, it is because of political realities outside the text. The opposition to the happy end comes from the preceding events, but also, Nowell-Smith suggests, it comes *from the viewers who know the odds of one outcome over another based on their own expert knowledge of social life.*[56] This comment, one of the few direct references to reception to be found in all of the British melodrama theory from the 1970s, allows that aesthetic excess is not just a matter of auteurist insight or the text's formal properties. A reader is required. Further, as this theory of the imperfect happy ending has been interpreted, the opposition to neat closure has to do with the audience's estimation of the character's chances for happiness in bourgeois society.[57] The epilogue to *The Scar of Shame,* with its union of Alice and Alvin and the uplift benediction delivered by the corrupt lawyer Hathaway, Alice's father and Louise's client, is ill-fitting. The death of Louise is an unsatisfactory condition of uplift and the marriage an unsatisfying solution. In a racist society, these bonds may prove brittle.

What of my original question regarding the position of the viewer in the domestic melodrama produced for black audiences? I do not see that *The Scar of Shame* offers the black "reader" the privileged place that is offered, for instance, in such novels as *Iola Leroy,* which shows black characters as morally superior to whites and mulatto characters choosing black society over white. More needs to be done on this question, and the research is complicated by the fact that so few black-produced films from this period remain. To some degree, we also have to admit that merely seeing images of black life on the screen in a motion picture theater would have been affirming for the 1927 audience. Beyond that, we still need to consider the therapeutic function of melodrama theorized by feminists analyzing romance fiction, gothics, and soap opera, which shows how readers may be invited to rehearse their own victimization and its reversal within the same plot.[58] The feminist reevaluation that sees the domestic melodrama as meaningful confrontation rather than escape and avoidance suggests that the end of *The Scar of Shame* could simultaneously fan smoldering resentments and convey hope: "Happy endings do not necessarily ignore issues; rather melodrama places the most profound problems in a moral context and thereby makes them manageable. By insisting on the ultimate triumph of social and personal justice, melodrama is able to provide consolation and hope without denying the social reality that makes goodness and justice so fragile."[59] For black readers, then, domestic melodrama would have made the cruel irrationality of social and political disenfranchisement seem manageable; cast in personal terms, injustice could almost seem to be dealt with finally and absolutely. Ideals of fairness and equality could appear to win out at least temporarily over bigotry, heartlessness, and malevolence. The advantage of this argument is finally the way in which it credits the audiences of *The Scar of Shame* who might have viewed the film in these terms.

With ingenuity the viewer could also glean some political satisfaction in seeing these domestic melodramas produced for black audiences but projected with whites looking over their shoulders. I even imagine the black viewer in 1927 performing a kind of transposition that would go beyond seeing the upper class as effete and impotent. The title of the film identifies a central metaphor and a peculiar inversion. Before the black pride movement, blacks in the United States might have seen color as a stigma either carried by and projected onto themselves, or tied up in some way with interracial conflicts. *The Scar of Shame*, however, carefully shows that Louise is stigmatized as the result of *intraracial* class strife. Like the drop of black blood, Louise's scar, although not visible, still dooms her to a life of dissipation, a strange harkening back to the loose mulatta from earlier antebellum literature. Intraracial class distinction in 1927 might well have been experienced and understood in similar terms as interracial black–white differences. Class difference within black society was then analogous to caste difference between races in the United States, and, therefore, the term *caste* in a metaphoric and slightly exaggerated sense would stand for all such invidious distinctions, and would function characteristically in melodrama to stir emotions and touch raw nerves.

NOTES

1. After the advent of sound and the Depression, this product was a mix of genres—comedy, Western, musical, as well as melodrama. In the black turn-about melodramas, black heritage is generously rewarded, as in *By Right of Birth* (1921), in which a California coed is forced to leave school when she finds she is part Negro. She later inherits a fortune in land, and is reunited with a lost parent. *Call of His People* (1922) holds up a light-skinned hero whose success in the business world is certain as long as his race is undetected, but the darker-skinned woman he loves and her brother dramatize the choice he must make between his black birthright and his career. His decision to acknowledge his race is rewarded by a seeming miracle—his employer turns out to be unexpectedly liberal. The best source for these plot descriptions is Harry T. Sampson, *Blacks in Black and White: A Source Book on Black Films* (Metuchen, N.J.: Scarecrow Press, 1977).

2. See, for instance, Janice Radway, *Reading the Romance: Women, Patriarchy, and Popular Literature* (Chapel Hill: University of North Carolina Press, 1985). Jane Tompkins, "Sentimental Power: *Uncle Tom's Cabin* and the Politics of Literary History," in *The New Feminist Criticism: Essays on Women, Literature, and Theory*, ed. Elaine Showalter (New York: Pantheon, 1985), 81–104, analyzes the power position of the weak in abolitionist literature.

3. Exceptions to this pattern of condemnation are Henry Gates Jr.'s "Introduction" to Harriet E. Wilson, *Our Nig; or, Sketches from the Life of a Free Black* (1859; rpt. New York: Random House, 1983), which he discusses as part sentimental fiction and part slave narrative. Barbara Christian, in "The Use of History: Frances Harper's *Iola Leroy, or Shadows Uplifted*," in *Black Feminist Criticism: Perspectives on Black Women Writers*, ed. Barbara Christian (New York: Pergamon Press, 1985), 165–70, discusses the first novel published by a black woman in the United States as a popular form, but in her earlier *Black Woman Novelists: The Development of a Tradition, 1892–1976* (Westport, Conn.: Greenwood Press, 1980), 43, she criticizes Jessie Fauset because "her plots seldom rise beyond the level of melodrama."

4. Thomas Cripps, in "'Race Movies' as Voices of the Black Bourgeoisie: *The Scar of Shame*," in *American History/American Film*, ed. John E. O'Connor and Martin A.

Jackson (New York: Ungar, 1979), 49–50, says that the "title cards refer frequently to 'caste' when they must be 'class.'" Cripps called my attention to this article after I had already written my composition. He has a similar explanation for the use of the term *caste,* although this is not central to his argument.

5. Cripps, "Race Movies," 42, 46.

6. David Gordon Nielson, *Black Ethos: Northern Urban Negro Life and Thought* (Westport, Conn." Greenwood Press, 1977), 76, 51, 53, 61. I am also indebted to Thomas Cripps for this important reference, which contains one of the few attempts to construct a sociology of black society in the 1920s.

7. Geoffrey Nowell-Smith, "Minnelli and Melodrama," *Screen* 18 (Summer 1977): 115.

8. Martha Vicinus, "'Helpless and Unfriended': Nineteenth-Century Domestic Melodrama," *New Literary History* 13 (Autumn 1981): 152.

9. Here I am drawing on John Cawelti, *Adventure, Mystery, and Romance: Formula Stories as Art and Popular Culture* (Chicago: University of Chicago Press, 1976), and Peter Brooks, *The Melodramatic Imagination: Balzac, Henry James, Melodrama and the Mode of Excess* (New Haven: Yale University Press, 1976).

10. Vicinus, "'Helpless and Unfriended,'" 141.

11. Technically, William Wells Brown's *Clotel, or The President's Daughter* is the first novel written by a black American. (Published in England in 1853, it went through several different versions: *Miralda: or, the Beautiful Quadroon* and *Clotelle; or, The Colored Heroine: A Tale of the Southern States.*) Then Frances E. W. Harper, *Iola Leroy, or Shadows Uplifted* (1895; rpt. Boston: James H. Earle); Nella Larsen, *Quicksand* and *Passing,* ed. Deborah McDowell (New Brunswick, N.J.: Rutgers University Press, 1986); Jessie Fauset, *Plum Bun* (New York: Fredrick Stokes, 1928); Jessie Fauset, *There is Confusion* (New York: Boni and Liveright, 1924). Thanks to Kenny Williams for originally leading me to this fiction.

12. Kristin Herzog, *Women, Ethnics, and Exotics: Images of Power in Mid-Nineteenth Century American Fiction* (Knoxville: University of Tennessee Press, 1983), 125; Barbara Christian, "Shadows Uplifted," in *Feminist Criticism and Social Change,* ed. Judith Newton and Deborah Rosenfelt (New York: Methuen, 1985), 190.

13. Jim Pines, *Blacks in Film* (London: Cassell and Collier Macmillan, 1975), 37. See T. E. Perkins, "Rethinking Stereotypes," in *Ideology and Cultural Production,* ed. Michelle Barrett et al. (London: Croom Helm, 1979), 134–59, for an especially rich theory of stereotyping that understands these popular images as, like ideology, both true and false.

14. Christian, "Shadows Uplifted," 209.

15. Ibid., 190.

16. In conversation with Ed Hill, director of the Mary Lou Williams Black Cultural Center, Duke University, Durham, N.C.

17. See my "White Privilege and Looking Relations: Race and Gender in Feminist Film Theory," *Cultural Critique* 4 (Fall 1986), for some discussion of the shifting definitions of black women's sexuality and the implications this has for feminist theory.

18. Christian, "Shadows Uplifted," 192.

19. Research Report, Andrew C. McKay (June 22, 1973) in *The Scar of Shame* file, Museum of Modern Art Film Library.

20. Distributed by Black Filmmaker Foundation, 1 Centre St., New York, NY 10007. Also distributed by BFF is Denise Oliver and Warrington Hudlin's *Colour* (1982), 30 min., a contemporary black-produced film dealing with color caste.

21. Thomas Cripps, *Slow Fade to Black: The Negro in American Film, 1900–1942* (New York: Oxford University Press, 1977), 198; Pines, *Blacks in Film,* 38.

22. Other films the Colored Players are known to have produced are *A Prince of His Race* (1926), *Ten Nights in a Bar Room* (1926), and *Children of Fate* (1928).

23. Cripps, "Race Movies," 48–49; idem, *Slow Fade to Black*, 195; idem, "Black Films and Film Makers: Movies in the Ghetto, B. P. (Before Poitier)," *Negro Digest* (February 1969): 25; idem, *Black Film as Genre* (Bloomington: Indiana University Press, 1978), 67; Stephen Zito, "The Black Film Experience," in *American Film Heritage: Impressions from the American Film Institute Archives*, ed. Tom Shales and Kevin Brownlow et al. (Washington, D.C.: Acropolis Books, 1972), 65.

24. Daniel J. Leab, *From Sambo to Superspade: The Black Experience in Motion Pictures* (Boston: Houghton Mifflin, 1975), 74, quotes this title as: "If only she had turned her mind to the higher things in life." This mistake in the transposition may account for his uncritical acceptance of Norman Kagan's interpretation of Louise as destroyed because of her "base instincts" ("Black American Cinema," *Cinema*, 6, no. 2, as quoted in ibid., 3).

25. This diffused villainy is consistent with the historical development of melodrama in which the earlier villainy of the natural disaster or the slimy character was replaced by social institutions. Michael Walker, in "Melodrama and the American cinema," *Movie* 29/30 (Summer 1982): 35, suggests that as patriarchal laws and class structures took over for the villain, prohibition replaced wickedness:

> The prohibitions and repressions which these generate are in place of the villain's wicked deeds. And such a shift inevitably introduces problems. On the one hand, the ideology endeavours to affirm the laws of patriarchy, the class and gender de-termined positions, as "good," and punishes transgressions; on the other, audience sympathy is usually with the transgressing characters. When the punishments, often directed against fe-male characters, lead to the same sort of sufferings as in trad-itional melodrama, the ideology is unconsciously func-tioning as the villain.

26. E. Franklin Fraser, *Black Bourgeoisie* (1955; rpt. New York and London: Collier Macmillan, 1975).

27. Cripps, in "Race Movies," 42, suggests these other indicators of status.

28. Pines, *Blacks in Film*, 38.

29. Nielson, 76, quotes Rayford Logan, "The Hiatus—A Great Negro Middle Class," *Southern Workman* 58 (December 1929): 53, on this scapegoating:

> The lower classes resent being used as a stepping stone to help the lawyer or doctor or teacher to remove himself from their intellectual society, and economic orbit; the upper classes con-demn the lower for "making it hard for us." The professional class approach the masses with the typical twentieth century "uplift" psychosis; the masses have the perfectly natural re-action of suspecting ulterior motives on the part of their self-professed friends.

30. Thomas Elsaesser, "Tales of Sound and Fury: Observations on the Family Melodrama," *Monogram* 4 (1973): 3; rpt. in *Movies and Methods II*, ed. Bill Nichols (Berkeley: University of California Press, 1985), 167–94.

31. Vicinus, "'Helpless and Unfriendly,'" 129.

32. See Julia Lesage, "Artful Rape, Artful Violence," *Jump Cut* 26 (December 1981): 51–55, for an analysis of rape and incest in *Broken Blossoms*.

33. Walker, "Melodrama and the American Cinema," 8.

34. "Griffith's Family Discourse: Griffith and Freud," *Quarterly Review of Film Studies* 6 (Winter 1981): 79.

35. Cripps, in "Race Movies," 51, attributes this action to Louise. Where my analysis differs significantly from his is in the interpretation of Louise.

36. *After Freedom: A Cultural Study in the Deep South* (New York: Viking Press, 1939), 334–35.

37. See Vincent Jubilee, "In the Shadow of Harlem," *The Pennsylvania Gazette* 79 (May 1981): 37–40, for one of the few descriptions of the Black Opals, Philadelphia's literary answer to the Harlem Renaissance.

38. Joseph Wilson, *Sketches of Higher Class of Colored Society in Philadelphia* (Philadelphia: Merrihew and Thompson, 1841), 66–67.

39. W. E. Burghardt Du Bois, *The Philadelphia Negro: A Social Study* (1899; rpt. New York: Schocken, 1967), 317, 177.

40. John Dollard, *Caste and Class in a Southern Town*, rev. ed. (Garden City, N.Y.: Doubleday, 1949), 449, 62.

41. Ibid., 63, 74; see also W. Lloyd Warner, "American Caste and Class," *American Journal of Sociology* 22, no. 2 (1936): 234–37, for the first scholarly treatment of caste in the United States that established the usage in American sociology.

42. Joseph R. Washington, *Marriage in Black and White* (Boston: Beacon Press, 1970), 99, 101, 102.

43. Sterling Brown, in *The Negro in American Fiction* (Washington, D.C.: The Association in Negro Folk Education, 1937), 149, comments on this in what remains one of the most insightful discussions of the representation of color and class in black literature.

44. Charles S. Johnson, *Growing Up in the Black Belt: Negro Youth in the Rural South* (Washington, D.C.: American Council on Education, 1941), 274.

45. Washington, *Marriage*, 105.

46. Nowell-Smith, "Minnelli and Melodrama," 118, describes this subversive opportunity melodrama provides: "The importance of melodrama (at least in the versions of it that are due to Ophuls, Minnelli, and Sirk) lies precisely in its ideological failure. Because it cannot accommodate its problems, either in a real present or in an ideal future, but lays them open in their shameless contradictoriness, it opens a space which most Hollywood forms have studiously closed off."

47. Elsaesser, "Tales of Sound and Fury," 6.

48. The phrase is Sirk's, as quoted in Paul Willemen, "Distanciation and Douglas Sirk" in *Douglas Sirk*, ed. Laura Mulvey and Jon Halliday (Edinburgh Film Festival, 1972), 26. For one of the most important attempts to theorize melodrama, cinema aesthetics, and black suffering in a discussion of the 1959 version of *Imitation of Life*, see Richard Dyer, "LANA: Four Films of Lana Turner," *Movie* 25 (Winter 1977–78): 40–52.

49. Jane Feuer, in "Melodrama, Serial Form and Television Today," *Screen* 25 (January–February 1984): 6, makes this point about authorship in her discussion of British melodrama theory, along with the point that another problem with the "space" theory is that the other discourse can only be read by "an elite audience already committed to subversive ideas."

50. Elsaesser, "Tales of Sound and Fury," 2–3.

51. Terry Eagleton, *Criticism and Ideology* (London: Verso, 1978), 43.

52. Ralph Matthews, "Too Light for the Movies," *The Afro-American Week*, March 25, 1933; Ray Buford, "Color in Hollywood," Los Angeles, Calif., December 21, 1934 (clippings file, Schomburg Center for Research in Black Culture, New York Public Library).

53. The Hollywood film that is most notorious for using skin color variation to create types is *Carmen Jones*, and the indictment of it is James Baldwin, "*Carmen Jones*, The Dark Is Light Enough," in *Notes of a Native Son* (New York: Dial Press, 1964), 50–51.

54. Nowell-Smith, "Minnelli and Melodrama," 117.

55. Christine Gledhill, in "Recent Developments in Feminist Criticism," *Quarterly Review of Film Studies* 3 (Fall 1978): 483, makes a similar point. Reprinted in Mary Ann Doane, Patricia Mellencamp, and Linda Williams, eds., *Re-Vision: Essays in Feminist Film Criticism* (Frederick, Md.: University Publications of America, 1984), 18–45.

56. Nowell-Smith, "Minnelli and Melodrama," 117.

57. Christopher Orr, in "Closure and Containment: Marylee Hadley in *Written on the Wind*," *Wide Angle* 4, no. 2 (1980): 28–35, considers Marylee's future; and Feuer, "Melodrama, Serial Form," 12, in reference to the same scene, suggests that the audience may have some concern about Mitch and Lucy's future.

58. See Tania Modleski, *Loving with a Vengeance: Mass-Produced Fantasies for Women* (New York: Methuen, 1984).

59. Vicinus, "'Helpless and Unfriended,'" 132.

Tommy L. Lott

A No-Theory Theory of Contemporary Black Cinema

When film scholars are asked to decide which are best among a body of films they identify as "black," what is at stake is something more than merely the aesthetic question of what counts as a good black film. Indeed, they must consider a more fundamental definitional question regarding the nature of black cinema, a question that raises deeper issues concerning both the concept of black identity and the concept of cinema itself. I suspect that film criticism has not offered much assistance in clarifying the concept *black cinema* because there exist no uncontested criteria to which an ultimate appeal can be made to resolve these underlying issues. This scholarly morass must be understood in terms of the inherently political context in which the concept of black cinema has been introduced.

In his book *Black Film as Genre*, Thomas Cripps demonstrates how difficult it is to provide an adequate definition of black cinema. He employs a notion of black cinema that refers almost exclusively to theater films about the black experience that are produced, written, directed, and performed by black people for a primarily black audience (3–12). But this leaves us wondering what to do with a well-known group of films about black people by white filmmakers. Although Cripps displays a rather tenuous allegiance to his initial statement of an essentialist paradigm, he has nonetheless presented an idea that lends credence to those who would exclude films such as King Vidor's *Hallelujah*, Shirley Clarke's *The Cool World*, Michael Roemer's *Nothing But a Man*, Charlie Ahearn's *Wild Styles*, and John Sayles' *The Brother from Another Planet* from the newly emerging black canon. On strictly aesthetic grounds, however, these films may strike some critics as being better than many others that would more adequately satisfy Cripps's essential criteria.

Some black film catalogers have sought to avoid the essentialist problem of being overly restrictive by opting for all-inclusive criteria. Klotman's *Frame by Frame: A Black Filmography* and Parish and Hill's *Black Action Films*, for instance, seem to identify films as black if they

Originally appeared in *African American Review* (formerly *Black American Literature Forum*) 25, no. 2: 221–36. Reprinted by permission of the author.

meet *any* of Cripps's several criteria. As might be expected, some critics have complained that not all of the films they list ought to count as black cinema.[1]

Missing from both the narrowness of essentialist criteria and the broadness of nonessentialist criteria are criteria that would account for the political dimensions of black filmmaking practices. Although audience reactions may vary from film to film, black people have a deep-seated concern with their history of being stereotyped in Hollywood films, a concern that provides an important reason to be skeptical about any concept of black cinema that would include works that demean blacks. Some would seek to abate this concern by specifying a set of wholly aesthetic criteria by which to criticize bad films about black people by both black and white filmmakers. Unfortunately, this approach contains undesirable implications for black filmmaking practices. We need only consider the fact that low-budget productions (e.g., *Bush Mama*, *Bless Their Little Hearts*, and *Killer of Sheep*) frequently suffer in the marketplace, as well as in the eyes of critics, when they fail to be aesthetically pleasing, or the fact that a film's success will sometimes be due largely to its aesthetic appeal, despite its problematic political orientation (e.g., *Roots* or *Shaka Zulu*).

For this reason, such commentators as Teshome Gabriel and Kobena Mercer ("Diaspora") have urged film critics to address the politics of black filmmaking practice with an awareness that what is often referred to as "aesthetics" is linked with important issues pertaining to the control of film production and distribution. Incorporating aesthetics into a more politicized account of black filmmaking practices would seem to allow critics to evade the narrowness of the essentialist view, but there is some reason to wonder whether this move toward aesthetics would allow the accommodation of a strictly cultural criterion for the definition of black cinema without invoking a notion of "black aesthetics," on which some reconstituted version of biological essentialism may again be reinstated.

The political aspects of the notion of aesthetics in film theory are sometimes shielded by the latent connection between biological essentialism and issues of control in film practice. We can, for example, see a tendency to racialize the political concern with control of the black film image in August Wilson's recent demand for a black director for the movie version of his play *Fences:* "Let's make a rule. Blacks don't direct Italian films. Italians don't direct Jewish films. Jews don't direct black American films. That might account for about 3 percent of the films that are made in this country" (71). Although Wilson's claim might be taken to commit him to accepting any director who is biologically black, he clearly would not want a black director who lacked the cultural sensibility required for a faithful rendering of his play. But if even a black director could prove unsatisfactory for aesthetic reasons, how do we make political sense of Wilson's demand for a black director, given that there could be some white director who might be more suitable from a cultural standpoint?

I want to advance a theory of contemporary black cinema that accords with the fact that biological criteria are neither necessary nor sufficient for the application of the concept of black cinema. I refer to this theory as a no-theory, because I want to avoid any commitment to an essentialized notion by not giving a definition of black cinema. Rather, the theoretical concern of my no-theory is primarily with the complexity of meanings we presently associate with the political aspirations of black people. Hence, it is a theory that is designed to be discarded when those meanings are no longer applicable.

The Aesthetic Critique of Blaxploitation

The history of black cinema can be roughly divided into four periods: Early Silent Films (1890–1920), Early Soundies and Race Films (1920–45), Postwar Problem Films (1945–60), and Contemporary Films.[2] With regard to the history of black cinema, the so-called blaxploitation period is a relatively recent, and short-lived, phenomenon. Although there has been a siphoning off of black audiences since the early days of race films, nothing approximating the Hollywood onslaught of the early 1970s has occurred at any other time.

The term *blaxploitation* has been used to refer to those black-oriented films produced in Hollywood beginning in 1970 and continuing mainly until 1975, but in various ways persisting until the present (Miller; Pines, "Blaxploitation"; Ward). However, in addition to its being a historical index, the term is a way of labeling a film that fails in certain ways to represent the aesthetic values of black culture properly.[3] Mark Reid, for instance, expresses this view in his account of the shortcomings of blaxploitation era films:

> Having established the fact that there was a young black audience receptive to thoughts about violence, it should have been possible to create black action films that appealed to this audience while satisfying a black aesthetic. The commercial black action films of the 1970s, however, never reached this ideal because they were not independent productions or because black independent producers relied on major distributors. (25)

Although, as I shall indicate shortly, Reid's criticism rests on a misleading dichotomy between independent and nonindependent films, his remarks inherently acknowledge the role that production and distribution play in shaping the aesthetic characteristics of a film. At a time of financial exigency, some Hollywood studios discovered that there was a large black audience starving for black images on the screen. This situation provided an immediate inducement for them to exploit the box office formula of the black hero (first male, later female) which, subsequently, became the earmark of the blaxploitation flick.[4]

Although there are many issues raised by blaxploitation era filmmaking that deserve greater attention, I want to focus on the problem of commercialism in order to highlight the influence of the market on certain aesthetic characteristics of black movies.[5] First, it needs to be stated, and clarified, that not all blaxploitation era films conformed to the box office formula. Some were not commercially oriented, while others were very worthwhile from a social and political standpoint.[6] To reduce them all to the hero formula, provided somewhat inadvertently by Van Peebles' *Sweet Sweetback's Baadasssss Song,* is to overlook their many differences in style, audience orientation, and political content.

Second, given the history of black cinema, there is a certain logic to the development of the box office formula. The idea of depicting black men as willing to engage in violent acts toward whites was virtually taboo in Hollywood films all the way through the 1960s. But once the news footage of the 1960s rebellions, along with the media construction of the Black Panther Party, began to appear, mainstream films such as *In the Heat of the Night* made an effort to acknowledge (albeit to contain) this "New Negro" (Ryan and Kellner, 121–29). Even within these limits, however, what had made Malcolm X appear so radical to mainstream television audiences at that time was the fact that he had *publicly* advocated self-defense.

When *Sweetback* was shown in 1971, it was an immediate success with black audiences because it captured an image of self-defense that gave on-screen legitimation to violent retaliation against racist police brutality. Black heroic violence against white villains rapidly became a Hollywood commodity, and literally dozens of films were produced for black audiences that capitalized on this new formula. It is worth noting here that it was, in many respects, a Hollywood-induced taboo that created a need for such images in the black audience, a need that was then fulfilled by Hollywood. The ultimate irony is that, once these films began to proliferate, there was an organized effort in the black community to demand their cessation (see Miller, 149).

It is also worth noting that *Sweetback* provoked a critical response that varied among different political factions within the black community, as well as among film critics. Community-based activists who opposed the film's image of black people ranged from cultural nationalists, who wanted a more culturally educational film, to middle-class black protesters, who wanted a film that projected a more positive image of the race (Reid, 29). As Mark Reid has noted, the film's political orientation, quite interestingly, received both "high praise" from Huey

Newton and the Black Panther Party newspaper in Oakland and "denunciation" from a Kuumba Workshop nationalist publication in Chicago (30). Although Newton was not alone in giving the film critical praise, his allegorical interpretation of the film's sexual imagery was not widely shared among critics, especially feminists concerned with its portrayal of women (Bowser, 51).

The critical controversy around *Sweetback*'s image of black people is not amenable to resolution on strictly aesthetic grounds, for *Sweetback* clearly represents some version of the black aesthetic. A political debate seems to have transpired between the film's supporters and detractors in an attempt to make the case for either accepting or rejecting the film. Indeed, some critics have argued that *Sweetback* lacks a politicized image (Reid, 26), while others have argued that it politicized the image of black people to the point of lapsing into propaganda (Pines, "Blaxploitation," 123).

With regard to the role of aesthetics, blaxploitation era films pose a rather peculiar problem for a theory of contemporary black cinema. Can a film count as black cinema when it merely presents a blackface version of white films, or when it merely reproduces stereotypical images of black people?

Commentators have maintained quite different views in answer to this question. James Snead has argued for a very sophisticated notion of recording that requires of black cinema what he calls the "syntagmatic" revision of stereotyped images through the selective use of editing and montage ("Recording Blackness," 2). According to Snead, the syntax of traditional Hollywood cinema must be reworked to recode the black image effectively. However, against the backdrop of Hollywood's pre-blaxploitation era stereotype of black men as sexually castrated buffoons, what rules out the less sophisticated blaxploitation practice of substituting a highly sexualized black male hero who exercises power over white villains as an attempt to record the Hollywood image of black men? Mark Reid asserts, with little hesitation, that "blacks who would find psychological satisfaction in films featuring black heroes have just as much right to have their tastes satisfied as do whites who find pleasure in white heroes such as those in Clint Eastwood and Charles Bronson films" (30). If the creation of black heroic images through role reversals can be considered a recoding technique utilized by blaxploitation filmmakers, then how does this practice compare with other, more avant-garde recoding practices of black independent filmmakers?

It can be quite troublesome for a theory of black cinema that relies too strongly on aesthetics to give an account of the influence of blaxploitation films on subsequent black independent films (see Taylor, "We Don't Need," 84–85). Given that aesthetic-based theories, such as Snead's want to contrast black independent films with Hollywood-produced films about black people, where do blaxploitation films fit into such a juxtaposition? How do we make sense of the charge, brought by a black independent filmmaker, of a fellow black independent filmmaker's having irresponsibly produced a blaxploitation film?[7] The fact that the charge was made suggests that black independent filmmaking is not immune from the aesthetic pitfalls of blaxploitation cinema.

For present purposes, I am less interested in deciding the question of what films to count as blaxploitation than I am in the implication the appeal to aesthetics, inherent in the accusation, seems to carry for our understanding of the place of aesthetics in a theory of black cinema. To denounce a film such as *Sweetback* as exploitative is to suggest that aesthetic criteria provide the highest ground of appeal for deciding definitional questions regarding black cinematic representation, for the charge presupposes that there is some sense in which to produce a blaxploitation film is to have compromised black aesthetic values. What must be explained, however, is how such films stand in relation to independently made films that were not constrained to violate black aesthetic values in this way. Apparently, the term *independent* does not always mean what a filmmaker has eschewed market concerns. When a blaxploitation film is independently made by a black filmmaker for a black audience, however, to whom has the film's aesthetic orientation been compromised and, further, to what extent do such compromises affect a film's status as a black cinematic work?

Recently there has been a major shift toward independently produced blaxploitation films. This practice makes clear that the biologically essentialist view of black cinema (those films about black people, produced by a black filmmaker, for a black audience) is much too simplistic. One important implication of the aesthetic critique of blaxploitation is that certain aesthetic qualities of a film can sometimes count as much against its being inducted into the canon of black films as the filmmaker's race or the film's intended audience. While the insights derived from the aesthetic critique of black filmmaking practices are undoubtedly healthy signs of sophistication in black film commentary, we must not overlook the fact that these critiques also give rise to many difficulties connected with the problem of how film criticism should relate to a plurality of standards by which black films are evaluated.[8]

One such difficulty that must be faced by aesthetic-based theories of black cinema arises from the fact that, since the mid-1980s, there has been a growing interest in black-oriented cinema, especially black comedy, by white audiences. The success of black television sitcoms, as well as Arsenio Hall's nightly talk show, provides some indication that white audiences are more willing to indulge not so completely assimilated black people than network executives had previously supposed. Spike Lee's humorous social commentary has opened the door for other, similarly inclined, black filmmakers and television producers. All of this comic relief in the television and movie industry has been spearheaded, of course, by the mass appeal of Richard Pryor, Eddie Murphy, and Bill Cosby. Given their influence on the present context for black filmmaking, it seems that a theory of contemporary black cinema cannot postulate the black audience as a necessary ingredient.

A related difficulty that carries greater significance for our understanding of the influence of the crossover audience on the aesthetics of certain films about black people arises from the manner in which Eddie Murphy's attempt to signify on black minstrelsy has simply replaced the old-fashioned minstrel show. Murphy's success in Hollywood was quickly followed by that of his "black pack" cohort Robert Townsend, whose humorous criticism of Hollywood in his very popular film was largely reduced to a shuffle with a critique of itself.[9] As though the hegemony of the Hollywood industry were not enough to contend with, more politically astute filmmakers working in the realm of comedy, such as Spike Lee, are now challenged with finding ways to distinguish themselves from such neo-minstrelsy. Indeed, some filmmakers formerly aligned with the counterhegemonic practices of the post-1960s black independent movement seem to have allowed the white audience for black-oriented humor to so influence their filmmaking that we now have a new generation of blaxploitation cinema. This influence is displayed in the Hudlin brothers' film *House Party*, which seems rigorously to avoid dealing with certain very pressing issues raised in the film (e.g., police brutality) in order not to offend the potential white audience. Unlike Spike Lee's probing satire, which engages in a black-oriented humor that sometimes seems intended to offend white audiences, *House Party* is closer to mindless slapstick.[10]

Although some film commentators have attempted to acknowledge the disparity between the aesthetic values of black audiences and the aesthetic values of filmmakers and critics, film criticism generally tends to adhere to a top-down view of aesthetics, as though audiences have no role to play in the determination of aesthetic values. What the black audience appeal of blaxploitation films (old and new) indicates, against the wishes of many film critics, is that it is misguided to suppose that a filmic work of art, or entertainment, has black audience appeal simply because it aims for a black audience by promoting certain black aesthetic values. In the case of the black independent cinema movement of the 1970s in America, as well as the 1980s black workshop movement in Britain, the attempt to reclaim and reconstruct a black film aesthetics that would somehow counteract the influence of Hollywood's blaxploitation filmmaking has, by and large, not been well received by black audiences, although many of these films have been frequently presented at international festivals, in art museums, and in college courses devoted to film study.[11] How can we best understand the fact that films which aim to present a more authentic black aesthetic are largely ignored by and unknown to black audiences, while being extremely well-received in elite white film circles? Despite their admirable political orientation, such films seem to have achieved the status of art-for-art's sake, with mainly an all-white audience appeal.

This lack-of-a-black-audience problem shows the need to resist the tendency of aesthetic-based theories of black cinema to position the aesthetic values of the black artist above those of the black audience. In order for black film commentary to acknowledge more pluralistic criteria by which to assess the artistic value of cinematic works, some weight must be given to the viewpoint of black audiences, inasmuch as it is imprudent at best continually to posit a black aesthetic that very few black audiences share.

Some of these considerations regarding the audience crossover phenomenon in contemporary black cinema argue against the cultural essentialist attempt to define black cinema in terms of aesthetics. As the divisions between independent and Hollywood-produced films about black people begin to dissolve, as a result of the mainstream market for both, it has become extremely difficult to maintain that either a black filmmaker or a black audience is required for a film with a black orientation. To see this, we need only consider the fact that, in addition to his crossover status in the record industry, Prince is virtually neck and neck with Spike Lee as a filmmaker, each having four major releases. There is no reason to suppose that, despite a preference among commentators for Spike Lee's version of the black aesthetic, the aesthetic in Prince's movies has any less box office appeal to much of the same audience.[12]

The need for an essentialist theory diminishes, along with the idea of a monolithic black film aesthetic, once we realize that there is no monolithic black audience. There certainly are black-oriented films, some of which are much better than others, but not all of those approved by critics manage to touch base with black audiences (e.g., *To Sleep with Anger*) and many of those condemned by critics have become black audience classics (e.g., *Superfly*). These facts may be difficult to accept, but to advocate a "better" cinema that is significantly different requires a political argument. I will now turn to consider the argument I think is presently most viable in a politically confused era dominated by neoconservative ideology.

Black Identity and Black Cinema

Before I take up the question of how politics and aesthetics can be situated into a theory of black cinema, I would like to insert a word of clarification regarding the prevailing use of the term *cinema* to refer to films as such; for example, movies that were made to be shown in theaters. I believe that this restrictive usage is unfortunate, since some fairly good films about black people have been made for television.[13] The misconception that underlies this narrow focus on box office movies is exacerbated by the fact that some of the most innovative black filmmaking is presently occurring in music videos. Indeed, the dominant influence of television on black popular culture has some rather interesting implications for black film practices that no theory of black cinema can afford to overlook. Because black urban youth culture has been visually promulgated primarily through television, this segment of the black movie audience has been heavily influenced by black images presented on television. Added to this television orientation is a large black youth market for blaxploitation films on videocassettes. These influences are displayed quite regularly in what Nelson George refers to as "blaxploitation rap," for example, rap lyrics that have been heavily influenced by blaxploitation films.[14] It is, to say the least, perilous for filmmakers interested in reaching black youth to ignore the single most important medium of visually representing their cultural values.

In Britain, black filmmaking and television are much more structurally connected, since the workshops produce their films for Channel 4 (see Fountain; Pines, "Cultural"). Undoubtedly, this structural relation between filmmaking and television will eventually obtain in America once high-definition television is introduced since, with the advent of this new technology, movies as such seem certain to be superseded by television. For all these reasons, I think it wise at this point to expand the concept of cinema to include television.

With regard to politics, there is a very good reason that the biological version of the essentialist definition of black cinema will invariably fall short. Any definition that requires films to be made by black filmmakers in order to be included in the category of black cinema will simply not match the ambivalence engendered by having to place biological over cultural criteria in deciding questions of black identity. This does not mean that, generally speaking, most of us have no idea of what to count as a black film. Indeed, the definition of black cinema is a problem by virtue of the fact that, whether it is based on biological or cultural criteria, its viability can easily be called into question.

The Du Boisian worry about the adequacy of biological criteria as the ultimate ground of appeal when faced with questions of black identity poses the greatest difficulty for the essentialist notion of black cinema. For Du Bois, the problem stems from the fact that there is no agreement about how best to define a black person, although there is some sense in which we all operate with some ideas about what constitutes black identity.[15] We need only consider the manner in which we must still grapple with the age-old problem of the "non-black" black person, for example, the person who, though biologically black, does not identify with black culture. Although there can be little doubt that, in the context of the American system of apartheid, the question of whether a particular person counts as black is most often decided by skin color and physical appearance, there are numerous instances in which this honor is withheld strictly on cultural grounds. It is far too common for black people to feel the yoke of oppression at the hands of a white-identified black person. Consequently, as someone perceived to be disloyal to the group, an overly assimilated (Eurocentric) black person can sometimes lose his or her standing in the eyes of other black people. In such cases we can notice how the tension between biological and cultural criteria of black identity is resolved in terms of a political definition of black people.[16] It is for some reason such as this thta I am motivated to develop the concept of black cinema within the context of a political theory.

The Concept of Third Cinema Revisited

Without any pretense that I can offer a replacement for the essentialist definition of Black cinema, I want to suggest why I think the Third Cinema movement of the 1960s seems to have been on the right track, although in America certain mainstream cooptational factors have basically derailed it. According to various conflicting reports, the advocates of Third Cinema have come under heavy criticism lately for being, of all things, overly nationalistic.[17] Unfortunately, in an attempt to address this worry, some commentators tend needlessly to equate nationalism with the essentialist view.[18] But the concept of Third Cinema should not be saddled with the myopic vision of essentialists who are constrained by an overemphasis on biological criteria for resolving questions of national identity.[19] What makes Third Cinema thrid (i.e., a viable alternative to Western cinema) is not exclusively the racial makeup of a filmmaker, a film's aesthetic character, or a film's intended audience, but rather a film's political orientation within the hegemonic structures of postcolonialism. When a film contributes ideologically to the advancement of Black people, within a context of systematic denial, the achievement of this political objective ought to count as a criterion of evaluation on a par with any essentialist criterion.

The best way to meet the criticism that the concept of Third Cinema is too vague because it allows under its rubric many diverse cultural groups is to recognize that this objection misleadingly imputes an uncontested essentialist paradigm.[20] The Third Cinema movement represents a break with, and resistance to, the cultural imperialism fostered by the global expansion of the Hollywood industry. There is an important sense in which it aims to do what Hollywood has done—namely, to reach beyond national boundaries. There is no reason to deny that cultural diversity is a problem among the many ethnically distinct black people living together in America, much less a problem among various

Third World people from widely different backgrounds in faraway places. But clearly if Europeans, who for centuries have waged war against each other, and are still caught up in their own ethnic rivalries, can construct a concept of themselves as a globally dominant white group, how can it be so much more objectionable for non-white people to construct a global counterconcept by which to defend themselves? The white cultural nationalism of Hollywood's Eurocentric empire requires something like a Third Cinema movement to help non-white people survive the oppressive and self-destructive consciousness that empire seeks to perpetuate.

With regard to black filmmaking practices, the concept of Third Cinema provides the rudiments of a theory of black cinema that is most conducive to this political function. As a primarily oppositional practice engaged in resistance and affirmation, black cinema need not be presently defined apart from its political function (see Espinosa). I call this a no-theory theory because I see no need to resolve, on aesthetic grounds, the dispute over what counts as blaxploitation. Neither do I see a need to choose between realist and avant-garde film techniques.[21] I am more interested in understanding how any aesthetic strategy can be employed to challenge, disrupt, and redirect the pervasive influence of Hollywood's master narrative. To accomplish this decidedly political objective, black filmmaking practices must continue to be fundamentally concerned with the issues that presently define the political struggle of black people. Hence, I want to advance a theory of black cinema that is in keeping with those filmmaking practices that aim to foster social change, rather than participate in a process of formulating a definition of black cinema that allows certain films to be canonized on aesthetic grounds so as to occupy a place in the history of cinema. The theory we need now is a political theory of black cinema that incorporates a plurality of aesthetic values that are consistent with the fate and destiny of black people as a group engaged in a protracted struggle for social equality.

NOTES

1. Phyllis Klotman's black filmography prompted Gladstone L. Yearwood to complain that "to identify a black film as any film with black faces is to trivialize or nullify a definition of black film" ("Towards," 68–69). In his review of *Black Action Films*, Roland Jefferson takes Parish and Hill to task for including *Rocky I–IV* as black films (22).

2. Various periodizations have been offered by other commentators. See, for instance, Snead, "Images"; Taylor, "L.A."

3. In this sense, Fred Williamson's independently produced films (which have been continuous since his participation in the early phase of Hollywood blaxploitation) would count as a perpetuation of this style. Eddie Murphy's recent *Harlem Nights* is a throwback to Williamson's *Black Caesar* and *Hell Up in Harlem*. I would also include the recent spate of hip hop movies as a neo-blaxploitation genre, although, within this genre, we must again distinguish "positive-image" films such as Harry Belafonte's *Beat Street* from more violence-laden films such as Run DMC's *Tougher Than Leather*.

4. For a discussion of the cooptational use of black heroic characters to legitimate oppression, see Gladstone Yearwood's "The Hero." David E. James provides a wise bit of cautionary reflection on the bildungsroman narrative of *Sweetback* as a self-defeating contributor to the film's commodification into blaxploitation (135–37). And Clyde Taylor ("We Don't Need") takes issue with the master narrative in all of its various guises.

5. For instance, there is a need to examine more fully the transition period in the late 1960s as a precursor to blaxploitation era filmmaking, especially with regard to independently produced films about black people. Some attention should also be given to the carryover effect of blaxploitation era films on the image of black people in mass-audience films and to the intertextual influences of blaxploitation on television programming.

6. Several factors helped shape the movie industry's multifarious output of blaxploitation era films, but the most outstanding was the market orientation of each film. Given that some of the larger-budgeted productions (e.g., *100 Rifles*, *The Great White Hope*, and *The Learning Tree*) were intended for a mainstream audience, whereas low-budget productions (e.g., *Superfly*, *Blacula*, and *Coffey Brown*) were limited to box office showings in black communities, it would be a serious oversight to ignore the guerrilla tactics employed by Melvin Van Peebles to produce *Sweetback* and Bill Gunn to film *Ganja and Hess*. The avant-garde styles mastered by Van Peebles and Gunn owe much to the clandestine context in which their projects were pursued and contrast sharply with the more standard approaches displayed in mainstream productions such as *Claudine*, *A Hero Ain't Nothing But a Sandwich*, *The River Niger*, *Brothers*, *The Spook Who Sat by the Door*, and *Gordon's War*. These latter films, nonetheless, were a far cry from the more typical black action movies of the period.

7. See the text of the panel discussion on *Sweetback* with Melvin Van Peebles, St. Clair Bourne, Haile Gerima, and Pearl Bowser held at a conference on black independent filmmaking at Ohio State University in 1981 (Yearwood, "*Sweet*").

8. This point was brought to my attention in a fall 1987 lecture at Northeastern University, during which Clyde Taylor presented an analysis of the class differences in audience reactions to *Sweetback* as a methodological device by which to interpret the film. See the very interesting discussion of this issue by Mercer in his "Recoding Narratives," but also see Mercer and Julien, and Willemen.

9. In a similar vein, Keenan Ivory Wayans's *I'm Gonna Git You Sucka* and his television show "In Living Color" present a black-oriented variety of post–Eddie Murphy humor that relies heavily on the ridicule of white stereotypes of black people.

10. The social taboo against public statements regarding the media hype of Larry Bird as the greatest basketball player ever was quite deliberately violated by Lee in *She's Gotta Have It*. Lee seemed to rail against the de facto censorship of what many black people believe about Larry Bird by having his character Mars Blackmon flaunt anti–Bird jokes in the face of the audience that had witnessed Isiah Thomas's being coerced on national television to demeaningly recant his truthful comments regarding the racist commentary in sports broadcasting.

11. For a pointed discussion of this dilemma facing black independent filmmakers, see Taylor, "Black Films"; Gilroy. See also Larry Rohter's discussion of Charles Burnett's *To Sleep with Anger*.

12. Prince's films remain closer to Hollywood's assimilationist paradigm of "crossover" black cinema, whereas Spike Lee entered the crossover market with black-oriented films that are closer to the black independent tradition.

13. I have in mind here, specifically, films such as *The Killing Floor*, *Minstrel Man*, *The Autobiography of Miss Jane Pittman*, *Go Tell It on the Mountain*, and *The Women of Brewster Place*.

14. Some rap artists have characterized their cultural practice as "black America's TV station" (see Leland, 48).

15. Du Bois argued for a socially constructed concept of black identity that black people should "invent" to advance themselves (483–92).

16. Within the unspoken norms of African American culture, black people with a Caucasian appearance generally bear the burden of proving their loyalty, given that they have an option to "pass," despite their known biological heritage.

17. See the alternative accounts of Kobena Mercer ("Third Cinema"), David Will, Paul Willemen, and Clyde Taylor ("Eurocentrics").

18. Willemen displays this tendency when he attempts to utilize Bakhtin's thesis regarding sociohistorical specificity to reconstruct Gabriel's internationalist account of Third Cinema practice (see 23ff.).

19. While it would be inaccurate to attribute this view to Willemen, some of his declarations lend themselves to an interpretation along these lines. For instance, he maintains that "the question of the national cannot be divorced from the question of Third Cinema" (20) and that those engaged in black film practices must refuse "to homogenise every non-Euro-American culture into a globalised other" (29). But surely Willemen does not mean to deny the possibility of new social formations, perhaps international in scope, which stand opposed to neocolonial structures that are ultimately rationalized on biological notions of national identities.

20. Stuart Hall ("Cultural Identity" and "New Ethnicities") has advocated an extreme version of the nonessentialist view of cultural practice.

21. For a critical discussion of how black films that are modernist in style have gained a greater currency than those that are steeped in realism, see Williamson; Fusco. See also Valerie Smith's insightful commentary on what counts as an "experimental" black film.

WORKS CITED

Bowser, Pearl. "Sexual Imagery and the Black Woman in Cinema." Yearwood, *Black Cinema*, 42–51.

Cham, Mybe B., and Claire Andrade-Watkins, eds. *BlackFrames: Critical Perspectives on Black Independent Cinema.* Cambridge: MIT Press, 1988.

Cripps, Thomas. *Black Film as Genre.* Bloomington: Indiana University Press, 1978.

Davis, Mike, et al., eds. *The Year Left 2: An American Socialist Yearbook.* London: Verso, 1987.

Du Bois, W. E. B. "The Conservation of Races." In *Negro Social and Political Thought 1850–1920.* Ed. Howard Brotz. New York: Basic, 1966. 483–92.

Espinosa, Julio Garcia. "For an Imperfect Cinema." 1969. *Liberation, Socialism.* Vol. 2 of *Communication and Class Struggle: An Anthology in 2 Volumes.* Ed. Armand Mattelart and Seth Siegelaub. New York: International General, 1979–83, 295–300.

Fountain, Alan. "Channel 4 and Black Independents." Mercer, *Black Film*, 42–44.

Fusco, Coco. "The Other Is In." Mercer, *Black Film*, 37–39.

Gabriel, Teshome H. "Third Cinema as Guardian of Popular Memory: Towards a Third Aesthetics." Pines and Willemen, 53–64.

Gilroy, Paul. "Nothing But Sweat Inside My Hand: Diaspora Aesthetics and Black Arts in Britain." Mercer, *Black Film*, 44–46.

Hall, Stuart. "Cultural Identity and Cinematic Representation." *Framework* 36 (1989): 68–81.

___. "New Ethnicities." Mercer, *Black Film*, 27–30.

James, David E. "Chained to Devilpictures: Cinema and Black Liberation in the Sixties." Davis, 125–38.

Jefferson, Roland, Rev. of *Black Action Films*, ed. James R. Parish and George H. Hill. *Black Film Review* 5, no. 4 (1989): 21–22.

Klotman, Phyllis, ed. *Frame by Frame: A Black Filmography.* Bloomington: Indiana University Press, 1979.

Leland, John. "Armageddon in Effect." *Spin* 4, no. 6 (1988): 46–49, 76.

Mercer, Kobena, ed. *Black Film/British Cinema.* London: Institute of Contemporary Arts, 1988.

___. "Diaspora Culture and the Dialogic Imagination: The Aesthetics of Black Independent Film in Britain." Cham and Andrade-Watkins, 50–61.

___. "Recoding Narratives of Race and Nation." Mercer, *Black Film*, 4–14.

___. "Third Cinema at Edinburgh: Reflections on a Pioneering Event." *Screen* 27, no. 6 (1986): 95–102.

Mercer, Kobena, and Isaac Julien. "De Margin and De Centre." *Screen* 29, no. 4 (1988): 2–10.

Miller, James A. "From Sweetback to Celie: Blacks on Film into the 80s." Davis, 139–59.

Parish, James R., and George H. Hill, eds. *Black Action Films.* Jefferson: McFarland, 1989.

Pines, Jim. "Blaxploitation: 'Ethnic Adjustment' in Hollywood." In *Blacks in Films: A Survey of Racial Themes and Images in the American Film.* London: Studio Vista, 1975. 118–27.

___. "The Cultural Context of Black British Cinema." Cham and Andrade-Watkins, 26–36.

Pines, Jim, and Paul Willemen, eds. *Questions of Third Cinema.* London: British Film Institute, 1989.

Reid, Mark A. "The Black Action Film: The End of the Patiently Enduring Black Hero." *Film History* 2 (1988): 23–36.

Rohter, Larry. "An All-Black Film (Except for the Audience)." *New York Times* November 20, 1990: B1.

Ryan, Michael, and Douglas Kellner. *Camera Politica.* Bloomington: Indiana University Press, 1988.

Smith, Valerie. "Reconstructing the Image: The Emergent Black Woman Director." *Callaloo* 11 (1988): 709–19.

Snead, James. "Images of Blacks in Black Independent Films: A Brief Survey." Cham and Andrade-Watkins, 16–25.

___. "Recoding Blackness: The Visual Rhetoric of Black Independent Film." In *Circular for The New American Filmmakers Series 23.* New York: Whitney Museum of American Art, 1985, 1–2.

Taylor, Clyde. "Black Films in Search of a Home." *Freedomways* 23 (1983): 226–33.

___. "Eurocentrics Vs. New Thought at Edinburgh." *Framework* 34 (1987): 140–48.

___. "The L.A. Rebellion: A Turning Point in Black Cinema." In *Circular for The New American Filmmakers Series 26.* New York: Whitney Museum of American Art, 1986, 1–2.

___. "We Don't Need Another Hero: Anti-Theses on Aesthetics." Cham and Andrade-Watkins, 80–85.

Ward, Renée, "Black Films, White Profits." *Black Scholar* 7, no. 8 (1976): 13–24.

Will, David. "Edinburgh Film Festival, 1986." *Framework* 32/33 (1986): 197–209.

Willemen, Paul. "The Third Cinema Question: Notes and Reflections." Pines and Willemen, 1–29.

Williamson, Judith. "Two Kinds of Otherness." Mercer, *Black Film*, 33–37.

Wilson, August. "I Don't Want to Hire Nobody Just 'Cause They're Black." *Spin* 6, no. 7 (1990): 71.

Yearwood, Gladstone L., ed. *Black Cinema Aesthetics: Issues in Independent Black Filmmaking.* Athens: Ohio University Center for Afro-American Studies, 1982.

___. "The Hero in Black Film: An Analysis of the Film Industry and Problems in Black Cinema." *Wide Angle* 5, no. 2 (1982): 42–51.

___. "*Sweet Sweetback's Baadasssss Song* and the Development of the Contemporary Black Film Movement." Yearwood, *Black Cinema*, 53–66.

___. "Towards a Theory of a Black Cinema Aesthetic." Yearwood, *Black Cinema*, 67–81.

Wahneema Lubiano

But Compared to What?: Reading Realism, Representation, and Essentialism in *School Daze, Do the Right Thing,* and the Spike Lee Discourse

> *Brothers and Sisters, we need to talk.*
> —*Joe Wood, "Looking for Malcolm"*

> *Underneath it all, the posse don't know. Who, in fact, are "our people"?*
> —*Joe Wood, "Self-Deconstruction"*

I

> *One of the first things to do is to think through the limits of one's power. One must ruthlessly undermine . . . the story of the ethical universal, the hero. But the alternative is not constantly to evoke multiplicity; the alternative is to know . . . that this is a limited sample because of one's own inclinations and capacities to learn enough to take a larger sample. And this kind of work should be a collective enterprise. Other people will do some other work.*
> —*Gayatri Spivak, "In a Word"*

I am an African American feminist, with fragments of a recalcitrant cultural nationalism still in my veins, working primarily in the area of African American narrative, and I am interested in cultural studies; those four things account for the nature of my interest in Spike Lee. When I agreed to write this essay, I felt considerable frustration, because if there is one African American filmic who has gotten press, media, and

Originally appeared in *African American Review* (formerly *Black American Literature Forum*) 25, no. 2, 253–82. Reprinted by permission of the author.

academic attention to the point of saturation, Spike Lee is that one.[1] My frustration arose also from knowing that the mass media and its discourse around Spike Lee might not be accessible to a critique, for example, of that which makes him a totem. On the other hand, despite my misgivings about leftist and liberal fetishization of Lee,[2] as well as my distaste for the regressive and ultimately useless criticism from reactionary critics and commentators concerned with "negative images,"[3] I think that he and his work represent a problematic through which the political difficulties that inhere in African American cultural production in this moment can be usefully discussed. The Spike Lee discourse and his production offer a site for examining possibilities of oppositional, resistant, or subversive cultural production as well as the problems of productions that are *considered* oppositional, resistant, or subversive without accompanying analysis sustaining such evaluation.

I do not want to be misunderstood. I am not criticizing Spike Lee for his representation of what some have called "damaging" or "negative" images of African Americans, images that drove Stanley Crouch to froth at the mouth in print. I want to consider instead the tendency (and the implications of that tendency) among the majority of critical commentators to uncritically laud Lee's films—especially *Do the Right Thing*—and Lee's presence in African American filmmaking. *She's Gotta Have It* and *School Daze* do raise complicated issues despite both films' masculinist representations and the rampant homophobia of *School Daze*. I don't address *She's Gotta Have It* in this essay because so many other feminist critics, bell hooks preeminent among them, have said everything (and some more besides!) that I would have said about that film. While I find *School Daze* a more interesting film for my own close reading and, therefore, address it here, I also include *Do the Right Thing* because of the importance of that film to what I'm calling the "Spike Lee discourse."

The first part of my title—"But Compared to What?"—is taken from a Gene McDonald lyric (sung by Roberta Flack on her album *First Take*)—"trying to make it real but compared to what?"[4] The unvoiced of my title, of course, is the "trying to make it real." Trying to make *what* real? Lee's films' cultural product? Trying to make real African Americans' complicated existence in the minds of others, real in their own minds? Trying to make real the possibility of a counterhegemonic discourse on race, a critique of race? Trying to make real or concrete a set of abstractions that achieve concrete form in material practices embodied in a film, in language about a film, in the effects of a filmmaker's presence in the cultural domain? And what is race in the United States if not an attempt to make "real" a set of social assumptions about biology?

But compared to what? Compared to what is not real? Compared to other things both real and unreal? Compared to whatever else exists, has existed, or might be able to exist within the present terms of cultural production, or under terms that might be changed by our examination of what is real? Compared to who else exists, has existed, or can exist within the specific histories—past and present—of Black people across the diaspora engaged in filmmaking? *Compared to what?* might just mean compared to whatever you have.

What do issues of realism, representation, and essentialism have to do with the Spike Lee discourse and Lee's films? I am concerned with the difficulty of thinking and saying anything at all about Lee and his work without contextualizing his work's possibilities and problems as well as what Lee himself has come to mean in the current cultural/political climate. Yet much of the Lee discourse has been insufficiently contextualized. And when I say *political,* I mean political in the sense of discourse and cultural production concerned with issues of power. In order to talk about these things, I examine Lee's evaluation of his work (specifically *School Daze* and *Do the Right Thing*),[5] others' evaluations of his work, the problems raised by Lee's place in film production and discourse, and the films *School Daze* and *Do the Right Thing* themselves.

Gayatri Spivak, in the interview to which I refer in the epigraph above, addresses the possibilities of politically engaged criticism in the academy. I evoke her language here to consider another kind of politically engaged work: African American film production within the constraints of Euro-American film discourse. She describes an interventionist political cultural project: doing one's "sample" while others, presumably, do theirs. The problem of Spike Lee's "sample," his place in the sun, is that his presence, empowered by Hollywood studio hegemony and media consensus on his importance, can function to overshadow or make difficult other kinds of politically engaged cultural work, not because it is impossible for more than one African American filmmaker to get attention at a time, but because of the implications and manifestations of the attention given to his work.[6] Further, the availability of different strategies of representation is foreclosed by the pressure many African Americans place on any artist to "speak" for the community, a pressure against which countless African American critics have inveighed, but a pressure to which Lee himself contributes when he claims to have "told the truth."

Spivak's discussion can serve to remind us that the *context* of the "samples," their availability or unavailability, and the process of their reception, determine how centered, unitary, or authoritative Lee's work becomes. Were a variety of African American filmmakers framed with such a profile, such a salience, critics and commentators (both African Americans and others) might be less likely to insist that Lee's work is the "real thing" and celebrate it so uncritically. That is to say, the recognition of multiple filmic possibilities, created from variant points of view by various filmmakers, could function to preempt the unitary authority of any one of them. This is not to say that the *rhetoric* of the "real thing" would disappear under these conditions, but a reductionist African American representational hegemony would be more difficult to maintain. In other words, the combination of the increasing financial success of Lee's films and the media's fairly general deification of him functions to marginalize other African American filmic possibilities—possibilities, for example, such as those offered by independent African American women filmmakers.[7]

II

School Daze and *Do the Right Thing* are both engaged with problems of race and racism (external and internalized) in the context of a nation where race *as a construction* is not much talked about outside academic circles and where the idea of racism as intellectual, systemic, or concrete individual practice is cause for far more anger than theory, more recrimination and defensiveness than focus. Against this background, Stuart Hall's reading of the possibilities of Antonio Gramsel's work theorizes race and racisms and enables us to focus on the ways in which race and racisms are historically specific and inconsistent, to understand that manifestations of both change across time and across the complexities of the social formation. Hall argues that, while race is consistently related to class, it is not always the *result* of class difference (nor, I want to add, is race consistently *mediated* by class difference). The political consequences of specific moments of racism differ. At one moment and geopolitical locale racism manifests itself in colonial enclaves; at another, in slavery; at another, Bantustans; and, at still another, in something referred to as an urban "underclass" ("Gramsci's," 23–25).

This general line of theory offers a vantage point for connecting more specific arguments about constructions of "blackness" in the U.S. context, including Henry Louis Gates Jr.'s arguments about the metaphorical nature of "blackness" in Western metaphysical discourse. Anthony Appiah's work on the construction of race, and Frantz Fanon's arguments about the effects on blacks of the construction of "Negroness."[8] I am not taking any of these arguments to Manichean extremes and suggesting that there is no biology for, as Spivak cogently asserts, "biology doesn't just disappear"; it simply ought not to be the "ground of all explanations" (148). Hortense Spillers, for example, warns against the ideological manipulations of racialized biology (65–66). In her close reading of the Moynihan Report, she remarks on that text's confirmation of "the human body as a metonymic figure for an entire repertoire of human and social arrangements" (66).

What has not changed in the history of race in the United States is its centrality within our culture, the importance of it to our socialization as produced and reinforced by schools, organizations, family, our sexual lives, churches, institutions—all of which produce a racially structured society (Hall, "Gramsci's," 25). Race is a cultural factor of overwhelming importance. I raise these issues not only because Lee's work renders visible the African American presence within the terms of Euro-American dominance, but because he sees himself and his work in terms of racial, and hence political, engagement: he is quoted by Salim Muwakkil as saying, "Someone has to force America to come to grips with the problem of racism" ("Doing," 18). Additionally, Lee and his co-producer Monty Ross told an audience at the University of Texas at Austin that they wanted to make films with a message and would try to make entertaining what was also thought-provoking; they insisted that they would "tell the truth."[9] Aware of the need to make changes in the film industry by bringing in African Americans, Lee has indicated that he is proud of the part that he plays. As part of his production deal for *Do the Right Thing*, he has made his films vehicles for African American employment and entrance into film craft unions: two folks off the streets of Bedford-Stuyvesant are now part of a union because of him (Lee, Presentation; Tate, 85). Being a voice for the "real," effecting "reality," then, is the way that Lee sees his cultural mission.

His confidence that he has been able to force the United States to come to grips with the problem of racism is repeated in his insistence (in response to questions at the University of Texas) that he can retain his intellectual and political independence and still be financed by the studios as long as he continues to make money. In the first instance, however, he mistakes the media noise around race, racism, and his film for evidence that this country has "come to grips" with race. In fact, he must have realized at some point that his confidence was misplaced; in an article in *Mother Jones* he says that white people were more upset over the destruction of Sal's property than they were over Raheem's death (Orenstein, 34). In the second instance, his belief that profit might not be somehow tied to how much a mass-distributed film can make itself acceptable to vast numbers of U.S. citizens is simply naive; he needs to consider that, if a production has to return a profit in the millions of dollars, the likelihood of that production's remaining oppositional or subversive with regard to race might well be in inverse proportion to the extent the film relies on the support of a large (of whatever races), politically uncritical audience to turn a profit. I do not want to argue that studio funding *always* means that a compromise in form and content is inevitable—profits have been made with more politically adventurous material—nor do I want to argue that the relationship between funding and content is a simple one. In fact, in a session at the 1989 MLA convention, Ann Cvetkovich and I argued that, if one wants to engage politically with the majority of African Americans or any other marginalized group, one has to be prepared to think seriously about working in the mass culture (and, more to the point, mass distribution) arena (Lubiano and Cvetkovich, 13).[10] But I do want to insist that Lee's confidence needs to be mediated by a *complicated* awareness of market pressure.

In that vein, James Snead has argued that "without the incessant and confining restraints of box-office considerations, studio agenda, and censoring boards, the range of artistic choice in *independent* films is potentially *widened,* rather than *restricted*" (17). I don't draw on Snead here in order to absolutize independent production as always politically empowered and empowering; I do not want to romanticize the coercive nature of inequitable access to the means of film production, something Sankofa Film/Video filmmaker Isaac Julien addresses in the black British context.[11] (He and the other members of black British video collectives became involved in separatist projects, opting for ethnically or racially based organizations, because of their exclusion from "white" institutions [Fusco, "Fantasies," 8].) Nonetheless, I think such consideration of the possible costs of studio/institutional support is especially timely when one sees critics such as Nelson George writing in the *Village Voice* about the economics of African American film production: he points out that, while some of Lee's investors have been African American, some of the most crucial have not and, therefore, that it is time for African American filmmakers to learn how to sit down and talk to studio money people because the *"Black Enterprise* crowd" would still rather invest in real estate than in African American cultural production (37).

George's thinking raises a number of other questions. Would the financing from African American capitalists necessarily be more politically adventurous than that from Euro-American capitalists? I am not so sanguine, not so sure that black nationalism breaches *class* walls. Black nationalist economics raise yet another issue: both Spike Lee and Keenan Ivory Wayans talk about the necessity for African Americans to be in particular positions of power in relation to African American cultural production; Lee is "appalled by the dearth of black executives in Hollywood," and Wayans thinks that "the destiny of black art rests on black people and black corporate America" (Greenberg, 23). To that last bit, "black corporate America," I can only reply that if our cultural production rests on anybody's *corporate* America, then God/Goddess help us.

It is to Lee's dominant position as and his forthright claim to be a "political" filmmaker that I want to return for the next section of my essay. My impetus for thinking about Lee in this way had its genesis in my reading of Manthia Diawara's article "Black Spectatorship: Problems of Identification and Resistance." I found his argument that Eddie Murphy's character in *Trading Places, 48 Hours,* and *Beverly Hills Cop I* and *II* is first allowed to appear threatening, then "deterritorialised from a black milieu and transferred to a predominantly white world" (71) helpful in considering containment and domestication strategies for certain other kinds of characters. It spurred me to consider similar phenomena within what is at least represented as African American milieux—those depicted in *Do the Right Thing* and *School Daze.* How might one account for the domesticating processes of particular kinds of representations unless one rethinks the politics of what constitutes the possible "territory" of a "black" milieu?

I find the idea of Lee as a politically radical or progressive filmmaker troubling for a number of reasons: (1) the politics of race, gender, class, and sexuality in *Do the Right Thing* and *School Daze* are inadequate to the weight that these films and Lee carry within the discourse of political cultural work, and (2) having Lee and his work deified by the media and critical establishment, especially (as far as my own interests are concerned) by members of the leftist and African American media and critical establishment, is bad news to other African American filmics who remain overshadowed by the attention granted to Spike Lee and bad news also to the larger possibility of more politically progressive and complex film production focused on African American culture or issues of race.

To return to the questions that I raise at the beginning of this essay, any evaluation of Lee's work as radical or counterhegemonic has to be run past the question, *Compared to what?* Against the underdeveloped, stymied state of discussion about race, racism, and racialization in the United States at this moment and against the paucity of productions about African Americans that we could invoke to situate Lee's work and stylizations, evaluations of his and his films' politics require considerably more analysis than has been available.

III

School Daze and *Do the Right Thing* were films discussed by most reviewers on the grounds of realism, authenticity, and relation to the "good" of the community represented in them. Many of the arguments that addressed the issue of *reception* fell into the trap of reducing the complexities of hegemony to simple polarities—white versus black audiences or black middle-class versus black lower-class audiences—as though these categories are completely understood and separately distinct.[12] That is to say, the blurred lines between unstable categories of people were firmly and falsely redrawn in the Spike Lee discourse. Omitted from discussion were the ways in which aspects of U.S. culture are internalized and contributed to (in some degree) by most of us (after all, how else does hegemony function?), as well as the ways in which culture constitutes contested ground—contested by different groups even within racialized communities under different circumstances. The complex problems of realism, representation, and essentialism were as apparent in the discussion around Lee and the films as they were in Lee's presence and in the films themselves.

Most of the reviews and articles written began, were imbued with, or concluded with references to how very realistic or authentic the films were; how much they captured the sounds, rhythms, sights, styles, and important concerns of African Americans.[13] Armond White tied the film's politics to its depiction of "Afro-American cultural style as triumphant opposition strategy" ("Scene," 46). As Michael Kamber, writing about *Do the Right Thing* in *Z Magazine* points out, "He's so authentic!" seemed to be the refrain among liberal whites. That refrain, however, came from all corners—liberals, progressives/leftists, and even some conservatives and reactionaries (as troubling as such critics found the film's "reality"), and from the political range of African Americans. It came from organs as ideologically dissimilar as the *Guardian*, the *New York Times*, and *Ebony*. More important, whether the critic/commentator was heaping encomia on Lee for attempting to portray African American culture without the "distortions" to which we have all grown accustomed (Muwakkil, "Doing," 24), questioning whether or not the characters were "real" (Staples, 9), or spouting vitriolic accusations of Afro-fascism because of what one critic saw as Lee's "fantastical" (i.e., "not real") distortions (Crouch, 74), "realism" (or its lack) and the effect of the films' representation of the real have been the keynotes of an incredible array of commentary about them.

Realism as the bedrock of narrative is inherently problematic. Realism poses a fundamental, long-standing challenge for counterhegemonic discourse, since realism, as a narrative form, enforces an authoritative perspective. According to Raymond Williams, while *real* has denoted the actually existing as opposed to the imaginary since the fifteenth century and, at the same time, was contrasted with *apparent*, by the nineteenth century the word additionally established the difference between the "true" or fundamental quality of some thing or situation and the "false" or mistaken quality, while at the same time marking the difference between concrete and abstract (216–17).

Reality, as Suzette Elgin puts it, is established via the consensus of a particular group and marks the "real world, the actually existing, true and concrete world" preserved by the absence of existing alternatives (30–31). Kobena Mercer argues that the "reality effect produced by realist methods depends on the operation of four characteristic values—transparency, immediacy, authority[,] and authenticity—which are in fact aesthetic values central to the dominant film and media culture." By adopting this practice as a "neutral" or "instrumental" relation for the means of representation, black filmmakers seek to "redefine referential realities of race through the same codes and forms as the prevailing film language whose discourse of racism" they seem to contest (Mercer, 53).

Mercer goes on to argue that, "in short, black film practices which incorporate these filmic values are committed to a mimetic conception of representation which assumes that reality has an objective existence 'out there,' that the process of representation simply aims to correspond to or reflect" (53).

Deployed as a narrative form dependent on recognition of reality, realism suggests disclosure of the truth (and then closure of the representation); realism invites readers/audience to accept what is offered as a slice of life because the narrative contains elements of "fact." Realism, then, temporarily allows chaos in an otherwise conventional or recognizable world, but at the end the narrative moves toward closure, the establishment of truth and order. As Michael Kamber puts it, the morning after the riot (in *Do the Right Thing*) the neighborhood is "back to normal, . . . and the feeling is that, were Sal to rebuild his pizzeria"—and, I would add, slap some pictures of Malcolm X and a few others on the wall—"and were the cops to avoid killing anyone in the immediate future, everyone would go on back and eat there. Ignorant and apolitical, letting the system roll on" (40).

Realism used uncritically as a mode for African American art implies that our lives can be captured by the presentation of enough documentary evidence or by insistence on another truth. The graffiti on Sal's pizzeria asserts, "Tawana told the truth." The implication is that her story was real, was actual and concrete, was *the* story of rape. The problem presented then is further cathected: must *Tawana* be telling the truth for us to believe the larger truth about sexual abuse of African American women by Euro-American men? Is this "truth" compared to the "truth" of their abuse by African American men? Compared to what other African American women say? Compared to what Alice Walker, for example, says about African American men?[14] Compared to what Jade is saying, or trying to say, to Mookie?[15] In the name of preserving the "truth" of Tawana and her reality, is it okay for Mookie to *insist* that he *knows* the truth?[16]

Realism establishes a claim to truth, but it also presents the ground for its own deconstruction—somebody else's truth. Telling it like it is, as John Akomfrah notes, "has to be said with a certain amount of skepticism, because ultimately one needs to challenge the assumption that you *can* tell it like it is" (Fusco, "Interview," 53). Telling it like it is, for example, can be claimed by narratives that are politically regressive. Shelby Steele, the new African American conservative media superstar, in his numerous attacks on the victims of racism (available in a newspaper/magazine near you) claims to be "telling it like it is" from his reality (Applebome, 18). "Reality" is promiscuous, at the very least.

Why the historically consistent demand for and approval of realism in African American cultural production? Fanon argues that the "natives,"[17] in the face of the colonizer's big lies about the history and culture of the colonized, make a conscious attempt to reclaim their history and aspects of their culture (*Wretched,* 206–12). Against the constant distortions of Euro-American ethnocentric dismissal and burial of the African American presence, we respond with an insistence on "setting the record straight," "telling the truth," "saying it like it is." The Harlem Renaissance intellectuals, artists, and writers went to cultural war with each other over accurate depictions of the African American community; the black aesthetic critics in a subsequent period built a political and intellectual movement around an assertion of a countertruth against the distortions of cultural racism; and, because the distortions have not ended, African Americans are presently preoccupied with the need to intervene in the dominant culture's construction of African Americanness. Nonetheless (and it is here that I am most concerned with the salience of Lee and his "truth"), despite the weight of a will to counter "lies," a marginalized group needs to be wary of the seductive power of realism, of accepting all that a realistic representation implies because of its inclusion of some "facts."

The reasons for "real" as a positive evaluation are tied, of course, to scarcity, the paucity of African American presentations of *facts* and *representations* as well as the desire for more of the first category, which in turn allows the second category to have its "selectiveness" forgotten in the rush to celebrate its mere presence. It is, however, because of the salience of Lee's representations that he and they warrant *critical* attention. In order to give them that attention, we have to first acknowledge that they are not *generally* "real" (however "factual" any part of the content might be) but *specifically* "real"—and that that specific "real" might be criticizable. If Lee's strength is a certain ability to document some of the sounds and sights of African American vernacular culture— its style focus—that vernacularity cannot guarantee counterhegemonic cultural resistance. One can be caught up in Euro-American hegemony within the vernacular, and one can repeat the masculinism and heterosexism of vernacular culture. Vernacular language and cultural productions allow the possibility of discursive power disruptions, of cultural resistance—they do not guarantee it. The particular politics of the specifics of vernacular culture that Lee represents are problematic. The films' presentation of and the critics' acceptance of these politics without a challenge encourages audiences to consider these representations as African American essences.

Telling the "truth" demands that we consider the truth of something compared to something else. Who is speaking? Who is asking? And to what end? I don't think that the problem of addressing the construction of reality can be answered by more claims to realism without considering how and why both hegemonic realism and resistance to or subversion of the realism are constructed. Reality, after all, is merely something that resounds in minds already trained to recognize it as such. Further, what happens in the shadow behind the "real" of Spike Lee—once it becomes hegemonic for African Americans? In other words, what happens when this "representation" is accepted as "real"? What happens to the construction of "blackness" in the public discourse?

According to Roland Barthes,

> Representation is not directly defined by imitation: even if we were to get rid of the notions of "reality" and "verisimilitude" and "copy," there would still be "representation," so long as a subject (author, reader, spectator, observer) directed his [or her] *gaze* toward a horizon and there projected the base of a triangle of which his [or her] eye (or his [or her] mind) would be the apex. (90)

Representation refers to images that are selected from what we recognize as reality; they are tied to and have meaning within particular settings. They come "from somewhere" (Barthes, 96) and have meaning insofar as "there are differences of meaning" (Culler, 83). Akomfrah argues that representation "is used to simply talk about questions of figuration. How one places the black in the scene of writing, the imagination, and so on. Others saw it in more juridic terms. How one is enfranchised, if you like, how one buys into the social contract" (Fusco, "Interview," 43). In other words, we need to consider how one constructs identity through the vehicle of representation. And compared to what? If Lee is working in a small field, if too much rides on the few African American filmmakers working in this cultural domain and this pressure to variously "represent" cannot be met, how might we reconsider the possibilities of African American filmmaking?

In *Invisible Man*, Trueblood tells a white philanthropist a story explaining his incest, his daughter's pregnancy, and his wife's. The unnamed narrator is shocked by Trueblood's frankness in relating his story and wonders, "'How can he tell this to white men . . . when he knows they'll say that all Negroes do such things?'" (57). The question of representation and what anyone should say about his or her community is a constant pressure under which African American cultural workers produce. But it is a question that constantly disenfranchises even as it reinforces the notion of absolutes—absolutes such as the "African American" community, the non-African American or "Euro-American" community, or notions of the author or filmmaker as the one who does "something" that a reader or an audience then simply consumes, resists, or appropriates. Further, if one is enthralled by the idea of absolute representations, then "good" or "real" cultural production is impervious to reader or audience misbehavior (misreading), and "bad" or "nonrepresentative" or "unrealistic" cultural production comforts racist Euro-Americans, or can be appropriate by them, or misleads African Americans. Believing and acting on these assumptions means deifying or demonizing African American cultural production or producers. In other words, it is as foolish to say that Lee has produced "appropriation-proof," *real* African American art as it is to say that he has produced "Afro-fascism" that distorts reality.

Lee is himself to some extent cognizant of how he is placed within the discourse of representation; on the other hand, he also produces representations that suggest particular Euro-American hegemonic politics. His *Do the Right Thing* is imbued with the Protestant work ethic: there is more language about work, responsibility, and ownership in it than in any five Euro-American Hollywood productions. The film insists that, if African Americans just work like the Koreans, like the Italians, like the Euro-American brownstone owner, these problems could be averted; or, if you own the property, then you can put on the walls whatever icons you want; or, if you consume at (materially support) a locale, then you can have whatever icons you want on the walls. And its masculinist focus could be distilled into the slogan that screams at us throughout the film: "real men work and support their families." These representations compared to what? Within the representations of *Do the Right Thing*, what are the ideologies being engaged here, or critiqued here, or, more to the point, not critiqued here? Contrary to Salim Muwakkil's assertion that "Lee's refusal to make clear his judgments has limited his popularity among audiences weaned on formulaic narrative" ("Doing," 24), I find *Do the Right Thing* relentlessly formulaic in its masculinist representations and its conventional Calvinist realism.

To paraphrase Stuart Hall ("Gramsci's," 15–16), there is no law that guarantees that a group's ideology is consistent with its economic— or, I would add, its race—position, nor is there any guarantee that the ideology of a group *isn't* consistent with its economic or race position. For the purposes of thinking about representation and Lee's films, we might want to consider the assumption held by his lower-class characters that work is the "right thing," that it means always what we think it means. Drug dealers (absent from this picture) work; global corporate CEOs responsible for planetary and human degradation also work. Work or non-work, but compared to what? We (as audience) could consider this "work" emphasis to be parody, but the film uses "work" or "ownership" to justify intervention.

Or, to return again to identity politics, Hall writes "'black' is not the exclusive property of any particular social or any single discourse. . . . it has no necessary class belonging" ("Signification," 112). He is drawing on his experience in the Caribbean and British context, but it is an argument that has considerable force for race theorizing and the politics of racial representation within the U.S. context. What does "blackness" mean in *School Daze* or *Do the Right Thing*? *School Daze*, the Lee film that has received by far the least amount of national critical respect, suggests far more complicated *possibilities* around the idea of identity politics than *Do the Right Thing* (despite *School Daze*'s foul gender politics and horrific homophobia, issues to which I will return). It is with regard to identity politics that unselfconscious realism and representation within the distorted discourse of Euro-American hegemony lead inevitably to a profoundly unstrategic essentialism.

Essentialism is, as Diana Fuss defines it, "commonly understood as a belief in the real, true essence of things, the invariable and fixed properties which define the 'whatness' of a given entity" (xi). It assumes that certain characteristics are inherently part of the core being of a group. The idea of authenticity—a notion that implies essence—can derive from the idea that a particular group and individual entities of that group can be recognized by the ways in which they are shown with some measure of the "real" or authentic or essential qualities of that group. Fuss argues additionally, however, that because essentialism is not in and of itself progressive or reactionary, the appropriate question is: "if this text *is* essentialist, what motivates its deployment?" (xi, my emphasis). Because I am mindful of Fuss's careful complications of essentialisms, I want to make clear my consideration of specific problem sites of essentialism—Lee, the discourse about Lee, and two of his films.

Some African American critics have indicated their impatience with criticisms of essentialism. Henry Louis Gates Jr., for example, has stated his suspicions about this charge as part of his defense of African Americanist canon formation or reformation ("On the Rhetoric of Racism in the Profession").[18] He refers to the fact that African Americanists' "attempts to define a black American canon—foregrounded on its own against a white backdrop—are often derided as racist, separatist, nationalist, or 'essentialist'—my favorite term of all."[19] He argues that "you cannot . . . critique the notion of the subject until a tradition's subjectivity (as it were) has been firmly established" (15), but he is not clear about *who* cannot critique the subject at issue here, the African American subject, or *for whom* this subjectivity still needs to be established. I am mindful of the fact that Gates is skeptical of a *specific* charge of essentialism—that leveled against the institutionalization of an African American literary canon—and I agree with his arguments about the political usefulness at this moment of such defining. Attacks on African American "canons" are blind to certain political "realities." I am simply picking one small bone here: I think that it is possible to argue for the work of defining African American literary traditions without "saving" essentialism.

I find Gates's argument about the need to "establish" African American subjectivity a little inconsistent, given his tracing (in *Figures in Black* and *The Signifying Monkey*) of the complexity of the historical development of African American subjectivity (African Americans have been already at work developing subjectiv*ies*) and his deconstruction of the idea of a "transcendent black subject" (in "The Blackness of Blackness," 297). Part of the work of African American cultural criticism has been not only to claim, to insist on, African American subjectivity/

subjectivities, but also to elaborate and complicate that subjectivity/ those subjectivities by speculating on their varied and fragmented relations to their products—abstract or concrete, formalized or ephemeral.

Within the domain of African American cultural discourse, African Americans have been about the business of establishing that tradition's subjectivity and have been fighting about the terms of that subjectivity since the seventeenth century. Some African Americans, as various critics (among them Gates, Gloria Hull, Valerie Smith, Deborah McDowell, and Hazel Carby) have documented, historically resisted essences inscribed in African American cultural commentary, even when these essences were meant to counter essences held by the dominant culture. Vernacular culture, in fact, has allowed a space and mechanism for complicating essences. And in literature and literary critical discourse, Zora Neale Hurston, Nella Larsen, Pauline Hopkins, Jessie Fauset, W. E. B. Du Bois, Sterling Brown, Jean Toomer, and Langston Hughes (to some extent) have complicated notions of African American subjectivity even against the African American male cultural and political hegemony of the Harlem Renaissance.

In her interview with Spivak, Ellen Rooney states that

> to contextualize is to expose the history of what might otherwise seem outside history, natural and thus universal, that is the essence. . . . The problem of essentialism can be thought [of], in this way, as a problem of form, which is to say, a problem of reading. Context would thus emerge as a synonym for reading, in that to read is to demarcate a context. Essentialism appears as a certain resistance to reading, an emphasis on the constraints of form, the limits at which a particular form so compels us as to "stipulate" an analysis. (Spivak, 124)

I am moved to consider the particular situation of Lee by Spivak's warning against "anti-essentialism" as yet another form of essence: "to an extent, we have to look at where the group—the person, the persons, or the movement[—]is situated when we make claims for or against essentialism. A strategy suits a situation; a strategy is not a theory" (127).[20] Lee's films and his place in the discourse of African American and American filmmaking are situations that warrant my criticism of their essentialism; and even if what Lee does is a strategy and not an essence, it is still fair to be critical of that strategy and its power to essentialize within the context of Euro-American hegemony and African American cultural discourse. Lee's presentation of images that resonate with factual reality is glossed as the general truth. The deification of Lee as "truth sayer," and his production as "real," means that the indexing of his selections becomes the "essence" of "black authenticity"—and thus impervious to criticism.

I understand that to be authentically "African American" or "black" has, at various times in history and in the present, meant and sometimes means to be rhythmic; or to have a predilection for playing craps, drinking, using or selling drugs, or raping white women; or being a jungle savage; or being uninterested in marriage; or being on welfare—the list goes on and on. The resonances of authenticity depend on who is doing the evaluating. But I want to foreground the problematic of authenticity and its relationship to essentialism.

Coco Fusco has argued that "the tenet of authenticity is virtually incompatible with the strictures of narrative drama, since 'typical' experiences are presumed to stand for every black person's perception of reality" ("Fantasies," 8). To that I would add only that, when further strengthened by facticity, "typicalness" homogenizes differences. Being different within such a narrative economy, then, is read as "white" or "middle-class" or whatever the current sign used to signify "not black." In any event, dramatic "play" or manipulation (and its political possibilities) is constrained. Authenticity becomes a stranglehold for political analysis and cultural practice beyond the strictures of narrative drama. When Michele Wallace asserts that "intrinsic oppositionality c[an] not be attributed only to the so-called Other" (Fusco, "Fantasies," 9) and Akomfrah asserts that "blacks are expected to be transgressive" (Fusco, "interview," 55), they, along with Fusco, point to the specific problem of essentialism in the context of black film production. If, as Akomfrah argues, we fall into the trap of Kant's categorical imperative—that categories carry with them their own imperatives, and following that, that the category *black* carries with it an essential obligation to oppose, to transgress constantly in specific ways—then we are "saddled with the assumption that there are certain transcendental duties that black film-making has to perform, . . . [that] it has to work with the understanding that it's in a state of emergence, . . . [and that] its means always have to be guerrilla means, war means, signposts of urgency. . . . the categorical imperative imprisons" (Fusco, "Interview," 53). "Black" essence can come to be read from its activity of transgressing another, even less elaborated essence—that of "whiteness."

The categorical imperative is essentialist, whether imposed by dominance or volunteered for under the terms of Euro-American political or African American cultural hegemony. If we fail to problematize the notion that being African American *always* means *only* being embattled, that African American film is political only insofar as "someone" empowered to make the evaluation recognizes its political "reality" and calls the shots on its transgressiveness, and that "authenticity" is always already known and can therefore be proven, then we have fallen into the trap of essentialism. Both the celebratory and the hostile Spike Lee discourse have been amazingly, although not entirely, uncritically essentialist.

There are "honorable" exceptions: bell hooks and Michael Kamber writing in *Z Magazine*, Herb Boyd writing in the *Guardian*, Mike

Dyson writing in *Tikkun,* and some of what J. Hoberman wrote in the *Village Voice*—all regarding *Do the Right Thing*—as well as parts of the multivoiced exchange on *School Daze* that went on in the *Village Voice,* not only moved past celebration or dismissal based on explicit language about "reality" and "authenticity," but also managed to critique assumptions of progressive or radical cultural politics based primarily on representations of African Americans on the screen in practices that too many of us have been trained to identify as "transgressive."

When I ask "Compared to what?" I am asking that we consider a larger domain of possibilities than the Spike Lee discourse has made available. The end of such inquiry is not to lead simply to a fuller explication of his films or his "presence" in cultural production—although that's not a bad side effect—but to enable us to think about the terms of African American cultural production and practice generally, and African American film production and practice specifically, without falling back on an uncritical and unstrategic essentialist celebration of any representations—on screen or embodied in a particular filmmaker.

IV

Although *Do the right Thing* received far more positive press than *School Daze,* perhaps because its working-class subjects seemed more "authentic" to critics[21] than the middle-class subjects of *School Daze,* I contend that *School Daze* is the more complicated movie. While both films are masculinist, and *School Daze* is also explicitly and viciously homophobic, *Do the Right Thing* stays, for the most part, comfortably within the boundaries of static and essentialist propositions about racial identity, and about the relationship of wages and ownership to qualities of responsibility, "manhood," and freedom.[22]

Do the Right Thing makes manhood synonymous with having a job (and being able to take care of one's monetary responsibilities). When one of the block's hip hop young men taunts Da Mayor for his drinking and other problems, Da Mayor returns (as explanation) an account of his inability (in the past) to feed his children because he had no job. The teenager sneers back that Da Mayor put himself in that position. Unlike Da Mayor, we are given to understand, the young man would make sure that he had a job and could take care of his kids; in other words, *he* would be a *man.* In this vein, Mookie's wages make him responsible enough—or man enough—that he can abjure others to "get a job," enable him to make some feeble attempts to provide for his child, and give him the standing to tell Jade what she needs to know about sexual oppression. Jade tries to make him back down by participating in the "wages = right-to-speak" discourse: "You can hardly pay the rent and you're gonna tell me what to do?" Mookie responds, "I get paid." When Jade returns with "You're getting paid peanuts," the point, I suppose, is that were Mookie to have higher wages, *then* it would be all right for him to tell her what to do. At the same time, Mookie is excoriated by Sal and Pino to do the work for which they are paying his wages/his peanuts.

Against, I suppose, the long-held racist charge that African Americans neither work nor want to work, this film spends much of its running time assuring its audience that African Americans in Bed-Stuy certainly do value work! (By its end, I am so overwhelmed by its omnipresent wage labor ethos that I find myself exhausted.) I am not anti-labor; however, this film makes no critique of the conditions under which labor is drawn from some members of the community, nor are kinds of labor/work differentiated. Instead, without any specific contextualization, work is presented as its own absolute good, because work and ownership are what empower *men* to make decisions, to exercise freedom. The Euro-American brownstone owner need only reply to the block's hip hoppers that he "owns" his house to have the last word in the encounter; Sal need only respond that he "owns" his pizzeria in order to maintain his freedom over decor; and Sweet Dick Willie is able to have the last word in a discussion of Korean ownership by insisting that since he has his *own* (or *"owned"*) money, he has the freedom to ignore any form of critical analysis on the part of his buddies or Buggin' Out and patronize the grocery store and the pizzeria, respectively.

"I own," however, complicates neighborhood boundaries and identity politics. The gentrifier both "owns" his house and was born in Brooklyn and, thus, can be said to "belong" in the neighborhood (if not on this particular block). And, ironically, the critique of the Korean grocery store owners because they don't "belong" in the neighborhood is begun by M.L., who is himself an immigrant, as his buddies are quick to remark. Yet, while Sal "owns" his pizzeria, Pino reminds him again and again that "this" is not "their" neighborhood; they don't "belong" here. Still, no one really needs to think about what might be at stake in these contradictions; it is enough to have the money: "When you own your own pizzeria, then you can put your own pictures up."

In these contradictions, *Do the Right Thing* raises an interesting issue: what is the difference, if any, between a person "born" (and thus able to lay some kind of claim to "belonging") in a neighborhood and a gentrifier who lays claim by "buying" his belonging? Further, the gentrifier's presence—as both "born in" (and therefore "native to") Brooklyn and as "buyer" in this block—raises the larger context of the relations of racial bodies, real estate and bank practices, and class issues.

Early on, the film promises a class critique of sorts in the discussion of Sweet Dick Willie and his buddies on the corner. M.L. begins with a complaint that the Koreans, like so many other immigrant groups, move into the neighborhood and seem immediately to "make it," only to lose the focus of his critique. The men make no mention of differential capital bases or accesses to bank loans—and there is no reason to think that vernacular language could not handle that analysis. M.L. concludes his discussion (simplistically): "Either them Korean motherfuckers are geniuses or you black asses are just plain dumb." The either/or proposition is reductionist: genius or dumb ass.

The discussion around, and the tensions raised by, the behavior of the Korean grocery story owners/employees as well as their economic relationship to the rest of the block degenerates completely when the film shows the rioting crowd suddenly stop seeing the Koreans as economically privileged and allow them instead to claim the common oppression of race: we are all colored (and therefore essentially equal) together. A moment's class hostility and film critique of stratification are disrupted and traded in for simplistic race unity without any of the complications of such change represented.

Nonetheless, it is in the realm of identity politics—of place and race—that the film both raises possibilities of complicated representation and undermines them. "Stay black" is the keystone phrase for the neighborhood, although it seems to refer to something ineffable. "Blackness" is what? Perhaps it is the roll call of musicians on the radio, the DJ's rap, the sounds and sights of vernacular culture, the claims of female genetic "tender-headedness." Yes. But "blackness" is also nailed down without specifics in the exchanges between Buggin' Out and Mookie, Mookie and Raheem, Raheem and Buggin' Out. Jade is "down for something positive" and black—and neither she nor Buggin' Out feels the need to specify exactly what the "black positive" is. "Blackness" is Malcolm X, although, as Smiley's picture and Lee's quotes after the conclusion of the film remind us, "blackness" is also Martin Luther King Jr.; "blackness," then, is reduced to the sacredness that inheres in the proper icons.

As Joe Wood asserts, "In the ever-evolving vernacular, Malcolm X has come to mean the real (black) thing, the authentic (black) thing, as close to (black) integrity as close can be. . . . Malcolm [is] the Essential black man" ("Looking," 43). Wood goes on to argue that, if Malcolm (or, I might add, Martin Luther King Jr., for that matter) is to be treated as a symbol of blackness, then we've backed ourselves into a religion of "essential blackness" and away from a historical analysis or exploration of its complexities, its constructedness. Iconography and fetishization is no substitute for history and critical thinking. The film offers no consistent critique of "pictures"—as icons, as fetishes—except for Jade's discussion with and aborted interruption of Buggin' Out's crude analysis. But the movie diminishes her intervention because, after all, within its terms, who is Jade by a sister who ought to but doesn't know when some white man is hitting on her and who has to be warned both by her brother and by the Tawana truth lurking behind and against her back?

Brothers and sisters, we *do* need to talk.

Blackness also seems to demand images that suggest African American males are prone to death by police violence—as bell hooks reminds us (31).[23] In fact, Lee dedicates this film to victims of the police, the dramatic high point of the film being Raheem's murder by the police (hooks, 31). Lee has waxed indignant about that murder's dismissal on the part of some Euro-American viewers (Orenstein, 34); on the other hand, Lee has said also that, if Raheem had just turned down the radio, none of this would have happened—so much for any representation of systemic racist oppression. What are we to make of identity politics within the domain represented by this film? For a filmmaker who claims the mantle of transgression, cultural opposition, political righteousness, and truth-telling, the political ambitions of this film are diffuse and, by its end, defuse into nothingness.

It is the film considered less politically ambitious (but equally masculinist and heterosexist), *School Daze,* that offers the possibilities of greater political depth—it at least raises interesting questions about identity politics "within the group." Although the film is undermined by its homophobia and sexism, it is within the terms of a consideration of these areas that identity politics and essentialism are, in fact, deconstructed.

School Daze is sloppy but complicated. It shows us frat hegemony-forging in action: "Q Dogs, that's what we want to be" is the refrain that bonds. "Q-Dogs are real men because it takes a real man to be a Q-dog"—tautological, yes, and therefore full of the comfort implied by unproblematized allegiances. This refrain, however, is followed by insistences that have no basis in absolutes, that could be read as critical of absolutes, having meaning only by stating differences. A "real" man is *not* a virgin, *not* a "fag." Men know themselves by virtue of their comparisons to "others"—gay men and those individuals in states of presexual being, untouched. Women, too, have their absolutes: "He's a man, he's sneakin'!" is clearly exegesis on the nature or essence side of the argument about the ontology of male being. Nonetheless, the women also have their moments of comparison and acknowledgments of constructedness: some sororities are not "bad," and Rachel wants to "become" a Delta even though she is *not* a wannabee.

The film offers some poststructuralist comforts. Half-Pint begins the film firmly centered: "I'm your cousin, your blood." But he ends it reconstructed and differently centered (however problematically): "I'm a Gamma man *now*" (my emphasis). That new insistence marks a historicized difference. The film offers additional critiques of identity politics. Possibilities include the town-gown split, an explicitly political one that manifests its implicit politics in aesthetics as well: the townies, who are working-class and, therefore, under some rubrics "blacker" than the middle-class college kids, are also the ones with the "jeri curls" (generally recognized as evidence of aesthetic *disaffection* with "blackness") protected by shower caps. And a concern with international politics—South Africa and apartheid—gets read by "wannabee" Julian as evidence that the male jigs really aren't "black," because "blackness" originates in and is concerned with U.S. geopolitical sites only—like Detroit.

The film's failing, of course, is that it does not explore the ways in which its (male) politics are also tied to its own forms of aesthetization. Males are not only socialized by the *behaviors* of their groups, whether within fraternities or within male-oriented, internationally focused political practices such as protests, marches, or rallies, but they are participants in the aesthetization of these practices. The film, unfortunately and myopically, presents aesthetics as formal matters of physical appearance in which women only participate.[24] Men *do:* they dance the beautifully choreographed Greek stomps, or the fellas' clever parody stomp, or make careful selections of political posters and other room decor items, and arrange that decor for sexual trysts.

Women, on the other hand, *show.* They wear or don't wear makeup; they straighten or don't straighten their hair; they show off the colors of the eyes with which they were born or show different eyes through the wonders of chemical technology. *School Daze* is incapable of making the connection between what the men do and what they are showing as their aesthetics, and the film is incapable of showing that women do anything other than look like components of male aesthetics. The film is allowed its specificity, but it could have chosen to selfconsciously represent male constructions of aesthetics; there is work to be done in this area. Still *School Daze,* while not recognizing its own attitude toward the gendering of its discussion of aesthetics, does make the issue available for critique.

The film's homophobia offers a similar site for examining historical identity and gender politics. In its retreat from and fear of homosexuality and the homosexual, it plays out the fear engendered during the course of African American history and concretized by Robert Park's assertion (in the 1920s) that "the Negro is the lady of the races" (280). The language around African American culture, intellectualism, and politics has been dominated by language analogous to that which has constructed and constrained women. Within a history that has used the same language to delineate the constructions of race *and* gender, that has insisted, against general Euro-American male privilege, that African American males can only share the space reserved for women, this film is a long commercial that reassures African American males that they *can* center themselves by asserting a salient difference: they are straight; all "real" men are straight; "blackness" is like real manhood—straight. So there, Robert Park.

Again, however, in defense of a critique of the specificities of this film's representations, the feeble excuse of "reality" comes into play. Lee has consistently defended his film against criticism of its homophobia by claiming and privileging its facticity, by defending realism: those (frat) guys really are that way. In so doing, he lets himself off the hook for the selection criteria at work in any representation. I respond as simply: yes, some African Americans are like that; some are not; therefore, to what particular end is this specific "real" content being mined? If it is intended as a critique of African American homophobia, "how" (in form and/or content) is the critique available?

V

I would like to end where I began. The historical moment and the attention given to Spike Lee by an entire spectrum of critics, commentators, and media fora; the effects of his presence and deification on possible productions of African American presences in the cultural domain; the reductionist tendency in any U.S. discussions about race and racism—all combine to make it imperative that we continue to think about the issues raised by Lee and his production. It won't hurt and might help to begin by refusing to consider Lee or his production simply within their own terms. Trying to make things "real" has been the problem. What might more contextual criticism of Lee and his production offer us?

The May 1990 issue of *Emerge* points to the recent successes of African American independent filmmakers at Sundance (White, 65–66). The news is cheering. But there were no African American women among their number and even more troubling, the critic writing the article said nothing about their absence from Sundance or from his discussion of African American filmmaking. Instead, he described and contributed to the uncritical veneration of the work of Melvin Van Peebles, a tradition in African American film criticism that ignores both formal infelicities in Van Peebles' films and issues of sexism and homophobia.

Within the terms of simple celebration of African American male filmmakers, there is no space for the criticism that any artist needs—especially, given present political constraints, artists from marginalized and racialized communities. Yet, as critics we are responsible for the work of analysis and thoroughgoing contextualization lest we run the risk of continuing, in the name of affirming our cultural production, disabling essentialisms. Representations are not "reality"; simple, factual reproductions of selected aspects of vernacular culture are neither necessarily counterhegemonic art nor anything else. They don't even "set the record *straight*" (pun intended). Therefore, in our critical considerations we do well to heed Fanon's warnings equally against nationalist nostalgia for a precolonial past and uncritical nativist celebrations in the present. While beginning with the question of context—Compared to what?—does not foreclose productive discussions, it does make it harder to rest on simple resolutions. And that's the truth, Ruth.

NOTES

1. Amazingly, the *New York Times*, not exactly famous for its in-depth analysis of African American cultural life or production, invited a group of people, including academics in literature, education, and sociology; a psychiatrist; an administrative judge of the New York State Supreme Court; and a film director (among others), to "explore issues raised by the film" *Do the Right Thing* (July 9, 1989). The editors of the *Arts and Leisure* section devoted almost two full pages to excerpts from this gathering ("*Do the Right Thing*: Issues and Images").

2. Included in this category are Pat Aufderheide, Vincent Canby, Jeremiah Creedon, Thulani Davis ("We've"), Barbara Day, Stuart Ewen, J. Hoberman, Stuart Klawans, Salim Muwakkil ("Doing"), and Greg Tate.

3. Included in this category are Stanley Crouch and Joe Klein.

4. The subtexts of the "compared to what?" are both dominant cultural production *and* the possibilities for politically engaged film explored by the black British film collectives—about which I do not write at any length (or in any depth) in this essay, but against which I look at Lee.

5. Lee sees himself and his work as politically engaged (see, e.g., Orenstein, 43); that is the reason that I take his political claims as well as the critics who deify him so seriously.

6. I focus only on Lee instead of including a critique of Eddie Murphy, Robert Townsend, Keenan Wayans, or the Hudlin brothers (all African American male filmmakers getting considerable attention from the general media and African American cultural commentators) to keep this essay focused and of moderate length.

7. This is an issue raised by Ann Cvetkovich and I in a coauthored paper presented at the 1989 MLA convention.

8. I refer to Gates's *Figures in Black*, Appiah's "The Uncompleted Argument," and Fanon's *Black Skin, White Masks*.

9. The truth of his vision was also the theme of his letter-to-the-editor response (to Joe Klein's hysterical attack) in *New York* magazine.

10. I do not think, however, that all African American cultural production has to be nationally distributed for it to be a site of resistance to the dominance of Euro-American cultural hegemony.

11. Cvetkovich and I have argued also against seeing a simple dichotomy between politically "good" independent and political "bad" commercial production and against as equally simple a dichotomy as the between "avant-garde" as an inherently elitist form and conventional narrative representation as an inherently popular form.

12. There were, for instance, those who thought Euro-Americans or *middle-class* African Americans needed to *learn* from *Do the Right Thing*. Consider the example of Barbara Day, who thought the movie was good because it was "as real as the nation's last urban insurrection." Middle-class people (of both races), she opined, "needed to see what the poor in New York City ghettos see too often: a Black or Latino Raheem being choked, feet dangling above the pavement." I could expend much ink and theoretical zeal on the tendency (need? pleasure?) on the part of many Euro-American commentators to romanticize African Americans represented at the most coercive sites, sites that bestow "authenticity," but I don't feel strong enough this time around. While there are differences among segments of the African American population, some circumstances of life in the United States for African Americans are fairly general. The existence of racist police practices is one such unifying factor. I will take issue, therefore, with another aspect of Day's myopia: the argument that racist police coercion is always lower- or

working-class oriented. Day connects "a Black or Latino Raheem being choked" with ghetto residents only, but one of the Miami "urban insurrections" was kicked off by the police murder of Arthur Little, a middle-class African American who worked in insurance. The violent tendencies of racist police are not unknown to middle-class African Americans: at the National Black Male Conference workshop on police abuse (Kansas City, Mo., July 13, 1990), the largely academic and middle-class African American audience was unsurprised when Don Jackson, an ex-police officer (made famous by the videotape of an LAPD officer pushing his head through a window), said that "almost everyone in this room looks like a criminal to police officers so inclined." Class does not necessarily mediate racism. Even most *middle-class* African Americans understand (and many have suffered from) some form of racist police violence or hostility.

13. Salim Muwakkil ("Doing"), Greg Tate, and Armond White ("Scene") were the most enthusiastic in this category, followed closely by Thulani Davis ("We've") and Barbara Day.

14. bell hooks examines the differences between critical responses to Alice Walker's representations of African American men and those of Spike Lee.

15. hooks also touches on this point (35).

16. How very much Mookie's insistence on the predatoriness of Euro-American males toward African American females echoes (while countering) Euro-American males' insistence on the myth of African American male predatoriness toward Euro-American females! Of course, one might argue, such insistences are meant to be counter-mythologizing, but such countering accepts the original structure—it does not transform or subvert it. Ironically, unlike the deployments of slippery indirections—the keynote of vernacular linguistic play—countermyths are as *direct,* as centered, as the racist myths they mean to displace.

17. Fanon argues that American blacks might also be considered "natives" in the sense of being part of an internal colony. In *The Wretched of the Earth* he states that the "Negroes who live in the United States and in Central or Latin America in fact experience the need to attach themselves to a cultural matrix. Their problem is not fundamentally different from that of the Africans" (215).

18. This defense might or might not be superseded—time will tell—by his more recent calls for a liberal humanist pluralism and attacks on social theory and critiques of race, class, and gender.

19. Gates is right to take issue with some pejorative descriptions of his work as essentialist. To this end, I disagree with Diana Fuss's argument, for example, that Gates' and Houston Baker's analyses inherently romanticize the vernacular (although some of their specific uses of vernacular analysis have done so—see Gates's media pieces on 2 Live Crew, for example) and that they speak *about* the vernacular and not *in* it. Such an argument is itself a romanticization, first, because it is not necessary to write in the vernacular to theorize about it. Most metacommentary systems employ their own jargon; theoretical discussions about fictional texts, for example, do not necessarily go on in the language of the texts themselves. More important, African American vernacular is *not* necessarily synonymous with "black English" or any form of black dialect (rural or urban), although the vernacular and vernacular users often employ black English or black dialects. African American vernacular is an attitude toward language, a language dynamic, and a technique of language use (see Baker's *Blues, Ideology, and Afro-American Literature,* Gates's *The Signifying Monkey,* and Claudia Mitchell-Kernan's "Signifying"). African American fiction writers such as Toni Morrison frequently "signify" in standard English. And both Baker and Gates have also used vernacular signifying practices from time to time in their oral and written presentations. Vernacularity is not simply a marker for African American working-class or "street" verbal practices. To attach it only to such sites is to be caught in a search for false authenticity.

Fuss further argues that "the quest to recover, reinscribe, and revalorize the black vernacular" is inherently essentialist (90). The vernacular is not in need of recovery or reinscription; it is alive and well—and multiclass within the African American group. To

Wahneema Lubiano

graph the specificities of African American cultural production, its textual theoretical possibilities, is not to go on a ghost hunt.

20. I refer to Gayatri Spivak's interview in *Differences*. While I am aware that exigencies of specific political moments and their attendant strategies have historically demanded essentialism on the large scale—nationalism—nonetheless, I want to think about unreflective essentialism as a problematic generally and specifically in regard to the Spike Lee discourse. I try to be very careful about the way that I use Spivak here because her interview is long and complex: I pick and choose parts of it because, while I think that her warnings about essentialism and anti-essentialism are very much to the point, working through the implications of all of her (and Rooney's) discussion would demand more time and space than I have here. I use, therefore, what seems to me to be most to the point. Spivak argues, among other things, that anti-essentialism risks being another form of essence, that anti-essentialism's insistence (in some quarters) on the primacy of "over-determinations" leads to paralyzing strategic anarchy. Further, she asserts, "essences . . . are just a kind of content. All content is not essence. Why be so nervous about it?" (145). I am nervous, however, because within the terms of Euro-American dominance, as far as African American cultural production and reception are concerned, there is no such thing as "just a kind of content."

21. Sarah Shulman is an exception to this generality, although I find problematic her article's insistence that Lee usurped "authentic" working-class voices and substituted his middle-class voice. I am not interested in taking sides on whether or not he does so; however, while I find much useful in Shulman's reading of the film, this issue of African American middle-class lack of authenticity versus African American working-class authenticity simply reinscribes another debate contained in terms of essentialism: who is the "real" black person? The insistence that only the working-class African American carries African American culture is one side of a pointless debate that has gone on for more than a century. All African Americans, in their complexity—of which class difference is a part—make up African culture. One need only watch Cornel West and Hortense Spillers (to name just two) make academic presentations in order to see variations of African American academic, middle-class, vernacular culture at work.

22. bell hooks, Michael Kamber, and Michael Dyson have all provided excellent extended readings of *Do the Right Thing*. My work here contributes to discussions they have begun.

23. The death of an African American male at the hands of police is a television and cinematic cliché, and bell hooks argues that Lee's representation of Raheem's death does not explode or remap that cliché. Further, as Michael Kamber also notes, despite the tragedy of the disproportionately high numbers of African American males killed by police, such murders are still fairly atypical—less than one percent of African American homicides (40). The vast majority of African American male and female homicides are committed by African American males, and the relationship of that fact to the representation of African American male homicide in *Do the Right Thing* is a fair enough question, since representation is the "practice" of the filmmaker's selection. Is the simplicity of murder by cops somehow more "real" than the complexities of murder by African Americans? I am not ranking factual horrors, but I am interested in the representation "selection" at work in this film. Does the specter of male socialization within African American communities and its participation in hegemonic violence and masculinism seem too "inauthentic" to be represented?

24. Vernon Reid, in the Thulani Davis et al. article on *School Daze*, touches on Lee's depiction of African American color line internalization as played out by women only.

WORKS CITED

Applebome, Peter. "Stirring a Debate on Breaking Racism's Shackles." *New York Times*, May 30, 1990, late ed.: A18.

Appiah, Anthony. "The Uncompleted Argument: Du Bois and the Illusion of Race." In *"Race," Writing, and Difference*. Ed. Henry Louis Gates Jr. Chicago: University of Chicago Press, 1986, 21–37.

Aufderheide, Pat. "Racial Schisms: The Daze of Our Lives." *In These Times*, March 16–22, 1988: 20.

Barthes, Roland. "Diderot, Brecht, Eisenstein." In *The Responsibility of Forms*. Trans. Richard Howard. New York: Hill, 1985, 89–97.

Boyd, Herb. "Does Lee 'Do the Right Thing'?" *Guardian*, July 5, 1989: 8, 24.

Canby, Vincent. "Spike Lee Tackles Racism and Rage." *New York Times*, June 30, 1989, late ed.: C16.

Cham, Mbye B., and Claire Andrade-Watkins, eds. *BlackFrames: Critical Perspectives on Black Independent Cinema*. Cambridge: MIT Press, 1988.

Creedon, Jeremiah. "That Cannes Can of Worms: Sex, Lies and the Right Thing." *In These Times*, October 18–24, 1989: 20–21.

Crouch, Stanley. "Do the Race Thing." *Village Voice*, June 20, 1989: 73–74.

Culler, Jonathan. *Ferdinand de Saussure*. Ithaca: Cornell University Press, 1976.

Davis, Thulani. "We've Gotta Have It." *Village Voice*, June 20, 1989: 67–70.

Davis, Thulani, et al. "Daze of Our Lives." *Village Voice*, March 22, 1988: 35–39.

Day, Barbara. "Spike Lee Wakes Up Movie Audiences, Confronts Questions of Black Power." *Guardian*, July 5, 1989: 24–25.

Diawara, Manthia. "Black Spectatorship: Problems of Identification and Resistance." *Screen* 29, no. 4 (1988): 66–81.

"*Do the Right Thing*: Issues and Images." *New York Times*, July 9, 1989, late ed., sec. 2: 1+.

Dyson, Michael. "Film Noir." *Tikkun* 4, no. 5 (1989): 75–78.

Elgin, Suzette. *Native Tongue*. New York: DAW, 1984.

Ellison, Ralph. *Invisible Man*. New York: Random, 1952.

Ewen, Stuart. "'Do the Right Thing' Is an American Movie in the Best Sense." *New York Times*, July 14, 1989, late ed.: A28.

Fanon, Frantz. *Black Skin, White Masks.* 201952. New York: Grove, 1967.

____. *The Wretched of the Earth*. 1961. New York: Grove, 1968.

Fusco, Coco. "Fantasies of Oppositionality." *AfterImage*, December 1988: 6–9.

____. "An Interview with Black Audio Film Collective: John Akomfrah, Reece Auguiste, Lina Gopaul and Avril Johnson." In *Young, British, and Black: The Work of Sankofa and Black Audio Film Collective*. Buffalo: Hallwalls/Contemporary Arts Center, 1988, 41–60.

Fuss, Diana. *Essentially Speaking: Feminism, Nature and Difference*. New York: Routledge, 1989.

Gates, Henry Louis, Jr. "The Blackness of Blackness: A Critique of the Sign and the Signifying Monkey." In *Black Literature and Literary Theory*. Ed. Gates. New York: Methuen, 1984, 287–321.

____. *Figures in Black: Words, Signs, and the "Racial" Self*. New York: Oxford University Press, 1987.

____. "On the Rhetoric of Racism in the Profession." *African Literature Association Bulletin* 15, no. 1 (1989): 11–21.

____. *The Signifying Monkey: A Theory of Afro-American Literary Criticism*. New York: Oxford University Press, 1988.

George, Nelson. "Shady Dealin'." *Village Voice*, February 23, 1990: 37.

Greenberg, James. "In Hollywood, Black Is In." *New York Times*, March 4, 1990. Arts and Leisure sec.: 1+.

Hall, Stuart. "Gramsci's Relevance for the Study of Race and Ethnicity." *Journal of Communication Inquiry* 10, no. 2 (1986): 5–27.

____. "Signification, Representation, Ideology: Althusser and the Post-Structuralist Debates." *Critical Studies in Mass Communication* 2, no. 2 (1985): 91–114.

Hoberman, J. "Pass/Fall." *Village Voice*, July 11, 1989: 59, 62, 66.

hooks, bell. "Counterhegemonic Art: The Right Thing." *Z Magazine,* October 1989: 31–36.

Kamber, Michael. "Do the Right Thing." *Z Magazine,* October 1989: 37–40.

Klawans, Stuart. Rev. of *Do the Right Thing. Nation,* July 17, 1989: 98–100.

Klein, Joe. "Spiked." *New York,* June 26, 1989: 14–15.

Lee, Spike. Presentation and Discussion. University of Texas at Austin, February 26, 1989.

___. "Spike Lee Replies: 'Say It Ain't So Joe.'" *New York,* July 17, 1989: 6.

Lubiano, Wahneema, and Ann Cvetkovich. "Black Film Production as Cultural Studies Problematic." Div. on Black American Literature and Culture, MLA convention. Washington, D.C., December 28, 1989.

Mercer, Kobena. "Diaspora Culture and the Dialogic Imagination: The Aesthetics of Black Independent Film in Britain." Cham and Andrade-Watkins, 50–61.

Mitchell-Kernan, Claudia. "Signifying." In *Mother Wit from the Laughing Barrel: Readings in the Interpretation of Afro-American Folklore.* Ed. Alan Dundes. Englewood Cliffs: Prentice, 1973, 310–28.

Muwakkil, Salim. "The Black Middle Class and Lee's School of Hard Knocks." *In These Times,* March 16–22, 1988: 21.

___. "Doing the Spike Thing." *In These Times,* July 5–18, 1989: 18, 24.

Orenstein, Peggy. "Spike's Riot." *Mother Jones,* September 1989: 32–35, 43–46.

Park, Robert. *Race and Culture: Essays in the Sociology of Contemporary Man.* Glencoe: Free, 1950.

Shulman, Sarah. "I Don't Like Spike." *Outweek,* August 7, 1989: 48–49.

Snead, James. "Images of Blacks in Black Independent Films: A Brief Survey." Cham and Andrade-Watkins, 16–25.

Spillers, Hortense. "Mama's Baby, Papa's Maybe: An American Grammar Book." *Diacritics* 17, no. 2 (1987): 65–81.

Spivak, Gayatri. "In a Word. *Interview.*" With Ellen Rooney. *Differences* 1, no. 2 (1990): 124–55.

Staples, Brent. "Spike Lee's Blacks: Are They Real People?" *New York Times,* July 2, 1989, late ed., sec. 2:9+.

Tate, Greg. "Burn Baby Burn." *Premier,* August 1989: 80–85.

White, Armond. "New Dawn at Sundance, Black Filmmakers Take Top Prizes." *Emerge,* May 1990: 65–66.

___. "Scene on the Street: Black Cinema from Catfish Row to Stuyvesant Avenue." *Mother Jones,* September 1989: 35, 46.

Williams, Raymond. *Keywords: A Vocabulary of Culture and Society.* New York: Oxford University Press, 1976.

Wood, Joe. "Looking for Malcolm: The Man and the Meaning Behind the Icon." *Village Voice,* May 29, 1990: 43–45.

___. "Self-Deconstruction." *Village Voice,* April 24, 1990: 79.

What Is This "Black" in Black Popular Culture?

I begin with a question: What sort of moment is this in which to pose the question of black popular culture? These moments are always conjunctural. They have their historical specificity; and although they always exhibit similarities and continuities with the other moments in which we pose a question like this, they are never the same moment. And the combination of what is similar and what is different defines not only the specificity of the moment, but the specificity of the question, and therefore the strategies of cultural politics with which we attempt to intervene in popular culture, and the form and style of cultural theory and criticizing that has to go along with such an intermatch. In his important essay, "The New Cultural Politics of Difference,"[1] Cornel West offers a genealogy of what this moment is, a genealogy of the present that I find brilliantly concise and insightful. His genealogy follows, to some extent, positions I tried to outline in an article that has become somewhat notorious,[2] but it also usefully maps the moment into an American context and in relation to the cognitive and intellectual philosophical traditions with which it engages.

According to West, the moment, this moment, has three general coordinates. The first is the displacement of European models of high culture, of Europe as the universal subject of culture, and of culture itself in its old Arnoldian reading as the last refuge . . . I nearly said of scoundrels, but I won't say who it is of. At least we know who it was against—culture against the barbarians, against the people rattling the gates as the deathless prose of anarchy flowed away from Arnold's pen. The second coordinate is the emergence of the United States as a world power and, consequently, as the center of global cultural production and circulation. This emergence is both a displacement and a hegemonic shift in the *definition* of culture—a movement from high culture to American mainstream popular culture and its mass-cultural, image-mediated, technological forms. The third coordinate is the decolonization

Originally appeared in *Black Popular Culture,* ed. Gina Dent (Seattle: Bay Press, 1992). Reprinted by permission of the author and Bay Press.

of the Third World, culturally marked by the emergence of the decolonized sensibilities. And I read the decolonization of the Third World in Frantz Fanon's sense: I include in it the impact of civil rights and black struggles on the decolonization of the minds of the peoples of the black diaspora.

Let me add some qualifications to that general picture, qualifications that, in my view, make this present moment a very distinctive one in which to ask the question about black popular culture. First, I remind you of the ambiguities of that shift from Europe to America, since it includes America's ambivalent relationship to European high culture and the ambiguity of America's relationship to its own internal ethnic hierarchies. Western Europe did not have, until recently, any ethnicity at all. Or didn't recognize it had any. America has always had a series of ethnicities, and consequently, the construction of ethnic hierarchies has always defined its cultural politics. And, of course, silenced and unacknowledged, the face of American popular culture itself, which has always contained within it, whether silenced or not, black American popular vernacular traditions. It may be hard to remember that, when viewed from outside of the United States, American mainstream popular culture has always involved certain traditions that could only be attributed to black cultural vernacular traditions.

The second qualification concerns the nature of the period of cultural globalization in progress now. I hate the term the "global postmodern," so empty and sliding a signifier that it can be taken to mean virtually anything you like. And, certainly, blacks are as ambiguously placed in relation to postmodernism as they were in relation to high modernism: even when denuded of its wide-European, disenchanted Marxist, French intellectual provenance and scaled down to a more modest descriptive status, postmodernism remains extremely unevenly developed as a phenomenon in which the old center/peripheries of high modernity consistently reappear. The only places where one can genuinely experience the postmodern ethnic cuisine are Manhattan and London, not Calcutta. And yet it is impossible to refuse the "global postmodern" entirely, insofar as it registers certain stylistic shifts in what I want to call the cultural dominant. Even if postmodernism is not a new cultural epoch, but only modernism in the streets, that, in itself, represents an important shifting of the terrain of culture toward the popular—toward popular practices, toward everyday practices, toward local narratives, toward the decentering of old hierarchies and the grand narratives. This decentering or displacement opens up new spaces of contestation and affects a momentous shift in the high culture of popular culture relations, thus presenting us with a strategic and important opportunity for intervention in the popular cultural field.

Third, we must bear in mind postmodernism's deep and ambivalent fascination with difference—sexual difference, cultural difference, racial difference, and above all, ethnic difference. Quite in opposition to the blindness and hostility that European high culture evidenced on the whole toward ethnic difference—its inability even to speak ethnicity when it was so manifestly registering its effects—there's nothing that global postmodernism loves better than a certain kind of difference: a touch of ethnicity, a taste of the exotic, as we say in England, "a bit of the other" (which in the United Kingdom has a sexual as well as an ethnic connotation). Michele Wallace was quite right, in her seminal essay "Modernism, Postmodernism and the Problem of the Visual in Afro-American Culture,"[3] to ask whether this reappearance of a proliferation of difference, of a certain kind of ascent of the global postmodern, isn't a repeat of that "now you see it, now you don't" game that modernism once played with primitivism, to ask whether it is not once again achieved at the expense of the vast silencing about the West's fascination with the bodies of black men and women of other ethnicities. And we must ask about that continuing silence within postmodernism's shifting terrain, about whether the forms of licensing of the gaze that this proliferation of difference invites and allows, at the same time as it disavows, is not really, along with Benetton and the mixed male models of The Face, a kind of difference that doesn't make a difference of any kind.

Hal Foster writes—Wallace quotes him in her essay—"the primitive is a modern problem, a crisis in cultural identity"[4]—hence, the modernist construction of primitivism, the fetishistic recognition and disavowal of the primitive difference. But this resolution is only a repression; delayed into our political unconscious, the primitive returns uncannily at the moment of its apparent political eclipse. This rupture of primitivism, managed by modernism, becomes another postmodern event. That managing is certainly evident in the difference that may not make a difference, which marks the ambiguous appearance of ethnicity at the heart of global postmodernism. But it cannot be only that. For we cannot forget how cultural life, above all in the West, but elsewhere as well, has been transformed in our lifetimes by the voicing of the margins.

Within culture, marginality, though it remains peripheral to the broader mainstream, has never been such a productive space as it is now. And that is not simply the opening within the dominant of spaces that those outside it can occupy. It is also the result of the cultural politics of difference, of the struggles around difference, of the production of new identities, of the appearance of new subjects on the political and cultural stage. This is true not only in regard to race, but also for other marginalized ethnicities, as well as around feminism and around sexual politics in the gay and lesbian movement, as a result of a new kind of cultural politics. Of course, I don't want to suggest that we can counterpose some easy sense of victories won to the eternal story of our own marginalization—I'm tired of those two continuous grand counternarratives. To remain within them is to become trapped in that endless either/or, either total victory or total incorporation, which almost never happens in cultural politics, but with which cultural critics always put themselves to bed.

What we are talking about is the struggle over cultural hegemony, which is these days waged as much in popular culture as anywhere else. That high/popular distinction is precisely what the global postmodern is displacing. Cultural hegemony is never about pure victory or pure domination (that's not what the term means); it is never a zero-sum cultural game; it is always about shifting the balance of power in the relations of culture; it is always about changing the dispositions and the configurations of cultural power, not getting out of it. There is a kind of "nothing ever changes, the system always wins" attitude, which I read as the cynical protective shell that, I'm sorry to say, American cultural critics frequently wear, a shell that sometimes prevents them from developing cultural strategies that can make a difference. It is as if, in order to protect themselves against the occasional defeat, they have to pretend they can see right through everything—and it's just the same as it always was.

Now, cultural strategies that can make a difference, that's what I'm interested in—those that can make a difference and can shift the dispositions of power. I acknowledge that the spaces "won" for difference are few and far between, that they are very carefully policed and regulated. I believe they are limited. I know, to my cost, that they are grossly underfunded, that there is always a price of incorporation to be paid when the cutting edge of difference and transgression is blunted into spectacularization. I know that what replaces invisibility is a kind of carefully regulated, segregated visibility. But it does not help simply to name-call it "the same." That name-calling merely reflects the particular model of cultural politics to which we remain attached, precisely, the zero-sum game—our model replacing their model, our identities in place of their identities—what Antonio Gramsci called culture as a once and for all "war of maneuver," when, in fact, the only game in town worth playing is the game of cultural "wars of position."

Lest you think, to paraphrase Gramsci, my optimism of the will has now completely outstripped my pessimism of the intellect, let me add a fourth element that comments on the moment. For, if the global postmodern represents an ambiguous opening to difference and to the margins and makes a certain kind of decentering of the Western narrative a likely possibility, it is matched, from the very heartland of cultural politics, by the backlash: the aggressive resistance to difference; the attempt to restore the canon of Western civilization; the assault, direct and indirect, on multiculturalism; the return to grand narratives of history, language, and literature (the three great supporting pillars of national identity and national culture); the defense of ethnic absolutism, of a cultural racism that has marked the Thatcher and the Reagan eras; and the new xenophobias that are about to overwhelm fortress Europe. The last thing to do is read me as saying the cultural dialectic is finished. Part of the problem is that we have forgotten what sort of space the space of popular culture is. And black popular culture is not exempt from that dialectic, which is historical, not a matter of bad faith. It is therefore necessary to deconstruct the popular once and for all. There is no going back to an innocent view of what it consists of.

Popular culture carries that affirmative ring because of the prominence of the word "popular." And, in one sense, popular culture always has its base in the experiences, the pleasures, the memories, the traditions of the people. It has connections with local hopes and local aspirations, local tragedies and local scenarios that are the everyday practices and the everyday experiences of ordinary folks. Hence, it links with what Mikhail Bakhtin calls "the vulgar"—the popular, the informal, the underside, the grotesque. That is why it has always been counterposed to elite or high culture, and is thus a site of alternative traditions. And that is why the dominant tradition has always been deeply suspicious of it, quite rightly. They suspect that they are about to be overtaken by what Bakhtin calls "the carnivalesque." This fundamental mapping of culture between the high and the low has been charted into four symbolic domains by Peter Stallybrass and Allon White in their important book *The Politics and Poetics of Transgression.* They talk about the mapping of high and low in psychic forms, in the human body, in space, and in the social order.[5] And they discuss the high/low distinction as a fundamental basis to the mechanisms of ordering and of sense-making in European and other cultures despite the fact that the contents of what is high and what is low change from one historical moment to another.

The important point is the ordering of different aesthetic morals, social aesthetics, the orderings of culture that open up culture to the play of power, not an inventory of what is high versus what is low at any particular moment. That is why Gramsci, who has a side of common sense on which, above all, cultural hegemony is made, lost, and struggled over, gave the question of what he called "the national popular" such strategic importance. The role of the "popular" in popular culture is to fix the authenticity of popular forms, rooting them in the experiences of popular communities from which they draw their strength, allowing us to see them as expressive of a particular subordinate social life that resists its being constantly made over as low and outside.

However, as popular culture has historically become the dominant form of global culture, so it is at the same time the scene, par excellence, of commodification, of the industries where culture enters directly into the circuits of a dominant technology—the circuits of power and capital. It is the space of homogenization where stereotyping and the formulaic mercilessly process the material and experiences it draws into its web, where control over narratives and representations passes into the hands of the established cultural bureaucracies, sometimes without a murmur. It is rooted in popular experience and available for expropriation at one and the same time. I want to argue that this is necessarily and inevitably so. And this goes for black popular culture as well. Black popular culture, like all popular cultures in the modern world, is bound to be contradictory, and this is not because we haven't fought the cultural battle well enough.

By definition, black popular culture is a contradictory space. It is a sight of strategic contestation. But it can never be simplified or explained in terms of the simple binary oppositions that are still habitually used to map it out: high versus low; resistance versus incorporation; authentic versus inauthentic; experiential versus formal; opposition versus homogenization. There are always positions to be won in popular culture, but no struggle can capture popular culture itself for our side or theirs. Why is that so? What consequences does this have for strategies of intervention in cultural politics? How does it shift the basis for black cultural criticism?

However deformed, incorporated, and inauthentic are the forms in which black people and black communities and traditions appear and are represented in popular culture, we continue to see, in the figures and the repertoires on which popular culture draws, the experiences that stand behind them. In its expressivity, its musicality, its orality, in its rich, deep, and varied attention to speech, in its inflections toward the vernacular and the local, in its rich production of counternarratives, and above all, in its metaphorical use of the musical vocabulary, black popular culture has enabled the surfacing, inside the mixed and contradictory modes even of some mainstream popular culture, of elements of a discourse that is different—other forms of life, other traditions of representation.

I do not propose to repeat the work of those who have devoted their scholarly, critical, and creative lives to identifying the distinctiveness of these diasporic traditions, to exploring their modes and the historical experiences and memories they encode. I say only three inadequate things about these traditions, since they are germane to the point I want to develop. First, I ask you to note how, within the black repertoire, *style*—which mainstream cultural critics often believe to be the mere husk, the wrapping, the sugar coating on the pill—has become *itself* the subject of what is going on. Second, mark how, displaced from a logocentric world—where the direct mastery of cultural modes meant the mastery of writing, and hence, both of the criticism of writing (logocentric criticism) and the deconstruction of writing—the people of the black diaspora have, in opposition to all of that, found the deep form, the deep structure of their cultural life in music. Third, think of how these cultures have used the body—as if it was, and it often was, the only cultural capital we had. We have worked on ourselves as the canvases of representation.

There are deep questions here of cultural transmission and inheritance, and of the complex relations between African origins and the irreversible scatterings of the diaspora, questions I cannot go into. But I do believe that these repertoires of black popular culture, which, since we were excluded from the cultural mainstream, were often the only performative spaces we had left, were overdetermined from at least two directions: they were partly determined from their inheritances, but they were also critically determined by the diasporic conditions in which the connections were forged. Selective appropriation, incorporation, and rearticulation of European ideologies, cultures, and institutions, alongside an African heritage—this is Cornel West again—led to linguistic innovations in rhetorical stylization of the body, forms of occupying an alien social space, heightened expressions, hairstyles, ways of walking, standing, and talking, and a means of constituting and sustaining camaraderie and community.

The point of underlying overdetermination—black cultural repertoires constituted from two directions at once—is perhaps more subversive than you think. It is to insist that in black popular culture, strictly speaking, ethnographically speaking, there are no pure forms at all. Always these forms are the product of partial synchronization, of engagement across cultural boundaries, of the confluence of more than one cultural tradition, of the negotiations of dominant and subordinate positions, of the subterranean strategies of recoding and transcoding, of critical signification, of signifying. Always these forms are impure, to some degree hybridized from a vernacular base. Thus, they must always be heard, not simply as the recovery of a lost dialogue bearing clues for the production of new musics (because there is never any going back to the old in a simple way), but as what they are—adaptations, molded to the mixed, contradictory, hybrid spaces of popular culture. They are not the recovery of something pure that we can, at last, live by. In what Kobena Mercer calls the necessity for a diaspora aesthetic, we are obliged to acknowledge they are what the modern is.

It is this mark of difference *inside* forms of popular culture—which are by definition contradictory and which therefore appear as impure, threatened by incorporation or exclusion—that is carried by the signifier "black" in the term "black popular culture." It has come to signify the black community, where these traditions were kept, and whose struggles survive in the persistence of the black experience (the historical experiences of black people in the diaspora), of the black aesthetic (the distinctive cultural repertoires out of which popular representations were made), and of the black counternarratives we have struggled to voice. Here, black popular culture returns to the ground I defined earlier. "Good" black popular culture can pass the test of authenticity—the reference to black experience and to black expressivity. These serve as the guarantees in the determination of which black popular culture is right on, which is ours and which is not.

I have the feeling that, historically, nothing could have been done to intervene in the dominated field of mainstream popular culture, to try to win some space there, without the strategies through which those dimensions were condensed onto the signifier "black." Where would we be, as bell hooks once remarked, without a touch of essentialism? Or, what Gayatri Spivak calls strategic essentialism, a necessary moment? The question is whether we are any longer in that moment, whether that is still a sufficient basis for the strategies of new interventions. Let me try to set forth what seem to me to be the weaknesses of this essentializing moment and the strategics, creative and critical, which flow from it.

This moment essentializes differences in several senses. It sees difference as "their traditions versus ours," not in a positional way, but in a mutually exclusive, autonomous, and self-sufficient one. And it is therefore unable to grasp the dialogic strategies and hybrid forms essential to the diaspora aesthetic. A movement beyond this essentialism is not an aesthetic or critical strategy without a cultural politics, without a marking of difference. It is not simply rearticulation and reappropriation for the sake of it. What it evades is the essentializing of difference into two mutually opposed either/or's. What it does is to move us into a new kind of cultural positionality, a different logic of difference. To encapsulate what Paul Gilroy has so vividly put on the political and cultural agenda of black politics in the United Kingdom: blacks in the British diaspora must, at this historical moment, refuse the binary black *or* British. They must refuse it because the "or" remains the sight of *constant contestation* when the aim of the struggle must be, instead, to replace the "or" with the potentiality or the possibility of an "and." That is the logic of coupling rather than the logic of a binary opposition. You can be black *and* British, not only because that is a necessary position to take in 1992, but because even those two terms, joined now by the coupler "and" instead of opposed to one another, do not exhaust all of our identities. Only some of our identities are sometimes caught in that particular struggle.

The essentializing moment is weak because it naturalizes and dehistoricizes difference, mistaking what is historical and cultural for what is natural, biological, and genetic. The moment the signifier "black" is torn from its historical, cultural, and political embedding and lodged in a biologically constituted racial category, we valorize, by inversion, the very ground of the racism we are trying to deconstruct. In addition, as always happens when we naturalize historical categories (think about gender and sexuality), we fix that signifier outside history, outside change, outside political intervention. And once it is fixed, we are tempted to use "black" as sufficient in itself to guarantee the progressive character of the politics we fight under the banner—as if we don't have any other politics to argue about except whether something's black or not. We are tempted to display that signifier as a device that can purify the impure, bring the straying brothers and sisters who don't know what they ought to be doing into line, and police the boundaries—which are of course political, symbolic, and positional boundaries—as if they were genetic. For which, I'm sorry to say, read "jungle fever"—as if we can translate from nature to politics using a racial category to warrant the politics of a cultural text and as a line against which to measure deviation.

Moreover, we tend to privilege experience itself, as if black life is lived experience outside of representation. We have only, as it were, to express what we already know we are. Instead, it is only through the way in which we represent and imagine ourselves that we come to know how we are constituted and who we are. There is no escape from the politics of representation, and we cannot wield "how life really is out there" as a kind of test against which the political rightness or wrongness of a particular cultural strategy or text can be measured. It will not be a mystery to you that I think that "black" is none of these things in reality. It is not a category of essence and, hence, this way of understanding the floating signifier in black popular culture now will not do.

There is, of course, a very profound set of distinctive, historically defined black experiences that contribute to those alternative repertoires I spoke about earlier. But it is to the diversity, not the homogeneity, of black experience that we must now give our undivided creative attention. This is not simply to appreciate the historical and experiential differences within and between communities, regions, country and city, across national cultures, between diasporas, but also to recognize the other kinds of difference that place, position, and locate black people. The point is not simply that, since our racial differences do not constitute all of us, we are always different, negotiating different kinds of differences—of gender, of sexuality, of class. It is also that these antagonisms refuse to be neatly aligned; they are simply not reducible to one another; they refuse to coalesce around a single axis of differentiation. We are always in negotiation, not with a single set of oppositions that place us always in the same relation to others, but with a series of different positionalities. Each has for us its point of profound subjective identification. And that is the most difficult thing about this proliferation of the field of identities and antagonisms: they are often dislocating in relation to one another.

Thus, to put it crudely, certain ways in which black men continue to live out their counteridentities as black masculinities and replay those fantasies of black masculinities in the theaters of popular culture are, when viewed from along other axes of difference, the very masculine identities that are oppressive to women, that claim visibility for their hardness only at the expense of the vulnerability of black women and the feminization of gay black men. The way in which a transgressive politics in one domain is constantly sutured and stabilized by reactionary or unexamined politics in another is only to be explained by this continuous cross-dislocation of one identity by another, one structure by another. Dominant ethnicities are always underpinned by a particular sexual economy, a particular figured masculinity, a particular class identity. There is no guarantee, in reaching for an essentialized racial identity of which we think we can be certain, that it will always turn out to be mutually liberating and progressive on all the other dimensions. It *can* be won. There *is* a politics there to be struggled for. But the invocation of a guaranteed black experience behind it will not produce that politics. Indeed, the plurality of antagonisms and differences that now seek to destroy the unity of black politics, given the complexities of the structures of subordination that have been formed by the way in which we were inserted into the black diaspora, is not at all surprising.

These are the thoughts that drove me to speak, in an unguarded moment, of the end of the innocence of the black subject or the end of the innocent notion of an essential black subject. And I want to end simply by reminding you that this end is also a beginning. As Isaac Julien said in an interview with bell hooks in which they discussed his new film *Young Soul Rebels,* his attempt in his own work to portray a number of different racial bodies, to constitute a range of different black subjectivities, and to engage with the positionalities of a number of different kinds of black masculinities:

> . . . blackness as a sign is never enough. What does that black subject do, how does it act, how does it think politically. . . . being black isn't really good enough for me: I want to know what your cultural politics are.[6]

I want to end with two thoughts that take that point back to the subject of popular culture. The first is to remind you that popular culture, commodified and stereotyped as it often is, is not at all, as we sometimes think of it, the arena where we find who we really are, the truth of our experience. It is an arena that is *profoundly* mythic. It is a theater of popular desires, a theater of popular fantasies. It is where we discover and play with the identifications of ourselves, where we are imagined, where we are represented, not only to the audiences out there who do not get the message, but to ourselves for the first time. As Freud said, sex (and representation) mainly takes place in the head. Second, though the terrain of the popular looks as if it is constructed with single binaries, it is not. I reminded you about the importance of the structuring of cultural space in terms of high and low, and the threat of the Bakhtinian carnivalesque. I think Bakhtin has been profoundly misread. The carnivalesque is not simply an upturning of two things which remain locked within their oppositional frameworks; it is also crosscut by what Bakhtin calls the dialogic.

I simply want to end with an account of what is involved in understanding popular culture, in a dialogic rather than in a strictly oppositional way, from *The Politics and Poetics of Transgression* by Stallybrass and White:

> A recurrent pattern emerges: the "top" attempts to reject and eliminate the "bottom" for reasons of prestige and status, only to discover, not only that it is in some way frequently dependent upon the low-Other ... but also that the top *includes* that low symbolically, as a primary eroticized constituent of its own fantasy life. The result is a mobile, conflictual fusion of power, fear, and desire in the construction of subjectivity: a psychological dependence upon precisely those others which are being rigorously opposed and excluded at the social level. It is for this reason that what is socially peripheral is so frequently *symbolically* central.[7]

NOTES

1. Cornel West, "The New Cultural Politics of Difference," in *Out There: Marginalization and Contemporary Cultures,* ed. Russell Ferguson et al. (Cambridge, MIT Press in association with the New Museum of Contemporary Art, 1990), 19–36.

2. Stuart Hall, "New Ethnicities," in *Black Film/British Cinema, ICA Document 7,* ed. Kobena Mercer (London: Institute of Contemporary Arts, 1988), 27–31.

3. Michele Wallace, "Modernism, Postmodernism and the Problem of the Visual in Afro-American Culture," in *Out There: Marginalization and Contemporary Cultures,* 39–50.

4. Hal Foster, *Recodings: Art, Spectacle, and Cultural Politics* (Port Townsend, Wash.: Bay Press, 1985), 204.

5. Peter Stallybrass and Allon White, *The Politics and Poetics of Transgression* (Ithaca: Cornell University Press, 1986), 3.

6. bell hooks, "States of Desire" (interview with Isaac Julien), *Transition* 1, no. 3, 175.

7. Stallybrass and White, *The Politics and Poetics of Transgression,* 5.

Nathan Grant

Innocence and Ambiguity in the Films of Charles Burnett

Wherever or whatever African Americans felt the "promised land" to be, it seemed certain that that promise would not be realized without the ethics and the values so carefully stored and taken from that place "back home."[1] Here were the beliefs and behaviors that could not be done without; they were the emblems of our survival in the new New World of asphalt and steel. But the urban background of today, against which much of black life has taken shape, reflects something quite other than the concerns at the end of the past century that our ethics would dissolve in the burgeoning metropolitanism of the present century, something much more urgent than the comparatively gentle fear of our losing our values forever in a wash of gin, bright lights, and jazz. In our own time in America's cities, privation, despair, and sudden death have formed part of our narrative. In this generation alone, the stereotype fashioned from these elements—the "bad nigger" of blaxploitation films—appeared to shelve the old values and confront a racism institutionalized in American temples of power with an ugly if not improbable force. The vexing reality behind this formula is that the veneer of black machismo had quickly faded with the closing credits, leaving behind only the pain that first called it into being. As well, those values nurtured in slavery and after which seemed to hold African Americans together during the period of migration—and after—because distorted by the landscape if not absent from it. That distortion became starkly evident in the rage of black Los Angeles after the alteration by some of even the simplest narrative to a different design, to a bizarre new notion that many thoroughly equipped and supported attackers had more to fear than one manacled and defenseless attacked. The man hogtied and huddled on the ground too easily resembled, in a time gone by, what father or uncle or brother or friend or lover we felt certain we were seeing for the last time. The bright flames that later engulfed the city suggested that whatever values had been capable of defending the spirit in such an instance were duly attenuated in this very different locale and in this kinder, gentler time.

In the fictions that reflect this reality—in the contemporary narrative instance, and especially in the powerful moment of film—we have been challenged to confront the city as a stiflingly narrow cultural space for African Americans, and accept that those once-sustaining precepts are now overwhelmed by the urgent situation of urban life in which they are now found.[2] In the films of Charles Burnett, that space is described, on one hand, with representations of innocence, and on the other, with figurations of ambiguity. By rough analogy, innocence would be to ambiguity as good would be to evil. Innocence represents an ingenuousness, a wholeheartedness inherent within which is an entire tradition of civilizing values that came out of the experience of slavery; these include everything from folk wisdom and religion to simple respect and fellow-feeling to faith in progress and mobility. These are the values with which grandmothers imbued their grandchildren, which perhaps points to the efficacy of children in Burnett's work as conduits of the experience of innocence. Even when they are merely being playful and solicitous, they are directing our attention to the dangers that threaten their lives and the lives of adults. These dangers are the facets of evil always appearing beneath the experience of innocence; as such they emerge with uncertainty and without warning, always producing dismay.

Often in Burnett ambiguity is simply the blind and vexing absurdity of everyday life, but the enduring representation of the ambiguous in his work is this instance of ambiguity coupled with the fact of the African American urban present, in which the aspects of crime (including black-on-black crime), betrayal, poverty, despair, and sudden death are distributed along life's contingent moments. The situation of the black city in Burnett's films finds innocence in constant conflict with ambiguity as each struggles for primacy, and whenever ambiguity pauses to gather strength, Burnett engages our concern.

Burnett's "wider shot"—the angle at which we no longer view just the narrower cultural milieu of urban African America but view instead America as a whole—seems to soften the harder edges of these master categories, but it nevertheless locates within them the issues and ideologies of a racialized society. *America Becoming* is a 1992 Burnett documentary about the growing immigrant presence in the United States and how both newcomers and natives coexist. Members of both groups in different parts of the country are interviewed, and all respond to the issues of their changing communities and their new and challenging social and economic realities. This film seeks to examine the ever-changing human landscape of the American macrocosm; the inevitable collisions of languages and castes in a multicultural society as well as efforts to maintain semblances of harmony are of moment here.

Burnett's focus on environs includes the long shot, a technique which, in this instance, guides its subject to an intriguing, if unsettling location. These shots, while capturing the multitudes, deliver a mannerist pose that can be described as being at once both innocent and ambiguous: they deliver a sense of sameness among individuals, whereas close-ups of workers moving toward the morning whistle or of congregations leaving church would doubtless capture difference. In contrast, Burnett's close-ups capture customs and mores and show how those human rules exclude. A Vietnamese woman quietly sits well outside a circle of men who are planning the funeral of a departed friend; as a woman, however, she is not allowed to participate in this process. The close shot also focuses on how many foreign-language immigrant parents customarily speak through their children, trustingly but haplessly leaving the task of deciphering *and* conveying meaning to even the very young. Burnett's choice not to edit out the jumping-up into view of an African American child in Chicago while his father was being interviewed may itself have been indicative of Burnett's own sense of proleptic irony: in its own way, this brief instance can be said to describe—innocently and enigmatically—the whole life of the African in the West, the very matter of *being seen*. Throughout this film the revelations and concealments of Burnett's lens mirror the increasing tensions within an America becoming more broadly immigrant and diverse. Life from beyond America's borders, the camera consistently shows, should not, for immigrants or for natives, dissolve into life at the margins.

When Burnett confronts the narrowly configured, sharply demarcated environs of black Los Angeles, he confronts the American microcosm, focusing again on the inner life of exclusion. Black Los Angeles is home to Burnett; it is a region demanding a vision that is not only mindful of history and heritage, but which seeks as well a mapping of its having been situated somewhere between blaxploitation and Rodney King. Burnett writes about his home:

> One of the features of my community is that it does not have a center, does not have an elder statesman, and more important, does not have roots; in essence it is just a wall with graffiti written on it. Life is going to work, coming home, making sure every entrance is firmly locked to keep the thugs out, thinking on how to move up in the world or being a member of a street gang standing at neighborhood corners, thinking about nothing and going nowhere. In both cases what is missing is not only the spiritual but mother wit.[3]

He moved to Los Angeles with his family from Mississippi when he was three years old, and grew up playing in the vacant lots that are very like the cherished grounds of the children in *Killer of Sheep* (1977). His days as a film student at UCLA in the late 1960s and early 1970s coincided with the era of black radical political ferment as embodied by the Panthers and the Muslims, and it coincided as well with the period of blaxploitation in which ridiculous and demeaning images of African Americans were meant to signal the newly sublime. Burnett and the other young filmmakers to whom he became close at this time—Haile Gerima, Julie Dash, Billy Woodberry, and others—had and projected a vision of the black milieu that, in defining itself, rejected the unreality of black exploitation and exposed the immediate reality of communities at risk—a risk that, in the specific case of Los Angeles, has matured into the conflagration ignited by injustice.

Killer of Sheep is the story of Stan, a worker in a Los Angeles area slaughterhouse whose life, suddenly and inexplicably, has become insipid and mundane. His deteriorating state of mind becomes a stark reflection of the state of his community. The film opens with the music of innocence: a woman and a child singing the lullaby, "My Curly-Headed Baby," is the background for the chastising of a child by his parents for his not having defended his brother in a fight. After a tongue-lashing from his father and then a slap in the face from his mother, the women's voices are replaced by the somber voice of Paul Robeson, whose deep and sonorous tones somehow demonstrate the sadness of the child's loss of dignity as well. The song's lyrics ("Do you want the stars to play with / And the moon to run away with / They'll come if you don't cry"), in contrast with the harsh words of the father ("You are not a child anymore. You will soon be a goddamn *man!* Start learning about what life is about *now*, son"), suggest that part of the difficulty of growing up inheres in having to fight before one is ready, having to face a mean world without support, and often without love.

Children, who figure prominently in Burnett's films, are, as he says, "a means of telling a story. As one element of the story they are witnesses."[4] But they appear often to be more than witnesses, if witnesses are not somehow also unconscious conveyers of an ethic, of high conscience, are not themselves the bearers of innocence. That these characters appear only here and never again in the film (though the actors appear in other roles) would seem to construct a tableau of innocence and ambiguity whose themes so thoroughly permeate the narrative. The slap, which ends the scene and returns us to the remaining beginning credits, is itself a crisp depiction of a loss of innocence, of a sense that violence in any form is the most powerful and enduring factor of human development in this setting.

We next meet Stan Junior (Jack Drummond) for the first time. He is peeking out now and again from behind an old piece of wood. Friends of his are throwing rocks at him and some other friends as this war of children goes on in an old railyard, and this seems not at all dangerous an activity but for the rocks being thrown. Here innocence and ambiguity dovetail continuously into each other; what begins as a child's game appears much more serious as suddenly, one of the children seems to be hurt. But when it is soon discovered that he has been faking it, the boys revert to roughhousing, once again invoking the ambiguity of desultory yet dangerous play. A long shot from the freight train at which they throw rocks suggests their descent upon it like rail bandits of an earlier time; there is talk of going to a red-light district to watch prostitutes come out of a building; one boy lies under the wheels of a standing freight car while exhorting others to push it over him (they cannot, of course). Their insouciance is ironic, as it is that their grandfathers could have worked these lines with the consciousness of race conjoined to a constant threat of danger. But some perhaps far more unsettling idea is at work here. In just these few scenes of adolescent play, Burnett manages to cohere sex, violence, and death: in the games and idle talk of these children, these elements are reified, becoming the dossiers of their young adulthood, and all of it takes place in an abandoned railyard, a playground much like that of Burnett's own youth.

In next deciding to warn two thieves that someone has seen their burglary and intends to call the police, Stan Junior demonstrates that he has begun to make the wrong choices for his community as well as for himself. Music again becomes portentous as Cecil Gant croons "I Wonder" ("I wonder / My little darlin' / Where can you be / Again tonight / While the moon is shining bright . . .") in the background while the boy drags home through the alley, and the thieves drag their booty ahead of him. Nothing of his son's waywardness is felt or even understood by the senior Stan, who, when we meet him for the first time, is almost literally sunk "down the drain" as he pulls his head from under the kitchen sink he has been repairing. Everything we have seen before meeting Stan describes the world in which he and his family live and the future that is his and that of his children. He tells his friend Oscar, "I'm working myself into my own hell. I can't get no sleep at night . . . no piece of mind." Oscar, like most of Stan's friends, is blithely unhelpful: "Why don't you kill yourself?" he rejoins. For Stan, Burnett's master categories of innocence and ambiguity actually sum up his life. Although there comes a point at which he believes it to be the case, it is not his job at the slaughterhouse that is responsible for his state of ennui. Lack of connection with all that is around him, a being out of touch, appears to have gained control. "Back home"—a theme that echoes again and again in Burnett's work—is a place that Stan cannot reach just now, or perhaps ever. It is in his answer to Oscar's question as to his last visit to church, and both are revealed as places set in a time long ago if only because his present environment is precarious in its every manifestation. Again and again, his friends prove unsympathetic: in an effort to pull himself up with even the smallest pleasure, Stan reminisces with friend Bracy (Charles Bracy) over a cup of coffee that the steam from the cup feels like the warm forehead of a woman while making love. But Bracy's remark, "I don't go for women who got malaria!" simply destroys the effort for Stan, perhaps allowing him only to sink even deeper. At that very moment, the throaty growling and loud barking of what is perhaps a huge and vicious dog disrupts the silence, causing both men to pause and look toward the camera. But then, because such an occurrence is itself so natural in this landscape after all, both men wordlessly resume sipping.[5]

The obvious irony of the slaughter of innocents is but a metaphor for Stan's own vulnerability, for since we never quite know the source of his pain—the sheep never quite know what hits *them*—we then understand that his salvation may be as present a condition as his destruction. His neglected wife (Kaycee Moore), who in one instance balefully checks her appearance in her reflection in the cookware, highlights the irony of Stan's reverie of lovemaking and steaming coffee: unlike his friends who mock him, a loving, caring woman actually seeks to cleave to him—yet he cannot reach out to her.

Some of the other men who know Stan are anything but supportive and understanding. Oscar, Bracy, and Ernie Cox are merely annoying, but the two men who later come to ask Stan to help commit murder are truly dangerous. In an almost heavy-handed way, Burnett first returns to the slaughterhouse to focus for a moment on more sheep about to be killed while Robeson's rendition of "Going Home" is the audio background. But this moment speaks to something larger than Stan's own defenselessness. Perhaps with only a scant preconsciousness of its implications, Stan is living his vulnerability as well as that of his friends. He is witnessing not only the threat to his own survival as that is made evident by the actions of his friends, but he is also watching his community's self-destruction. The men arrive at Stan's front porch, tell Stan their plans, and seek to secure his support. The old values of African American family honor and integrity now seek to take their place and reestablish equilibrium. As one man seeks to convince by saying, "Be a man, Stan, if you can," Stan's wife launches into a spirited defense of his manhood for Stan, and does so not solely because she is acting in the best tradition of the "good woman," but also because it is inherently right that she do so as she sees his own defenses flagging.

Stan's wife's anger may be read as a kind of emasculation of Stan, who sits while she argues with his friends, and is thus unable to come to *her* defense. But if this instance can be read as emasculation, it is really symptomatic of the more totalizing instance of Stan's vulnerability. Burnett appears to equate masculinity with will or purpose by presenting male characters whose dislocations from self and others subordinate purpose. In *My Brother's Wedding* (1983), Pierce so thoroughly shuns responsibility—if preferable, he so *wills himself out* of it—that the remarks made by his mother and other women about his manhood cannot be considered at all undeserved. The sacrifice of purpose is everywhere in Pierce's character. But while Baby Brother's treatment of his wife in *To*

Sleep with Anger (1990) is decidedly unmasculine (read unchivalrous or unpartnerly), the preservation of his manhood seems only adjunct to his real predicament—namely, a disengagement from family and from self brought about by his preoccupation with the acquisition of capital. He has lost his purpose without entirely having willed it away. Even as his family berates him for *his* lack of responsibility, Baby Brother can be seen to reside haplessly in a place beyond emasculation, a place in which he is otherwise otiose.

Similarly, Stan's difficulty is located in his disaffection for everything he had previously come to know as real, as genuine. This miasma is the horizon of every apparent expression of Stan's lack of masculinity, or of emasculations effected from without. His estrangement precedes—or even preempts—the efficacy of a desexualizing agent. His lack of sexual drive, for example, cannot be seen as something his wife, who wants him desperately, or any other woman has given him. In the instances of sex and sexuality following the scene on Stan's stoop, Burnett piles ambiguity upon ambiguity. The middle-aged, overweight white woman who owns the liquor store where Stan goes to cash his check is emasculating to the slightly built and soft-spoken black man who works for her, and is simply rude to the first man who comes in to cash his check. She is entirely solicitous to Stan, however, and overtly propositions him by offering him a job that would involve his working in the back of the store with her. Of course, Stan can easily avoid insulting her by invoking the fact of his marriage (he does not), and we do not know whether the reason for his refusal when first asked is genuine ("Liquor stores get held up, and I'd hate to get shot"). What seems to be of moment to Burnett is the presentation of possibilities that dissolve into ambiguity precisely because they are incommensurable with the elements of Stan's real dilemma. Though Stan is in a sense masculin*ized* by her advances, her relative unattractiveness (she is probably not the woman Stan had in mind in his talk over coffee with Bracy) and the face of her whiteness (Stan would risk the opprobrium of his community with such a liaison), might well preclude his acceptance of her proposition. But Stan's response to such things are not revealed to us because, ultimately, they do not matter. We cannot know if they would if, say, the owner were a woman of color with limitless sex appeal, and if her employee were as virile-looking as Stan, though I think we are led to believe that they would not. But with things as they are, Burnett conceals even these possibilities, and preserves the ambiguity of Stan's relationships with a component of absurdity.

The irrevocability of a reified emasculation makes resolution between the sexes in Burnett or anywhere else impossible. Resolution is clear in *Killer of Sheep* and *To Sleep with Anger;* men and women do come together at the ends of these films, and they do so because the issue of male existential estrangement is solved. But Pierce (who never had a meaningful relationship with a woman) is never reconciled, even with himself, and this is perhaps the clearest message at the end of *My Brother's Wedding*. Stan's and Baby Brother's masculine configurations are splintered, partly by the deep ambiguities of existence that confound them—and it is all the more intriguing that the master theme beneath these very differently constructed states is that of social class. Although class is an issue important both to *My Brother's Wedding* and to its protagonist, Pierce fails to respond actively in situation to any issue that threatens or overwhelms. He thus falls somewhere in the middle between Baby Brother's stultifying lack of awareness of his embarrassment of riches, and Stan's poignant lack of connection with his fragmenting community and its attendant poverty. For Stan, who sits on his stoop in despair and confusion, the challenge from his friend—"Be a man, Stan, if you can"—is layered with levels of indeterminacy that practically demand that someone come to his rescue.

The scene in which Stan's wife acts in true defiance actually reestablishes Stan's innocence and the integrity of his family, for the men's efforts are finally frustrated and they do leave. But innocence and integrity again fall victim to ambiguity as Stan's daughter (Angela Burnett), now shoeless, and his son, who chooses to address his mother in countrified style as "Ma dear," then immediately emerge from the house; both children are summarily chastised for these transgressions by both parents. The importance of tradition is now gently, but crucially questioned, for as is dramatized by the parents' irritation, tradition has just been overwhelmed. Suddenly, the force of the old values has evaporated, because while they have saved in the past, they cannot now sustain. This moment casts Stan's life in relief as what remain as his everyday experience are precisely those conditions that would allow the candor and the casualness with which a man's own friends would ask that he help them kill someone.

To help break at least the gnawing tedium of such an existence, Stan decides to buy a car. (He is eventually reduced to having to buy an engine for an existing car.) His pride is assaulted, however, when it is suggested to him that he cannot afford one. In defending fiscal solvency to friends, he protests that his relative freedom from poverty is demonstrated by his ability to give things to the Salvation Army. As discussed above, there is even an assault on the values of the home as the lecherous liquor store owner tries to get him to work for her. The form of innocence that has constructed parts of the film's message now begins to fragment and fall heavily, but sex and poverty (whether financial or spiritual) enter earlier as thematic substructures. When we first meet Stan, one of the more immediate symbols of innocence is his daughter's standing to the side of the kitchen wearing a dog mask. Chased out of the house by Stan Junior, she goes—innocently—to play with a little neighborhood boy. But the instance of innocence here is itself ambiguous, highlighted by the larger effect of *masking*. The considerable length of time spent on the girls' coyly approaching the boy may suggest a portentous, precocious sexuality. Precocious sexuality and single motherhood are recurrent themes in *My Brother's Wedding*, and these are played out as well in *Killer of Sheep*. In one instance, the little girl, who is the apple of Stan's eye, comes to Stan after his hard day at the slaughterhouse and rubs her father's shoulders; her mother, who has just been rebuffed again by Stan, watches the scene helplessly, even jealously, as mother's and daughter's eyes meet. Stan's daughter is able to command fatherly attention and playfulness while his wife remains unable to engage him sexually; in this more local, familial instance and in the larger community, of which early sexual experiences constitute a part, this sequence becomes deeply equivocal. The "mask of innocence" worn by the daughter in the earlier scene is contrasted to Stan's masking his poverty through Stan Junior's distorted face when the boy menacingly tells his sister: "I need some money!" What has Stan—and by extension, what has his community, in the very phase in which it exists—left behind as meaningful and valuable for Stan Junior and his sister? Stan's own defense against all of this, perhaps, is the visible wound he suffers when it is suggested to him that he is poor, and when he responds that he has at least enough worth to make a gift of charity every now and again. But he is rebuffed when he seeks repayment of a debt in order to buy the automobile engine, and the engine's ultimate uselessness when it falls from the truck, its block broken, only exposes more of Stan's hell, the quite ordinary waste and frustration of his life.

A startling cataleptic irony draws on the innocence/ambiguity theme for its power. As we return with Stan to his neighborhood, children dance across rooftops as a woman, turning back to look at the two babies in the apartment, holds her husband at bay with a pistol. The man peeks several times from behind the wall he keeps between himself and her bullets, which recalls the film's second scene, wherein Stan Junior peeks several times from behind a piece of wood he keeps between himself and the rocks being flung at him. By now, and in this same vein, innocence and ambiguity appear to be coming to a crisis. Another sequence at the slaughterhouse shows the debraining of sheep, as the heads are turned upside down on a stand, sliced along the jaw, and the tissue scooped out. We are led to understand that men, particularly black men, go often like sheep to their slaughter in a world of random violence, their heads being targets for any projectile. This ironic configuration of Burnett is completed through the end of Stan's day, as two children are doing headstands in front of the house while another counts, testing the ability of the first two. As Stan enters the house, he deliberately knocks the children over—perhaps in a liminal awareness of the possibility of sudden and horrific death—and in one of the final expressions of this construction of innocence and ambiguity in this film, one can feel Stan's frustration, especially as the camera holds the shot of the children as they resume headstanding after Stan closes the door.

Finally, however—although we are not sure, and it does not appear that Stan is sure—it is Stan's own community that pulls him out of his state. A gift of money and a can of peaches to a friend are simple gestures, but they are almost the first to put a smile on his face. He is still distant at a neighborhood house party, but a flat tire endured on a trip to the racetrack with family and friends probably points up something of the comedy of his existence as Bracy's mock outrage governs the scene. But though Stan's reemergence into the world appears to be the end, his son seems to be beginning his own departure from it: Stan Junior is hiding among nearby rooftops as his mother calls vainly for him. Stan Junior's growing delinquency, as well as the fates of all of the children in his neighborhood, is tied to both of the two final scenes of the film. A friend of Stan's wife, a woman on crutches, hobbles into the house to tell everyone about her pregnancy. She appears, however, to be unable to speak, which forces us to question what impact her disabilities will make on a motherhood that is already as infirm as is her environment. Her voicelessness—and the wide arc she makes over her womb with her hand—bring us *full* circle, back to the mother and child who sang the opening lullaby, back to the instance where innocence was first defeated. Stan himself is finally buoyant and smiling as he is next seen driving a flock of sheep into the pen—but they crowd and shove toward an uncertain fate, a fate not unlike that of the men and women who people Stan's neighborhood, nor is it unlike the fate of the smiling Stan himself.

Religion as a cherished value and its usefulness as a solution to the issues of the African American city is an interesting subtheme that begins *My Brother's Wedding,* and the irony Burnett creates with it in just the film's opening is itself compelling narrative. The film itself is about a man who, upon learning of his best friend's death, must decide whether his true responsibility is to that friend and his family, or to his own family, for it happens that the funeral takes place on the same day as his brother's wedding.

At the very beginning of the film, voiced music is as portentous as it is in *Killer of Sheep:* here, a man in a church is pictured humming the spiritual "Amazing Grace." But then he actually begins singing the words that lend a significantly ironic tinge to the crossing of the line between rural and urban, innocent and ambiguous: "was lost, but now, I'm found, / Was blind but now I see." His continuing his performance by playing another tune on the harmonica while a second voice reads from the Book of Matthew—"that man shall not live by bread alone, but by every word that proceedeth from the mouth of God"—alludes to old-time religion and the spiritual values of rural black folk as well as it signals the existence of class antagonisms among blacks, which is another important theme in this film. The rapid visual sequences include congregants being seized by the Spirit and ritual baptism; in the latter case, one baptism is of the baby of a woman whose sister is friend to the protagonist, Pierce Mundy (Everette Silas). As the camera focuses on the baby in her christening gown and then fades to her sleeping in her stroller, we suddenly become aware of two worlds: the time-honored world of religion, in which righteousness and faith are absolute values, and the urban arena, in which for the disenfranchised, these values are sorely tested. The doubt raised here is whether this child, now sanctified by ritual, can with equanimity face the life into which she has been born. Burnett appears to say no, as the dour aspect of the baby's mother holds the camera's attention, and as Pierce, while holding the baby, shows only his eagerness to be on his way.

As the story unfolds, Pierce's brother Wendell (Monte Easter), an aspiring young attorney, is preparing to marry the beautiful but also tiresomely upwardly mobile Sonia (Gale Shannon Burnett). As a man of the people, one of the "folk," Pierce represents the opposite of everything Wendell stands for. But Pierce fails as a potent, dynamic black male figure if, as a member of the community, he is to be seen, finally, as a folk *hero*, one who through his own inner aim seeks to improve the condition of his brothers and sisters. Pierce is a dutiful son—he works with his mother and father in the family dry cleaning store (truly, they support him), and he takes care of his grandparents when asked—but we are made keenly aware of the fact that Pierce, at age thirty, devoutly avoids responsibility. Pierce is unmarried; his relationship with a married woman provides him with the sexual satisfaction he seeks without his ever having to face the obligation of commitment. Although the playful wrestling matches between father and son are cute in their way, they suggest Pierce's infantilization by his parents, a nurturing of his avoidance of responsibility; as well, there is Angela (Angela Burnett), the nubile adolescent who flirts with Pierce without shame, and to whom Pierce—though he may be hiding his ardor under an "older man's cool"—appears to pay something more than just polite attention.

Innocence and ambiguity figure in this film in their ability to further shape Pierce's character. His mother's indirect disdain of him doesn't help; that she so indulges him makes equivocal Pierce's status as a man. In one instance, she even shoos away the nymphet Angela from the store—as if Pierce needed protecting! As one regular customer begins speaking to Pierce, and asks: "Say, boy—you don't mind me callin' you boy, do you—," what preserves innocence in this instance is that both men are black, thus exposing some absurdity in the questioning, as well. The ambiguity, however, nevertheless suggests the importance of race in that Pierce, in the instant, urgent situation of his community, has not acquitted himself as a man—has not met the challenges of responsibility and self-sufficiency. One stony-faced man who enters the store seeking work at least appears to be seeking to assess his manhood through labor while Pierce and his father are roughhousing in back; when he asks whether he is needed, Mrs. Mundy (Jessie Holmes) just says dryly, "No thanks; I've got two grown men out back to do everything."

Neither has Wendell escaped the numbing effects of infantilization by his parents. He is accomplished and successful; he is in just the proper position socially and financially to attract a woman like Sonia. He is, however, remote and even one-dimensional; while it seems clear that he loves, or at least tolerates Pierce, his ultimate class fantasies hold him at a genuine (and ever-increasing) distance from both Pierce and their parents. Wendell and Sonia compose all of a piece: they are sterile and self-hating African Americans, having cherished their status as buppies even to the extent of telling each other demeaning office jokes about blacks. Both he and Sonia are blinded by their attitudes toward class differences, as they treat the rest of the black world as a world entirely apart: after one of many tense meetings between the families before the wedding, Sonia asks Wendell: "Is Pierce retarded?" to which Wendell answers, "No, just ghettoized."

Despite the fact that this remark is forged in Wendell's own innocence (i.e., his ignorance), it nevertheless reveals the deeper ambiguity about Pierce and his environment, and thus becomes the true background in which his story is set. Pierce's best friend Soldier Johnson (Ronald E. Bell) is about to be released from prison, and Pierce has promised Soldier's mother that he will look after him and try to find him steady work. Soldier, however, has proved himself so practiced a pariah that no one in the neighborhood will do Pierce the favor of securing a job for his friend. Pierce's demonstrated inability to handle responsibility hampers him from the start, for this is one thing that he has not been able to do for himself. This reclamation project also appears doomed as Burnett again works the metaphor of mobility—or the lack thereof—into his tale. On the day that Pierce is scheduled to meet Soldier at the bus station, he is forced to take a bus himself. The ride covers only a portion of the distance, thus necessitating his running through a large part of downtown Los Angeles. Pierce's excuse to Soldier for not having driven is that his own car was vandalized. Burnett's own words come sharply into focus here, as an apt metaphor given shape to the face of "thinking about nothing and going nowhere." The car-as-trope, in which its drivers, potential or actual, do go nowhere, figures with two-dimensional interest in Burnett's work. The automobile engine that never gets installed in *Killer of Sheep*, as well as the flat tire endured by Stan, Bracy, and Gene on the way to the racetrack, Baby Brother's inability to leave his BMW in his moment of crisis in *To Sleep with Anger*, and Soldier's death in an automobile are all indicative of the stasis in the lives of many urban African Americans. The complexity in contemporary terms is made manifest in that the particular location of this inactivity is the Los Angeles area, a vast, sprawling expanse in which the automobile is a valued necessity. Burnett appears to give rein to irony by casting and then inverting these men's roles: they are now predators, now quarry. Earlier in the film, Pierce is warned by some neighborhood people that Soldier may be a marked man because he has roughed up one of their associates. Later, Pierce and Soldier are confronted by a would-be assassin, unsuccessful only because his gun jams. The ensuing long chase scene in which Soldier and Pierce pursue the assailant helps emphasize the bond between the friends, for Soldier soon afterwards learns from Pierce not only that another of their old buddies has been killed, but also that because of this, they are perhaps the only two who remain. So quickly do they go from being the hunters to being, finally, the hunted.

If familial support is Burnett's resolution in such an obviously bleak landscape, as is the case in *Killer of Sheep,* or where bleakness is interiorized and behavioral, as in *To Sleep with Anger,* then the young Black men in *My Brother's Wedding* appear irretrievably lost as every instance of family is fragmented. Pierce's mother and father come down on opposite sides of the issue of Christian charity versus hard work, albeit in comic fashion. While Pierce has simply disappeared somewhere between these two positions, Wendell's development is no more than stunted, for in shunning his father's extreme philosophy of hard work and embracing his mother's class aspirations, he has forsaken the larger family, the larger black community, thus raising the question as to his—and Soldier's—future contribution to African American well-being.

The cavalier treatment in this film of women by men is especially indicative of an irremediable breakdown of family and the impossibility of the resolution of conflict through the means of family. Soldier's character makes this observation seem quite ordinary, but it is within a sequence of events that the horror of this fragmentation becomes available to us, and it again appears within the master complexity framed by Burnett, that of innocence blended with ambiguity. On one day, a number of pregnant women come in to the shop to pick up clothing. Again, Burnett uses this device to structure the same doubt as at the film's opening, and also as at the ending of *Killer of Sheep:* into what are these children being born? Pierce denigrates the pregnant woman who asks him why at age thirty he remains unmarried, but he cannot win in this repartee; the woman joins forces with his mother to further unman him.

Shortly before Mrs. Mundy leaves for her prayer meeting, Soldier walks in with his date. The women nod cordially to each other, but Soldier's remark—"Everybody knows what you been doing"—is a master stroke of ugliness, which succeeds only in insulting both the woman and his date. After Mrs. Mundy departs, he further demeans his date by forcing her to have sex on the floor in the back of the shop. Pierce snoozes at the counter while these two are engaged, and when on two occasions Soldier asks for a glass of water and then some aspirin for his girlfriend,

Pierce walks in on the naked couple as would a waiter to a table. Soldier notices that the woman's forehead is cool, not warm, and Burnett, in this extrafilmic joke, harks back to Stan's pleasurable reverie in *Killer of Sheep*, and in so doing, perhaps makes his own indictment of Soldier as being an unfulfilling (i.e., lousy) lover. The comic urge here is fulfilled by the premature return of Mrs. Bundy, in search of the prayer book that Soldier's girlfriend has managed to find on the floor in her distress. But the sex comedy of the young and the restless takes an even nastier turn as the woman, now deeply shamed, tries to run from the scene, as Soldier commands her to return and Pierce momentarily struggles with her. She throws her shoe at them in a fit of frustration as she then hobbles down the boulevard. Neither man a Prince Charming, Pierce picks up the shoe as both men laugh and run in the other direction. It is indeed Soldier's own rejection of family in his rejecting Pierce—which is presumably the only family he really trusts—that coincides with his death, if it does not lead to it. Rather than wait for Pierce, Soldier and his next sexual interest leave him behind. The unfortunate result is an automobile accident in which Soldier is killed, and here is the most compelling instance of Burnett's idea of the car as being an element of life ironically inimical to the mobility of African Americans. Soldier's death in this manner is only the most unsettling testimony to the fact that he, as were so many others before him, seemed really to be going nowhere in particular.

Now, however, family disintegration as a motif continues for Pierce. He must decide between being the best man at Wendell and Sonia's wedding or being the eulogist at Soldier's funeral, and in so deciding, he must determine whether he will risk embarrassing his family and Sonia's—and the class interests they represent—or whether he will risk insulting not only Soldier's family, but the larger community, those everyday folk who knew both Pierce and Soldier best. Burnett magnifies this dilemma for Pierce by emphasizing it in terms of dress; when Pierce asks his friend Walker (Charles Bracy) whether he can attend as a pallbearer, he replies that he may have to borrow some clothing for the task. Another man must put in so many hours at his plant that it is impossible for him to take time off from work. No such difficulties hamper the wedding guests, who are of course dressed in all their finery; Sonia, her mother, and the wedding party can be seen fussing and primping, striving for perfection. In sharp contrast, Soldier's funeral is attended by poorer folk, one of whom, as pallbearer, is wearing the uniform shirt of the beer company he drives for. The rolled-up sleeves over the muscular arms, the shirttail hanging languorously at the flank, attest perhaps to his getting just enough time off to bear this burden. Pierce, now torn between duties to two families—and two sensibilities—decides finally to escape the wedding and try to get to the funeral on time. Again the metaphor of the "motionless" car comes into play; though Pierce actually does borrow a car from one of the guests at the wedding, Burnett winks at us as Pierce is told that there is not much gas in it. The car, a small sports model, moves at considerable speed with the attendant irony that Pierce, when meeting Soldier at the bus station, ran mostly on foot to meet a man who was probably impatient, but stationary and very much alive. But now, despite Pierce's comparably improved mobility, Soldier, in a very different state, is unable to wait. The funeral is over, the procession has left the parlor. Pierce arrives very late, his responsibilities to both groups having collapsed, and in his consternation, he takes from his pocket and fingers the wedding ring, the circle of an eternal devotion now nowhere realizable. "Getting nowhere" has acquired a slightly different tone as Pierce has fallen helplessly between two choices, two families, two loyalties; his was a well-intentioned effort that was inextricably mired in both ambivalence and ambiguity.

In *To Sleep with Anger* (1990), Burnett remains with the twin themes of innocence and ambiguity as determining features of narrative, but with another slight difference in emphasis. Here, ambiguity, which has been effective in giving dimension to those valuations and sensibilities most often accepted as central or sacrosanct, such as religion, or motherhood, or sexual fidelity, more often trades places with masked evil, itself a species of ambiguity. In order for evil to retain its efficacy as evil, it must be insidious, it must be cloaked. This time, the setting is not the hardcore urban landscape of the other films, but rather a greener Los Angeles; while still African American, the tension between classes is played out within a fractured middle class.[6]

The film opens with Gideon (Paul Butler), the family patriarch, sitting serenely in a blue suit with matching shoes. As he dozes, one arm is propped up on a table bearing a bowl of fruit, while the portrait of a colorfully clad, elderly black woman (presumably his grandmother) watches on. The bowl of fruit catches fire, as do his shoes and suit. The scene suddenly switches to Gideon seated in his own backyard, shoeless, wearing overalls and holding a copy of the Bible, and we realize that we have just witnessed Gideon's dream. Shoelessness here signifies the countrified, as it did with Stan's young daughter in *Killer of Sheep*, and the camera's fading from one attitude to another while remaining with the character himself or herself, thus signifying the ambiguity of that character's presence in two worlds, is a motif last seen at the christening of the baby girl that begins *My Brother's Wedding*. Here, at the opening of *To Sleep with Anger*, the religious values of Gideon's origins are exemplified by his holding the Bible as he awakens in a bewildered state. At least symbolically, Gideon has been thrown "back home," which, as the film soon demonstrates, is paradoxically the site of both the values that have a potential to sustain in the unforgiving, fragmenting, disillusioning city, and the elements of a clandestine, insidious evil that can forever mark us by turning our deepest fears and anger further inward. It is precisely this duality that Burnett examines in this film.

Like Pierce, Baby Brother (Richard Brooks), the younger of Gideon's sons, exhibits real difficulty in taking responsibility: he often has his parents babysit his son without returning at a reasonable hour, he doesn't attend church with his family, and he forgets his mother's birthday. Rather than be reminded by his father of his heritage as an African American, he prefers to be shown how to make more money. His wife Linda (Sheryl Lee Ralph) is of a similar mind, though as an in-law, she voices her prejudices less strenuously. She ordinarily avoids entering Gideon's home for fear of having to hear the family tales of the Old South: hard work, the railroads, the long journeys everywhere either by horse or on foot. Unlike Wendell and Sonia in *My Brother's Wedding*, Baby Brother and Linda represent Burnett's maturer vision of black bourgeois culture. Rather than being mere stock figures for the moral dialectic of class aspiration versus cultural identity, or icons of black upward mobility for its own sake, Baby Brother and Linda can be seen as having their class aspirations blended delicately with a conflict between genders: the independent, resourceful woman is diminished in stature as her husband, now becoming more consumed by the anger he has always harbored, seeks even more to abdicate his responsibility and relegate her to the status of maidservant. The interesting resolution at the end, however, has Baby Brother sleeping at Linda's feet. This is not another reversal of roles, but for all the trouble that has gone before, it is its own expression of harmony, of fine balance.

Gideon's loss of his ancestral talisman—his "tobie"—reflects, as such incidents in our lives usually do, on the structure and importance of faith and the value of self-reliance. In the sequence of events that describe these ideas, innocence and ambiguity are mightily potent. Gideon appears to be fond of telling uncomplimentary jokes about organized religion; in one instance he is telling one to Sunny (Devaughn Walter Nixon), his grandson and the son of Linda and Baby Brother. (Throughout the film, organized religion is shown to be effete, and comically so, in combating what the folk call "science.") Though at the tale's end Sunny insists on hearing another, his grandmother, Gideon's wife Suzie (Mary Alice), effectively silences Gideon by telling him not to tell any more such stories. Sunny is then enjoined by Gideon to tell a story of his own, but at the moment he starts, he is interrupted—checked into silent innocence—by a mysterious sliding of the broom that breaks the teapot, releasing the marbles that figure significantly near the film's end. Here Gideon remembers that he has not yet found his tobie, and thus this awareness of the absence of an anchor, of an "article of faith," coupled with the irreverence of mild blasphemy, makes him vulnerable to the advent of evil—the arrival of Harry.

Harry Mention (Danny Glover), whose character is probably derivative of that of Daddy Mention, the trickster hero of some of the folktales that were collected by Zora Neale Hurston for her book *The Sanctified Church*, is an old family friend from "back home."[7] His stated purpose for appearing at Gideon's door is that he simply became fatigued in traveling by bus from Chicago to Oakland, and just had to stop in Los Angeles for a rest. Truly, however, he is there to upset Gideon's household—specifically, to release the suppressed anger that the members of the family have been harboring against one another. When Harry and Sunny meet, Sunny first presents himself as the innocent child hero: perhaps mistakenly—or with the innocent consciousness of a child—he touches Harry with a broom, and appears to be the only one in the room (despite Gideon's insistence that he does know better) who has not learned that touching someone with a broom is considered bad luck. As Suzie dutifully brings out salt for Harry to sprinkle over his shoulder, some of the old values of folk culture are here reaffirmed and set things back into equilibrium. But in another scene, as Harry and Suzie are left alone after Harry displays good manners to Gideon, the exchange following ambiguously extols the virtues of that culture:

SUZIE: "You know, Harry, one can sure tell that you're from back home."

HARRY: "Well, you had to know how to act right where we come from. Now, you had to know how to say 'yes sir,' 'no sir.' You had to know your place."

SUZIE: "That's right. In those days you could always find something redeeming in the very worst person."

What is portentously evil in this exchange is the idea that "knowing one's place" certainly carries with it racism's demand that black folk observe proper behavior. This is an evil in itself that should of course make Harry and his manners suspect. Also ambiguous is Suzie's use of the word "redeeming," which has a curious religious significance in this context as it refers obliquely both to the smiles forced through the clenched teeth of southern whites and to what may have been Harry's ordinary acquiescence to those smiles (and to his own falseness) as well. Here Burnett casts a large shadow on the prescribed manners and forced gentility of the Old South, for so very often, the ground in which they were sown was itself already fertile soil for the managed indignity of African Americans.

Later, when Harry meets the rest of the family, Junior (Carl Lumbly) and his pregnant wife Pat (Vonetta McGee), Harry's shaking hands with Pat is precluded by the violent kicking of the fetus at each attempt. In this instance, Burnett bestows the duties of innocence even on the unborn, as the look of shock on Harry's face in this moment acknowledges the presence of that innocence. Another master opposition in this vein occurs in the appearance of Hattie (Ethel Ayler), who, after a checkered past, has found salvation in the church. Her mother ran a house of ill repute back home, and all that Harry can do is try to revive those memories. He is relentless, remarking at one point: "I remember when you weren't saved. That was way back when the Natchez Trace was just a dirt road." His reference recalls not only Hattie's sordid past, but through the hyperbole, the history of slavery as well, the Trace having been, among other things, an important route for escapees. Again, Harry emphasizes his role as agent of evil by managing to mark with unerring aim the deeper pain of the black past, thus calling into question the picturesqueness of life in the Old South, and suggesting that too often and too easily does the pain of millions become the stuff of romance. Hattie does remain firm, however, and demonstrates to Harry that her past is indeed the past and that this, her new life, is genuine.

The "old-fashioned fish-fry" that Harry orchestrates fails in seducing Hattie, as was his object, but it does resurrect many old friends from Harry and Gideon's shared past, and contributes to Baby Brother's spiraling descent. Harry is able to take Baby Brother's soul because Baby Brother has demonstrated his weakness—his love for money and his self-enforced alienation from family support. He resents his brother Junior because he feels that Junior received all of the advantages while growing up; Junior resents Baby Brother because he, Junior, feels that he has always had to work harder in order to cover Baby Brother's negligence. This enmity is broadened as Gideon resents his younger son's lack of responsibility and thoughtlessness, and it is this outsidedness, this determined exclusion from the protection of family, which makes Baby Brother vulnerable. Harry's trip through the woods with Baby Brother, not to mention the several gatherings with Harry's cronies that Baby Brother attends, is reminiscent of the New Testament tale of Jesus' journey through the wilderness. Harry takes a similar journey with Gideon along the railyards, weakens him with memories of the work crews, obliquely invokes Gideon's having the qualities of John Henry (an appellation Gideon is fond of using in reference to himself), and forces him to recall a physical strength he is now slowly surrendering. Gideon's own vanity about hard work is the very issue that Harry uses to disable Gideon as well as he uses it to alienate Baby Brother both from the family and from his wife, Linda. In the guise of the friendly, down-home Harry, Satan is the pilot on both these excursions, and his sinister power here nearly reaches its height.

Burnett has controlled the ways in which we value Biblical text by turning those ways to his narrative advantage. That does not mean that the Bible itself is being satirized. It is indeed the very thing that saves Mrs. Mundy from the third would-be assailant in *My Brother's Wedding*, as her reading of the beginning of Proverbs halts the thief at the door of the cleaning shop; the text of First Corinthians is what Pierce and his grandparents, Big Mamma and Big Daddy, read in the hours before Soldier's death. In both these instances, textual and mystical elements are blended, lending great narrative power to the film. What Burnett scrutinizes, especially in *To Sleep with Anger*, are those prescribed behaviors whose validity emanates not from Scripture, but rather from the priestly tradition connected to it, and the extent to which these behaviors govern our lives. Perhaps the most outstanding examples in this film are one scene in which the minister of Suzie's church chides her for using folk remedies to cure Gideon; this is preceded by a scene in which Harry attempts an animal sacrifice. In another scene toward the end, the same minister tries to claim credit for Gideon's recovery on behalf of prayer. But while he and his choir sing at the foot of Gideon's bed, the sounds of Gideon's secular past, namely the sounds of the railroad, fight with the sounds of his religious past, a past about which Gideon has already demonstrated his cynicism in his telling off-color jokes about preachers to Sunny. Neither religion nor our ordinary relationship to it is uniquely equipped to set things aright; only the support of family and its continuing issue, its children as witnesses, restore order—or in this case, perhaps, create it for the first time.

The deadly confrontation between Junior and Baby Brother forces Baby Brother's reclamation and their reconciliation as brothers—but not before Suzie grabs the blade of the knife that Junior has set just inches away from Baby Brother's throat. The blood she sheds to save them from death signifies as well the pain she bore to give them birth, and it is this cleansing that begins to repair this sundered clan; even the issue of innocence-to-be, Pat's unborn child, has something to say in this regard. It kicks violently at the very moment Pat tries to get lard for Suzie's wound, perhaps as proleptic warning against any furtherance of discord, perhaps in its own effort to have more of the cleansing blood flow, and perhaps both. The questing innocence of family reconciliation takes hold from this point, and prepares to challenge the evil that first provoked it.

During the fight between the brothers, the camera keeps cutting to Sunny, thus suggesting that his innocent conscience must again be engaged while he watches tremulously from under a table. The irony of an earlier scene in which Hattie and Suzie are discussing seriously for the first time Harry's insidious evil is manifest as Hattie warns: "You can't keep a wild animal [i.e., Harry] as a pet around children." But again, it is Hattie's religious sensibility speaking here, and given Burnett's ironic attitude toward religion, it is not surprising that Hattie's past with Harry would provoke at least a little Old Testament revenge: "If it were left up to me, I'd poison him," she says. But this is a resolution that would fight evil *with* evil, and that is not Burnett's formula. Easily, *To Sleep with Anger* becomes not a revenge *tragedy*, but a revenge *comedy*. Only the very reverse of Hattie's remark becomes true as it is that Sunny's spilling the same marbles that signaled Harry's coming now leads to Harry's fatal heart attack, thus emphasizing the final triumph of childlike innocence over the machinations of insidious, ambiguous adult evil. Harry's body, as it lies in the kitchen, produces a macabre chuckle, a strangely felicitous blending of good and evil, of life's active principles being juxtaposed to death's nonbeing. The bureaucracy of the country, making it unable to pick up the body in timely fashion, prompts one man to say: "Now if he was white, they'd a had him on his feet and outta here!"

"Let the dead bury their dead" is the Scriptural command now being heeded, for while Harry's body remains in the kitchen, Gideon's family and the entire neighborhood gather down at the park for a communal feast. Located here at the nexus of the community, the family, are the spiritual wit and the mother wit now so desperately needed, the seed for new roots in earth where roots have heretofore failed to hold. The texture of African American life today tests the old values and demands solutions through what remains the primordial valuation of the African American experience: the exposure and confrontation of inequity with the integrity and the probity of the whole soul. The vitality possible in this is not missed by Burnett, as, at his narrative urge, as the procession leaves the house, the small boy next door, who throughout the film has been shattering silence and all sense with the sour notes of his trumpet playing, suddenly blows sweetly, like Gabriel's announcement of the new beginning.

NOTES

1. Carole Marks, in *Farewell—We're Good and Gone: The Great Black Migration* (Bloomington: Indiana University Press, 1989), writes that as late as 1910, seven million blacks lived in the South as compared to less than one million in the entire rest of the country (15). For the decades after 1910, she concurs with Nicholas Lemann, who, in his example of Chicago, notes its dramatic growth in the population of African Americans "from 44,000 in 1910 to 109,000 in 1920 and then to 234,000 in 1930" (*The Promised Land: The Great Black Migration and How It Changed America* [New York: Knopf, 1991], 16).

2. I am thinking of novels like Wright's *Native Son* (1940) and its signifying counterpart, Ellison's *Invisible Man* (1953); these are works that might have fit an idea of black Adamism if such a construction had ever fully existed in the thinking of R. W. B. Lewis (see *The American Adam* [Chicago: University of Chicago Press, 1955], 195ff.). The protagonists in these novels continuously remake themselves not with materials from a treasured past, but with whatever is at hand. Baldwin's *Another Country* (1962) perhaps does the same thing, but differently; here, the city is the setting in which race, like class and gender/sexual orientation is foregrounded principally for the inhibition and corruption of love. Of course, there is also the postmodern expressiveness of Toni Morrison's highly evocative *Jazz* (1992), which brings a range of cultural fragments to bear on a summary, peremptory metropolitanism. In film, the most recent films and filmmakers come to mind; in Spike Lee's *She's Gotta Have It*, Nora Darling appears to connect in a less genuine way to Janie (Hurston's *Their Eyes Were Watching God*) Crawford's struggle to nurture and advance a voice at once independent, female, and grounded in essential folk wisdom than she does to her own contemporary (though no less important) urgency

to maintain an autonomy of the self (via an autonomy of the female body) in an urban, congested, and sexually turbulent present. Similarly, Lee's *Jungle Fever,* while casting significant light on folk wisdom and behavior, locates complexities (without an inclusion of interdependencies, as was often the case in Southern settings) of inter-racial sexuality in an urban environment. To the young protagonists in Matty Rich's *Straight Out of Brooklyn,* Red Hook and Bedford-Stuyvesant may represent the Mesopotamian wilderness, while Manhattan is analogous to Canaan.

3. Charles Burnett, "Inner City Blues," in *Questions of Third Cinema,* ed. Jim Pines and Paul Willemen (London: British Film Institute, 1989), 223–26.

4. Telephone conversation with Charles Burnett, June 17, 1993.

5. Though it is hard to prove, I would personally like to think that this dog's barking is somehow synchronous with the chase sequence in *My Brother's Wedding,* in which Pierce, Soldier, and the man they are pursuing are themselves momentarily pursued by a big fierce-looking dog; that Soldier and Pierce are really running by Stan's house in an extrafilmic pronouncement by Burnett of the absurdity of existence in this environment.

6. Jacquie Jones, in her article "The Black South in Contemporary Film" (*African American Review* 27, no. 1 [1993]: 19–24), notes that *To Sleep with Anger,* among many recent films, "is the only one that avoids entirely the overwhelming reality of today's urban ghetto, in explicit and implicit terms." She writes as well that Gideon's loss of his ancestral charm is symbolic of the consciousness of dislocation from family and community felt by many African Americans during the periods of migration.

7. Lynell George, *No Crystal Stair: African Americans in the City of Angels* (New York: Verso, 1992), 142–43. Daddy Mention comes, of course, from that long list of trickster heroes and conjure figures that are found everywhere in black folklore. Another longer catalog of these types and their exploits is Hurston's *Mules and Men* (1935).

David Van Leer

Visible Silence: Spectatorship in Black Gay and Lesbian Film

No one was surprised at the controversy surrounding the broadcast of Marlon Riggs' *Tongues Untied* on national public television's *P.O.V.* in the summer of 1991. The film had been in release for two years, applauded in America and Europe at festivals of black, gay, and independent films, and even telecast three times on local PBS affiliates. But Riggs' powerful celebration of African American gay male subjectivity with its attendant criticism of U.S. racism and homophobia was less likely to please a national audience. More than half of the 284 stations carrying the show canceled this episode, while others moved it to a less visible time slot. Nobody could have anticipated the specific criticisms from conservative politicians—Pat Buchanan's unauthorized use of footage from the film in a campaign commercial to illustrate George Bush's supposed sympathy for homosexuals; or Jesse Helms' citation of it in the U.S. Senate as a purported misuse of NEA funds (of which the film had very little, and none directly from the Endowment). But such hysteria and opportunism were of a piece with other attacks on experimental artists.[1]

In some senses the screening upstaged the film. Shifting attention from the particular invisibility of black male homosexuals to more general (less racialized) issues of pornography and government funding for the arts, the broadcast did not so much untie tongues as set them wagging. Decrying homosexuality as sin, fundamentalists substituted moral categories for the sociological ones the film used to explore a minoritized subculture within the predominantly white middle-class (and implicitly racist) gay ghettos of New York and San Francisco. Even liberal defenses dealt more with the abstract issue of discrimination than with Riggs' specific representation of it. Emphasizing the film's criticism of black heterosexuals and white homosexuals, straight white culture emerged comparatively unscathed. Public Broadcasting was deemed heroic and *P.O.V.*, a series not previously attentive to race or sexuality, established its concern for minority issues, while using the controversy to cancel future gay programs.[2]

Celebrity is a dubious distinction; to be lionized is to be domesticated. The acclaim that singles out Riggs as "first" or "best" reduces the many voices of *Tongues* to the lone cry of a solitary victim, who is then seen to speak for all gay African Americans. Such a reduction, unfair in itself, misunderstands the dynamic process by which minoritized filmmakers position themselves within cinematic traditions affording little space to issues of race or sexuality. However unique (and stable) his voice seems to the dominant culture, Riggs' work is in ongoing dialogue with representations of homosexual African Americans throughout film and culture. Endlessly interactive, his films can only be understood in terms of their adaptation of the generic conventions of the documentary to the tradition of black gay and lesbian self-representation of which they are a part.[3]

I

Like all doubly minoritized artists, black homosexuals must make choices about how to characterize their dual participation in an African American culture usually assumed to be heterosexual and a gay culture usually thought to be white. In part this choice is determined by those communities' willingness to receive them as equal participants. In this regard neither black or gay filmmaking has been especially receptive. The ruthless exclusion of images of black homosexuals from most films is matched by the careful regulation of those few depictions that do appear. And as preliminary to their own speaking out, homosexual African American directors feel it necessary to remind audiences how flawed are the representations of black gays and lesbians within both traditions.

The homophobia of straight African Americans is the more obvious (or more regularly denounced) of the two. In *Tongues Untied*, Riggs singles out the monologues of Eddie Murphy and the "Gamma/Fag" chant in Spike Lee's *School Daze* (1988) as particularly demeaning characterizations of gay men. Elsewhere he expands the list to include *In Living Color's* "Men on Film" skits, while other critics have called attention to the jailhouse sequence in Reginald Hudlin's *House Party* (1990).[4] Depictions of African American lesbians, though probably less frequent than those of gay men, are equally unsatisfactory. A particularly unflattering sequence in Lee's *She's Gotta Have It* (1986) introduces a lesbian only to suggest that homosexuality is not one of the things his heroine has to have. Even the most positive gay figures remain isolated from the community. The self-confident Lindy in Michael Schultz's *Car Wash* (1976)—who responds to a co-worker's taunts with the claim to be "more man than you'll ever be and more woman than you'll ever get"—is marginalized both by his effeminacy and by his irrelevance in a plot that grants to its other characters political or sexual lives outside work.

The evident homophobia of some African American films is matched by the less explicit racism of white gay films.[5] Many groundbreaking scripts—like Mart Crowley's *The Boys in the Band* (1970) and Harvey Fierstein's *Torch Song Trilogy* (1988)—use black characters only as window dressing, while the most mainstreamed gay film on AIDS—Norman René's *Longtime Companion* (1990)—includes no people of color, despite their statistical prominence in the lists of those gay men infected or dead.[6] Even those films that do acknowledge race as an element of gay sexuality rarely give a voice to the racialized other. Gus Van Sant's *Mala Noche* (1986) views skeptically its white protagonist's fascination with Mexican youth. Yet by denying access to the Latino youth's points of view, the film implies that their bisexuality is more circumstantial and less interesting than the hero's unambiguous homosexuality.[7]

More painful than these insensitive silencings and omissions is the way in which sexuality often subsumes color in apparently well-meaning white narratives. Some works treat sexuality and race as interchangeable. In *Home of the Brave* (1949), gay playwright Arthur Laurents rewrites his stage drama about an anti-Semitic slur within the military as a racial incident. Denying the black character a separate identity, Laurents' plot merely substitutes racism for anti-Semitism, which itself symbolizes the more important but unmentionable problem of homophobia.[8] Lesbian directors offer more subtle depictions of the intersections between race and sexuality. Unlike its gay male counterpart, white lesbian cinema regularly examines the role of blacks within the homosexual community, and films like Lizzie Borden's *Born in Flames* (1983) and Sheila McLaughlin's *She Must Be Seeing Things* (1987) afford central roles to lesbians of color. Yet although these works explore in detail the consciousness of their black characters, some viewers still experience the films' subordination of racial categories to sexual ones as a form of tokenism and fetishization.[9]

If silenced or objectified in fictional narratives about white sexuality, people of color regularly speak in white gay documentaries. Yet here too black speech is restricted by the predominantly white conversation surrounding it. In chronicling the pre-liberation history of homosexual culture, Greta Schiller's *Before Stonewall: The Making of a Gay and Lesbian Community* (1985) includes the testimony of at least five people of color, most notably that of poet Audre Lorde. Yet to assert the unity of homosexual culture, the film downplays the differences, treating the black gay subculture about which the blacks reminisce as if it were the same culture referred to by the whites. Lorde's tonally ambiguous critique of the appropriation of civil rights political tactics by white feminists and gay activists is juxtaposed to (and implicitly equated with) a white gay man's dewy-eyed recollections of voter registration campaigns in the South. Mabel Hampton's account of her partying with "Ethel, Bessie, and Alberta" and other performers "in the life" is followed by (and used to validate) an optimistic distinction between the white homosexuals welcomed in Harlem and the fashionable heterosexuals who went slumming there. Racial differences are reinforced by the mise-en-scène. Although the white characters are often depicted in groups and at recognizable locales, the blacks are (except for Lorde and her companion) photographed one at a time in anonymous rooms. Cut off from all visible markers of communal experience or social environment, they become merely deracinated images of gay white tolerance. However much they are in the life, that life is not in the film.

The ambiguity of gay black representations in white documentary derives less from directors' insensitivity than from the conventions of the genre itself. In disseminating knowledge, documentary affects an objective point of view. Such realism is of course manufactured through a host of fictive and cinematic techniques: narrative, juxtaposition, pacing, editing, framing, camera placement. Yet viewers too conscious of cinematic techniques might become distracted from a film's argument or even distrustful of it. To learn anything, audiences must repress the material conditions of the film's production and projection to accept provisionally what they see as reality. Bracketing questions of positioning, motivation, and evidence, and pretending to transparent and unmediated vision, documentaries implicitly argue that their testimony, while perhaps incomplete, is "realer" than the silence and ignorance it is offered to counter. In most cases this argument seems defensible, and we treat the filmmaker as unbiased and the camera as invisible.[10]

When the camera looks across boundaries, however, the gaze seems more embattled, the medium less transparent. The very act of looking that the documentary posits as neutral has historically been a tool of racial oppression.[11] Intended as an act of identification, documentary looking at others is epistemologically indistinguishable from the voyeurism with which racial bodies have traditionally been sexualized and controlled. Such differences in the politics of the gaze are articulated in and epitomized by the Mariposa Group's *Word Is Out: Stories of Some of Our Lives* (1977). An anthology if gay coming-out stories, the film crosscuts interviews with more than two dozen individuals to demonstrate the variety of homosexual experience. The white interviewees are characterized by differences of geographic region, class, politics, education, and occupation, as well as those of sexual orientation. These characters tell a wide variety of stories—about former marriages, child custody suits, adolescent sexual experiences. Although sympathetically portrayed, the people of color speak more narrowly *as* people of color, as if race *were* their story. The Latina whose interviews open and close the film is a compelling presence, but not a vocal one. Her individuality is established not through anecdotal narratives but through her accented speech, her halting rhythms, and finally her silence. Even Betty Powell, the black lesbian who resoundingly challenges her ability to "represent," speaking *of* her discomfort at being forced to speak *as,* cannot escape appropriation. Despite her objection in the film's first minutes, her subsequent appearances cooperate fully with the film's project of representation. Nothing follows methodologically from her initial protest, which becomes just one more instance of the film's inclusive "honesty."[12]

The moral ambiguity of racial looking and racial learning lies at the heart of Shirley Clarke's *Portrait of Jason* (1967). The film is surely the most complex white representation of a black gay male, and Jason the least silent homosexual in cinema. The film's 100-plus minutes are entirely filled with his nonstop musings, and his body is the only human image that appears on screen (until in the final seconds the director appears out of focus to call a halt to the filming). Jason is not in any simple sense objectified by the filmmakers' probing questions and unflinching gaze. Though the film is formally cinema verité, Jason himself characterizes that verité as a performance. Moving through a range of ironic voices—most notably black hip, white gay camp, and black gay camp— he dodges Clarke's wheedling and her (black) boyfriend's harangues, much as he recalls playing with his psychiatrists. He similarly theatricalizes his body, through costumes, cabaret turns, and flamboyant postures, in a frenetic dance that evades the camera's gaze. Yet ultimately Jason is captured on film, and in robbing Clarke of her control he may lose his as well. At the very least his diversionary tactics make for very uncomfortable watching, and this documentary fails to explain anything. For whom is Jason performing and why? Does the movie escape its manipulations by recording them at every step, zooming in on the drugs and liquor with which the filmmakers spur Jason on to greater self-revelation? And why do audiences watch—how can we bear to?

II

It is incorrect (even generous) to say that before the work of Marlon Riggs African American male homosexuality was invisible in U.S. film. The problem is not the lack of a tradition of black gay representation but what that tradition had taught. Hostility, neglect, tokenization, and objectification are Marlon Riggs' inheritance from previous black and gay films and his points of reference as gay black director. The meagerness of that inheritance marks not simply the moral biases of previous directors but problems of stereotyping and objectification built into the very concept of minority representation. Focusing on the tensions between seeing and knowing, Riggs' mature work plays the ideological limitations of what dominant culture is willing to see off against the epistemological limitations of spectatorship itself as a process of learning through looking.

His concern with representation as process was not immediately evident. Riggs' first full-length documentary, the Emmy-winning *Ethnic Notions* (1986), seems a conventional "realistic" survey of the stereotypic images by which white society constructed the "notions" of the African American that it used to authorize its brutality and to undermine black self-respect. Surveying a wealth of racist illustrations, photographs, films, music, and material objects, the film contrasts these "distortions" with the reality of black experience in the United States. Riggs himself has underscored this conventionalism by characterizing the film as dues-paying, a straightforward historicist reading of racism that prevented critics from rejecting his nonlinear argument and multivoiced narration in *Tongues* as just "a faggot going off."[13]

There is no reason to question Riggs' sincerity either in *Notions* or in his subsequent evaluation of the work as preliminary. Yet some of the visual contradictions Riggs will later examine explicitly are already implicit in this early piece. As in many works documenting cultural misrepresentation, the film's overt catalog of inaccurate images is at odds with its tacit assumption that its own images are accurate. The argument depends on a series of visual contrasts—between true images and false images, between false images and true narrative voice-overs, between false images and false musical backgrounds, between (usually) false drawings and (usually) true photographs, between historical images and living academic commentators. These dichotomies are neither equivalent nor stable. Although certain cinematic components, especially the narrative voice-over and the scholarly analyses, seem entirely reliable, there is no one-to-one correlation between modes of representation and accuracy of images. It is at least suggestive that the harshest charges of misrepresentation are directed against the genre that Riggs employs to tell truth—that of film itself.

In part these tensions merely suggest the trivial paradox of trying to take an accurate picture of an inaccurate picture. Yet the film's explicit claim that images are never innocent requires that its own images be examined. There is a tension between the film's politics and its aesthetics: racist cookie jars and children's books are lovingly photographed with the clarity and brilliant colors of a museum catalog. Even more ambivalent is the film's tone toward those performers who enacted cultural stereotypes. An earlier television documentary on a similar topic—*Black History: Lost, Stolen, or Strayed* (1968)—had been so dismissive of Stepin Fetchit that the actor sued CBS. Riggs' account is never so directly critical. Yet the clips of Fetchit and especially Hattie McDaniel display these accomplished performers at their worst. And the sequence crosscutting Ethel Waters' performance of the song "Darkies Never

Dream" with King's "I have a dream" speech judges the singer deficient by measuring her against an impossibly high standard.

The film's tendency to blame actors for their complicity with cultural stereotypes is matched by a complementary desire to mask its participants' function as performers. Although the commentators seem merely to present the truth, our acceptance of their truthfulness depends as much on how the scholars look as on what they say. Despite the film's clear insistence that contemporary images continue to remain politically problematic, the commentators act as if the problem of stereotyping has been solved—both through their exclusive focus on former representations and for the ease with which they can today explicate such errors. Particularly interesting in physical terms is the film's first—and most famous—commentator, the Berkeley historian Lawrence Levine. One of the most respected historians of African American culture, Levine speaks throughout the film with unimpeachable authority. Yet as one of the film's "token" whites, his own image is more complicated. White bodies in black documentaries do not stick out as do black bodies in white ones. Called "Larry" on the screen and "Lawrence" in the credits, Levine's folksy white presence does not need to examine its position, as did the black lesbian in *Word Is Out.* This very absence of difference among the scholars raises questions about how the images of the commentators misrepresent (or at least suppress) some of the very racial constructions the film studies. Watching Levine express impatience and dismay at the white entitlement that allowed Al Jolson without qualm to black his face for *The Jazz Singer,* the viewer is uncertain how to read the potential discontinuity between Levine's image and his words.[14]

Similar ambiguities inform the use of Esther Rolle, the film's narrator. Speaking her scripted part in measured tones that contrast with Levine's offhand analysis, she stands as the film's most commanding contemporary voice, as he is its most intellectualized contemporary body. Yet Rolle's invisibility, however traditional in such voice-of-God narrations, is itself an absent image. Rolle's voice-overs attacking the mammy figure cannot entirely erase the ways in which she herself has unwillingly perpetuated it. A classically trained actress who has performed Shakespeare, Hansberry, and Baldwin, Rolle is still best remembered (and recognized) as Beatrice Arthur's maid and Jimmie Walker's mom. Her career has been hampered by the same racial preconceptions that hurt McDaniel. There is even a visual continuity between the two. Rolle's stately carriage and personal demeanor recall the ways McDaniel in her public appearances distanced herself from her screen persona. And the absence of Rolle's image in the documentary marks the continuing difficulty film has in representing the black female.

The careful visual use of Levine, McDaniel, and Rolle suggests that the film's realism is not effortless. At three points, *Notions* admits the film's conventionality to be a pose, by examining its methods of representation. In the final credits, the film acknowledges its dual use of images as aesthetic objects and as markers of racism by praising Jan Faulkner, "whose collection of black memorabilia inspired this documentary." It is perhaps overscrupulous to worry that the characterization of the historian of material culture as "muse" reinforces the paradox of the true imaging of false images that underlies documentary realism. But it is surely true that the process by which demeaning stereotypes become "inspirational" collectibles defines the transformative power of representation—that images can themselves be framed and thus redefined.

Even more striking than this brief moment of methodological self-reflection are two scenes in which the film, anticipating the disjunctions between image and sound in *Tongues,* explicitly announces its performances to be performed. Throughout the film, the history of white actors' playing African Americans is rejected as demeaning, whether in the trivializing comedy of the minstrel show or the brutalizing melodrama of *The Birth of a Nation.* Morally more complex is the process by which black actors, to gain a hearing, themselves donned blackface and adopted the stereotypes of their white predecessors. As Leni Sloan sympathetically explains, the actors saw degradation as a doorway, and the perpetuation of stereotypes also created a new black workforce.

To illustrate the doubleness of this activity, Riggs employs—for the only time in this film—the distancing techniques associated with postmodern performance art. In the simpler of the two sequences, Sloan himself blacks up and performs a monologue in the voice of Bert Williams, the most successful of the blacks in blackface. The doubling effect, which treats Williams as image and imager, allows for the kind of sympathy not afforded Waters or McDaniel. As the one moment not scripted by Riggs, the passage calls attention to the sensibility elsewhere unifying the film's diverse images, introducing in Sloan's prose a voice not identical to (even at odds with) that of Riggs as documentarian. To underscore this difference director Riggs chooses an unusual camera angle, filming the scene over Sloan's shoulder into a mirror where Sloan's reflection talks as he blacks himself up to become Williams in the process of Williams' becoming his stage persona. This self-conscious staging of the subjectivity of viewpoint identifies as equally staged the film's unobtrusive use of traditional headshots to represent the truthfulness of its analysis.

If the staging of Sloan's monologue admits the fictiveness of Riggs' realistic presentation, the second scene questions our own complicity as spectators. Two black actors with clown-white lips (but no visible blackface) re-create the vaudevillian comedy of the minstrel dance. Their performance is crosscut with images of a third black musician—also in clown costume—slapping out a rhythm on his knees and chest.

Unlike the historicizing realism of the rest of the film, this sequence is clearly modern. The costumes blend period and modern styles. The music is a contemporary re-creation (rather than an archival recording as elsewhere in the movie). Though the knee-slap serves as sound track for the dance, the dancers do not coordinate their movements to its beats. The effect is surreal, more akin to the modernist choreography of Merce Cunningham or Alvin Alley than to minstrel dance. Internalizing the film's hostility within the dance, this reframed performance shifts our relation for the material. Usually the film encourages us to identify with the filmmaker, as if looking at an exposé of racism were the same as writing one. Here, however, we are asked not to be angered by the object but to become the audience for and object of its anger. This ethnic "notion" stares angrily back out at our gaze, to ask whether in watching Riggs' outrage we have not assumed ourselves innocent of discriminatory image-making.

III

In challenging the purported realism of the documentary tradition, *Ethnic Notions* avoids one of the pitfalls of minority art—what Kobena Mercer has called the "burden of representation."[15] As Betty Powell complains in *Word Is Out*, minority voices are expected not only to present their views, but to present them as characteristic of a group—the representation must also be representative. In his first full-length statement, Riggs evades such pigeon holing by offering as "his" view images of the ways in which blacks were viewed over time. Through the neutralizing conventions of the historical survey, Riggs prevents his account from being reduced to his positioning, and reading ethnicity as merely "notional"—someone else's idea of who you are—he implies that there is no group of which he can be taken as representative, virtually no thing for a representation to represent.

Such a deconstruction resolves only some of the difficulties in figuring race. A minority defined solely in terms of its images has no voice of its own. Those underrepresented within the group remain invisible, and in *Ethnic Notions* black gays appear only as stereotypes in white gay greeting cards. To give voices to both race and sexuality, Riggs' next film *Tongues Untied* abandons other people's notions for direct testimony. Riggs admits his polemic intentions:

> *Tongues Untied* is explicitly a point-of-view work. It does not attempt to address question of so-called "balance" or "objectivity." I am a black gay man. I made the work from that perspective. . . . *Tongues Untied*

tries to provide people growing up with an image of the possibilities of life. I want them to know it is possible to live life fully, happily, and joyfully with the full understanding and the full affirmation of who you are.

He further insists that to represent the diversity of black gay experience the film "crosses many boundaries of genre."

What I wanted to do with *Tongues Untied* was to start the dialogue, and preserve our lives in a form that people can see and address, not only now, but in years to come. People will see there was a vibrant black gay community in these United States in 1989.[16]

In speaking directly to black gay men, however, Riggs must negotiate carefully his relation to the "people" with whom he "dialogues" only indirectly—his white and straight black audiences. Autobiography is customarily the genre in which dominant cultures first permit minorities to speak. Yet untying tongues comes with strings attached, and the popularity of minority autobiography depends on empowered readers' limited expectations for it as a literary form. Traditional autobiography presents a narrative of individual triumph—how I became rich and famous, for example, or how I won the war—and implicitly promises that through imitation the reader may become as wealthy/celebrated/decorated as the author. Minority autobiography, however, asserts not one's achievements but only one's presence: though neither rich nor famous, I too exist. As representatives of a victimized group, minority autobiographers do not stand as models or exemplars but only as counterexamples; they instruct dominant culture not how it can become "like me" but how it remains irrevocably "not us." Minority autobiographers are repeatedly disassociated from their lives, defining themselves in terms of past oppressions rather than present accomplishments. "Slave" narrators, permitted to publish only under the supervision of white editors, were further required to prove their stories were "written by him/herself." Preconceptions about such authors' skill were so strong that success in self-presentation was occasionally offered as evidence that they could not be what they claimed.[17]

This "burden of self-representation"—minority autobiography's subordination of individuals to their positioning—lies at the heat of Powell's objection in *Word Is Out*. In refusing to "represent" others, she primarily celebrates the diversity of black lesbian culture; she cannot speak for all. Yet in objecting that she is not everyone, she also asserts that she is herself, an individual whose virtues are not reducible to her affiliations. The inability of minority autobiographers to serve as exemplars is not a function only of race. All the lesbians and gay men interviewed in the film are similarly representative; the subgroups they represent—debutante, sissy, butch—are just less clearly articulated than are racialized ones. Yet it is possible to wonder with Powell whether the visibility of people of color within gay documentaries is a virtue. What seems one minority's sympathy for comparable positions may mark only the extent to which minority autobiography has already internalized the sense of inferiority by which dominant cultures subordinate racial minorities.

Tongues Untied undercuts the self-deprecating implications of minority self-representation by divorcing voice from personality and representativeness. Riggs' refusal of autobiography is clear from the film's title. Recalling minority autobiographies' reversals of previous silences, the phrase "Tongues Untied" suggests that something has not yet been heard. Unlike the positioned statement with which a minority artist traditionally announces a new voice, however, *Tongues* pluralizes the noun, refusing to cast its account as an authenticating statement from a reliable "inside" source.[18] "Tongues Untied" is not "Black Elk Speaks" or even Frederick Douglass's *Narrative . . . written by himself.* From the opening chant of "brother to brother," voices layered on top of each other speak in a disorienting mix of genres—poetry, song, monologue, skit. There is little concern for narrative continuity. Voice-overs contradict images, which are themselves often superimposed on each other. Nor is there much correlation between narrators and authors: Riggs recites Hemphill's poetry, Hemphill recites Audre Lorde's prose, as if all the voices of black homosexuality were interchangeable.

Such multiple voicings dramatize the act of speaking up while frustrating viewers' desire for personal revelation. Although such layering might have rendered the individual voices anonymous, however, Riggs' performers retain their separate identities. Some of the conventions of the confessional documentary remain. Unlike the scholarly authorities of *Notions,* the speakers are not identified by title cards. The camera angles suggest immediacy: avoiding the three-quarter shot of traditional documentary, the performers often look straight at the viewer, a gaze usually reserved for intimate revelation (and commercial hardsell). Yet these personalizing tactics only underline the film's disinterest in the most important convention of the minority autobiography—the realistic reproduction of conversation and thought. In *Word Is Out* or *Portrait of Jason* the interviewees banter with the production crew, and even in *Notions* the academics make their analyses appear natural and offhand.[19] In *Tongues,* however, where voices often play over images of still lips and every word is self-consciously scripted, there is no illusion of spontaneity: all is performance. In the theatricality of their authority, the speakers of *Tongues* recall less the storytellers of *Word* than the scholars in *Notions,* using their credentials as black gay men to recite positions that may or may not be identically their own.

Tongues does not merely cast its "representatives" as authorities. It insists on their individuality as well. From the first we are reminded that the film's performers have identities outside this particular untying. The title cards read "Tongues Untied/by Marlon Riggs/featuring Essex Hemphill." Although Frederick Douglass had to prove that he wrote his own words, Riggs' anthology of many tongues is unambiguously "by" him. In openly acknowledging the poet Hemphill, the film alludes indirectly to its use of such other celebrated figures as dancer Willie Ninja, poet Donald Woods, playwright Reginald T. Jackson, and Brian Freeman, founder of the performance art troupe Pomo Afro Homos. These highly claimed individuals are not silenced or invisible, and the absence of the name cards *Notions* used to identify its authorities measures not the lesser importance of the performers in *Tongues* but their greater fame. Quite simply Essex Hemphill is more recognizable than Larry Levine and at moments, especially in the vogueing sequence, we are even encouraged to star-gaze. *Tongues* never degenerates into popular autobiography's self-congratulatory hints about how to become a famous poet or meet Madonna. Yet the film does admit, as *Before Stonewall* does not in its similar use of Audre Lorde, that Hemphill *is* famous.

The film's refusal to reduce its performers to the merely representative status of the minority autobiography is clearest in Riggs' treatment of his own image, voice, and words. In one sense, of course, his approach is autobiographical. Riggs is a black gay male and draws on his own experiences for voices and images. At the same time, it is not their autobiographical authenticity that makes the arguments true. Riggs' nude dance beneath the opening credits epitomizes the irony of his self-presentation. One of the film's few controversial images, the dance skillfully (and erotically) exposes a beautiful muscled body. Yet the choreography, in which Riggs' hands repeatedly cover his face, suggests that openness can mask as well as reveal, offering confidences merely to direct attention from the significant. Coming so early in the film, the scene implies that sexualizing the black body is a very preliminary way of breaking silence. And of course the penis—defining icon of male nudity and taboo of Hollywood censors—is only fleetingly visible in Riggs' underlit movements: in this film, lips—not genitals—are the visual focus of homoeroticism.

Riggs' theatricalization of his body explores the epistemological difference between exposure and revelation, nudity and visibility. Filming himself as if naked and natural, Riggs asks viewers to question the categories of realness or immediacy by which any autobiography is judged authentic. When Riggs reads from a poem about his adolescent love for a white boy while the camera slowly zooms in on a photograph of a blond youth, documentary conventions ask viewers to accept the photo as evidence of the event's reality. Yet our acquiescence mostly measures Riggs' craft as poet, actor, and filmmaker. His impassioned delivery of the poetic cadences makes us believe his account; and it is the relentlessness of the zoom more than the blandness of the photo that lends the moment its air of tragic inevitability. We do not believe the story from the evidence of a poem and a picture, or even because we have come to "trust" Riggs. We believe it because we are predisposed to the poem's moral. Images and narrative only add substance to what we have already accepted in principle.[20]

It is in the context of the film's resistance to autobiography that we must read the most controversial moment—the film's closing statement (both written and recited) that "BLACK MEN LOVING BLACK MEN IS *THE* REVOLUTIONARY ACT." Many have read the statement as an attack on interracial love, and the film's final transitions from AIDS to civil rights as Riggs' privileging of his racial identity over his sexual one. Some have pointed out the contradiction between the claim and Riggs' long-term relationship with a white partner, whose "loving support" is acknowledged in the film's final title card. Yet such debates misread the sentence, both linguistically and in terms of the film's use of speech. Not original with Riggs, the statement quotes Joseph Beam, who sees it as merely (in a phrase Riggs quotes) "an acknowledgment of responsibility" and (in phrases not cited) "an autonomous agenda for the eighties, which is not rooted in any particular sexual, political, or class affiliation."[21] Nor is it clear what Riggs means by italicizing Beam's "the": does black male love become "the" revolutionary act because it is a very radical activity or because it is the only acceptable one?

The controversy's narrow understanding of the relation between politics and sex is less troubling than its attempt to resituate the film within the very traditions of documentary realism and minority autobiography that Riggs explicitly rejects. To avoid the trivialization and fetishization that plague the genres, Riggs insists that there are many voices, none identically his. Viewers who emphasize one title card— "BLACK MEN LOVING BLACK MEN IS *THE* REVOLUTIONARY ACT"—over another—"and the loving support of Jack Vincent"—impose their own priorities on the film's multiple narratives, and the objection "But Jack is white" recasts a group performance as simple self-revelation. The film's truth does not depend on what a particular Marlon may be doing off-screen, and like the sex "scandals" that attend many performers whose public behavior is at odds with their screen personae (Pee-wee Herman and Woody Allen, to mention only the most recent), the debate marks the audience's overidentification with Riggs' screen image.[22] Perhaps what makes one kind of loving seem "the" revolutionary act lies less in the differing characters of acts than in society's strident claim that sex has no political content: it is the (anticipated) denial of Beam's statement that makes it both true and revolutionary.

However misguided, the "problem of Jack" reveals the film's manipulation of its audience's need to (mis)identify with its images. Traditionally the film viewer (implicitly white, male, and heterosexual) assumes the camera's eye to be his own. *Notions* questioned the moral complacency of this identification, implying that looking at misrepresentations was not the same as analyzing their inaccuracy. *Tongues* more simply denies that most of us are the camera. Minority autobiography teaches nonminority readers to know another culture; Riggs confronts them with their inability to read it. The film makes great demands on our knowledge: refusing to explain its images and words, it expects viewers simply to understand cultural settings and recognize the famous participants. Unable to fulfill these expectations, viewers are repeatedly brought up short by the incompleteness of their knowledge—misinterpreting the source of a passage familiar to gay African Americans, or invited to think an image means one thing when it really means another. Opening in the masculine black environment of the basketball court, the film reveals the sexuality of its images only after some straight male viewers have mistakenly identified with the homosexuals on the screen. Other moments, like the stock footage of the Castro Street Fair, similarly ask white gay audiences to see that purported images of sexual liberation actually record the absence of black bodies.

In looking "as" a black gay man, blacks and gays experience the errors of their spectatorship. For straight white viewers, the movie does not even offer the possibility of misidentification by which black straights and white gays are included in the conversation. Offering no coming-out narratives or debates about the psychosocial origins of sexual object-choice, the film refuses to reproduce the traditional arguments used to "explain" homosexuality to a mainstream audience. Ignoring white racism and homophobia, it forestalls the tendency of liberal guilt to refocus attention on itself by reducing minority experience to oppression by dominant culture. In Riggs' representations dominant culture is not the audience, the standard, or the villain, and to view his "other" images, white heterosexuals abandon the very spectatorial privilege whose primacy is the foundation of traditional cinema.[23]

Only when considering aspects of black gay culture familiar to the general public does the film acknowledge the existence of a straight white gaze—documenting how the appropriation of black gay male culture transforms untied tongues into marketable goods. Though a comic sequence, the "lesson in snap" at "the Institute of SNAP!thology" darkly hints that the desire to know black gays may only be the latest form of radical chic. Mimicking the conventions of television hucksterism—complete with title cards, "greatest hits" lists, everything but the 800 number—Riggs refuses to distinguish the cultural motives of PBS from those of the Home Shopping Network. Equally self-deflating is his presentation of vogueing, the most commercialized aspect of black gay culture. The photography's "realistic" vocabulary—street setting, grainy color, unsteady camera, lack of cuts—places the dance within a specific social context denied it in Madonna videos. Yet in finally employing the documentary style absent elsewhere, the sequence questions viewers' equation of visual crudity with minority truth. Like the blackface dancers in *Notions*, Willie Ninja in his staginess calls attention to our gaze, and his mimed powdering of his nose recalls Riggs' ambivalence toward the similarly mirrored depiction of Bert Williams in blackface. This most commercialized image in *Tongues* is also the most hostile and silent, asking viewers not only by what right they look but whether looking automatically silences.[24]

IV
___

New voices can be heard only when old views are obstructed, and in *Tongues Untied* the immediacy of speech is tempered by the self-consciousness of sight. To all but the black gay men identified as the film's primary audience, spectatorship offers an eye not I, and the film's overlooked images become visible only through resistance to established modes of looking. Yet Riggs' cautions have largely been ignored by the mainstream viewers they address, and the film absorbed by the very traditions it critiques. Debates around the work reinstate the dichotomies—gay/straight, black/white—attacked by the film's pluralist tongues. Riggs' alienating theatricalizations are recast as personal autobiography, and his eroticized men as quickly fetishized as had been Josephine Baker. After such a taming of *Tongues*, black gay and lesbian directors have sought more drastic strategies to make images irreducible as well as visible.

As we would expect, Riggs' subsequent work revises the misreadings of his position. Two short pieces explicitly continue *Tongues*, employing the same performers, narrative techniques, and even footage to modify its argumentation and appearance. A visually unassuming postscript to *Tongues*, *Affirmations* (1990) tempers the earlier film's most controversial arguments, offering in two brief episodes a more hopeful account of interracial love and a more pessimistic one of black solidarity. Reworking form rather than content, *Anthem* (1991) adopts avant-garde film techniques to recast the earlier film as a frenetic collage of sound and color. With narrative and characterization obliterated, movement and pacing take precedence, and sexual sequences that seemed perfunctory in *Tongues* are eroticized by the sensuality of the whole.[25]

Riggs' longer pieces since *Tongues* appear to reembrace documentary realism. Though not explicitly revisionist, however, these films exploit absence and the unsaid to challenge viewer expectations through ominous omissions. *Color Adjustment* (1991), his first full-length film after *Tongues*, surveys the development of television images of African

Americans—from the gross oversimplifications of "Amos and Andy" and "Beulah," through the incomplete liberalism of "Julia," "Good Times," and "Roots," to more complex incarnations like "The Cosby Show" and "Frank's Place." Yet, as Riggs knows, greater availability of minority images does not automatically solve the problem; his own appearance as the single most visible gay television image (black or white) encouraged voyeurism as fully as gay pride. Throughout *Adjustment,* the charge that television images do not portray the reality of the African American experience is overshadowed by a greater uncertainty about what would constitute an appropriate image. The accuracy with which an image shows our experience depends on who defines the constituency of the "our"; and the documentary's analysis is compromised by its exclusive focus on heterosexuality. Perhaps the praise of "Frank's Place" for its broad range of blacks need not worry the series' depiction of a New Orleans without homosexuality. But when one scholar asserts that "Cosby represents everyone's fantasy; everyone wants to live that way," it is hard to believe the tongues of Riggs' previous three films would agree.

The film critiques its silence about heterosexism in structuring its material. The narrative is framed by quotations from James Baldwin, a writer most famous for his dual identity as African American and homosexual. The failure to mention the homoeroticism of shows like "I Spy" may be unintentional, but Riggs' HIV status makes the film's fleeting allusions to AIDS all the more painful for being understated. Most important, a sexual bias informs the film's most original argument—its linking of racial stereotyping to the myth of the family. Treating the incorporation of black actors into the American dream family as a form of cooptation, the authorities and film clips demonstrate that the family has been the site of racial stereotyping. Riggs' narration pushes this observation further to insist that the fault lies less with the particular content of the images than with the choice of the social unity of the family to measure African American achievement. Although from "Beulah" to "Cosby" depictions of the black family have become more accurate, racial misrepresentation will continue as long as television locates its images "all in the family."

The documentary's implicit claim for the "natural" antipathy between race and the family originates in an argument about the documentable tension between the family, by definition heterosexual, and a homosexuality that purportedly foreswears procreation and seduces children. Although black culture is not itself anti-family, the normative use of the family model to define gays as abnormal bodies ill as well for any minority group. Despite his authorities' naive faith in the possibility of better black images, Riggs warns that television's transformation of (straight/white/male) social structures into (universal) oral norms prevents any serious consideration of cultural difference. Using a gay trope to unsettle (perhaps undo) a media analysis reproducing the sexual conventionality of that medium, Riggs argues that until minorities cooperate in rethinking all the structures of representation, the normalizing potential of imagery will betray each group in turn.

As *Color Adjustment* must be read in dialogue with its own heterosexism, so Riggs' final completed film—the beautiful but austere *Non, Je Ne Regrette Rien* (*No Regrets*) (1992)—can only be appreciated in comparison with AIDS representation more generally. Weaving together five interviews with seropositive black males, the film argues powerfully for our fellowship with those affected, while ending the silence that still ties tongues concerning African American losses (of, for example, designer Willi Smith and choreography Alvin Ailey). Combining high-gloss photography with the static camera of the "talking heads" format, the narrative reinvents traditional mise-en-scène to correct gay documentary's customary penchant for entertaining characterization and low production values. Presenting comparatively subdued figures, the film avoids the epigrammatic wit and the class and gender stereotypes—salty butch, drag savant, streetwise tough, smug capitalist—by which gay documentary from *Word Is Out* to *Paris Is Burning* has made its interviewees lovable. The photography similarly reconceives the conventional imaging of AIDS.[26] In contrast to the debilitating lesions and sunken cheeks marking the seropositive as "victim," the absence of visible illness in the film depicts the strength (and longevity) of those infected with a virus falsely read as death. To counter the erotophobia surrounding infection, the camera imitates pornography's fondness for close-up body parts, sexualizing its bodies without the depersonalization often attending such dismemberments. The film calls no attention to its revisions; Riggs does not wish technique to upstage the immediacy of the testimony. But the minimalism of his staging redefines what it means to look at the diseased body, challenging spectatorial presuppositions as completely as does the more confrontive postmodernism of *Tongues.*[27]

After the success of Riggs' *Tongues* (and black British director Isaac Julien's *Looking for Langston*), increasing attention has been paid to representations of African American sexuality by such talented U.S. directors as Aarin Burch, Christopher Leo Daniels, Cheryl Dunye, Thomas Harris, Melanie Nelson, Michelle Parkerson, Sylvia Rhue, Catherine Saalfield, Dawn Suggs, Jocelyn Taylor, Jack Waters, Yvonne Welbon, and Jacqueline Woodson. Although this work is too rich to reduce to a single analytic model (or a few pages), these films extend Riggs' critique of documentary realism and personal revelation by incorporating into their narratives self-conscious reflections on their cinematic antecedents, photographic methods, and modes of production. Jack Waters' *The Male Gayze* (1990), for example, addresses familiar problems of white appropriation and objectification in its tale of a black dancer whose nude photograph was illegally marketed by a European choreographer. The film's ambiguous images, however, stand in ironic relation to the straightforward narrative. Just as modern dance dissociates movement from music, the film's images proceed independently of its narration: some intersect with it, like the shots of a postcard that may be an incarnation of the offending photograph; others—of a father and a child, a family picnic, or grazing horses—have no discernible relation to the tale. The disjunction between sounds and images questions the process by which we unify the diverse elements of any cinematic gaze. Viewers equate the postcard with the photograph, just as they assume the narrator to be the dancer, the dancer to be the director, and the film to be autobiography. Yet nothing requires such an ordering of cinematic images, which uses spectatorial privilege to control the film's irregularities much as the older choreographer uses his power and position to seduce and commodify the young black dancer. According to the film's ironic title, not only can gay male desire reproduce straight racism, but any gaze may involve a similar "mastery" in its "male" unification of flickering light and noise into narrative.

Black lesbian directors have probably even less access to funding and audiences than do African American gay males. Not surprisingly, their work maintains close formal ties to the marketable genres of documentary and autobiography. Yet highly sensitive to the inequities of cultural positioning, these triply minoritized artists scrutinize the techniques of realism and immediacy by which they gain viewers.[28] Yvonne Welbon's *Sisters in the Life* (1993), for example, dramatizes a conventional reminiscence of "first love." Yet the contrast between the staged representations of the woman's adolescent memories and the improvised scenes in which Wellbon as director "interviews" the adult woman and a "grown-up" lover undermine the dichotomies of innocence/experience, past/present, actor/director, and fiction/truth on which such reminiscences depend. After an imagistic meditation involving isolation, violence, and a masculinized woman in *Chasing the Moon* (1990), Dawn Suggs in her subsequent *I Never Danced the Way Girls Were Supposed To* (1991) recasts the same anger as a running commentary on lesbian images by a comically bemused narration. Wondering whether lesbians have abnormal relations to shoes and sandwiches, the narrative comes to realize the arbitrariness of any attempt to define normalcy. Acceptable behavior depends on who judges, and by its end the film's opening footage of stereotyped lesbians has been comically redefined to gaze not with contempt but with envy.

In *Among Good Christian People* (1991), Catherine Saalfield and Jacqueline Woodson examine the intersection of religion with race and homosexuality, largely in terms of Woodson's recollections of her youth as a Jehovah's Witness. Yet the documentary's variety of narrative styles—archival footage framed by a black border, improvised interviews by anonymous choir members, Woodson's scripted autobiography—calls attention to the staged character of all such authenticating realism. Though endorsing Woodson's narrative as true, the film also admits the theatricality of that truth, offering alternative readings of the same lines of script, and photographing the same objects on contemporary videotape and artificially aged "archival" film stock. Bringing fiction and reality even closer together, Saalfield's *Bird in the Hand* (1993), codirected with Melanie Nelson, tells the fictional story of a breakup between a student (played and scripted by Nelson) and her filmmaker lover. Hyperrealistically photographed, the film walks a narrow line between narrative and polemic, using its slight plot to debate issues of spousal violence and codependency. In its preoccupation with cars and Manhattan streets, it initiates along with white director Su Friedrich's *Rules of the Road* (1993) a lesbian inversion of the buddy/road picture. And its epilogue offering a date with the (now available) filmmaker breaks through the wall narrative establishes between image and audience.

As signaled by *Bird in the Hand,* the return to narrative within black gay and lesbian film does not impede the tradition's scrutiny of its modes of representation. Employing the traditional cinematic vocabulary of commercial Hollywood, Michael Mayson's *Billy Turner's Secret* (1990) energetically recounts the learning and liberation resulting from an urban black's coming-out to his African American and Latino friends. The very conventionality of Mayson's storytelling makes his political innovations more effective. He imitates Spike Lee's verbal wit, multiethnic characters, and use of Brooklyn exteriors to tell the story Lee's films most fear, even like Lee casting himself in a pivotal role (as the homophobe). The film gets too much comic mileage out of ethnic and sexual slurs and reinscribes a masculinist ethos of violence in the climactic brutalization of the homophobe by homosexual characters. Yet Mayson not only preaches tolerance with more energy and wit than the solemn uplift of PBS's *American Playhouse.* The guilelessness of his hybrid position as the straight-identified actor/director in a gay-identified film expands traditional definitions of what makes cinema gay.

A more sustained examination of the limits of narration is evident in the films of Michelle Parkerson. Although Parkerson's work is primarily within documentary, her focus on singers in *But Then, She's Betty Carter* (1980) and *Gotta Make This Journey: Sweet Honey in the Rock* (1983) and especially on a male impersonator in *Storme: The Lady of the Jewel Box* (1987) has placed questions of performance and theatricality at the center of her realism. Her science fiction mini-epic *Odds and Ends* (1993) confronts directly the symbiotic relation between artifice and verisimilitude. Unlike science fiction novels, where imagination can roam to the very limits of language, sci-fi films are at the mercy of their production values. Yet the special effect only epitomizes the dependency of all cinematic images on technological manipulation, and

Parkerson's satire directs its deconstructive (not to say camp) gaze not only at Hollywood gargantuanism but at the more general exclusions of realistic narrative. Inverting the imperialism, and racism, and misogyny of traditional sci-fi plots, she tells a story of a galactic liberation from a culture of while male clones as undertaken by black females in the name of interplanetary Afrocentrism. Building on the gay absurdist techniques of Charles Ludlam's Theater of the Ridiculous and of Pomo Afro Homos, she experiments with fractured chronology and hyperbolic performance to loosen the stranglehold of realistic representation on plot and character as well. Thus while introducing new characters and ideas into a genre where they had been invisible, she continues to warn that old forms unmodified may not permit speaking the new.

Perhaps the most promising model for minority self-representation lies in recent work by Cheryl Dunye. In *Janine* (1990), Dunye recalls a troubled high school friendship with a patronizing rich white girl. An adept reading of how power inequities reinforce personal insecurities, the narrative, like Riggs' memories of the white boy in *Tongues*, leaves relatively unexamined the conditions of its retelling. In her *She Don't Fade* (1991), Dunye situates a similar consideration of lesbian relationships within a self-reflexive exploration of filmmaking in general. Appropriating the title, photography, mock documentary style, and character asides of Spike Lee's *She's Gotta Have It*, Dunye not only lambastes Lee's anti-Lesbianism, but explores more generally the interdependence of sexuality and narrative. Moving effortlessly between her personae as director Cheryl and character Shae, Dunye teases audience readiness to accept as authentic any personalizing narrative, whether of Shae or of Janine. White technician Paula, reluctantly acting the part of Shae's confidante Paula, dramatizes the arbitrariness of our markers of difference in her incoherent character accent, half Brooklyn Jew, half black snap queen. And the intimacy and solemnity viewers impose on all sex scenes is prohibited by the film's sound tract, in which crew members, including technician Paula, offer advice to the nude actresses until all collapse in laughter. In dialogue with Lee, storytelling, and audiences' needs for identification and verisimilitude, Dunye's *Fade* suggests that a romance can ironize its conventions without sacrificing in the final fade-out the narrative satisfaction of the passionate embrace.

Beginning with the work of Marlon Riggs, black lesbian and gay male directors have made homosexuality visible in film. They have done so not simply by imaging it through traditional modes of filmic representation but by using sexual invisibility to define what realism and autobiography are unable to represent. In these films speech both announces its former silencing and tests the boundaries of its newfound permission to speak. Their self-reflexivity marks not only an abstract commitment to theory but a practical instinct for survival. Those not aware how to address an audience will never appear before one; those inattentive to the conditions by which they are tolerated will be coopted by the very process of their screening. The methodological skepticism of the minority artists is a hard lesson to those for whom conventional representation has been adequate, because it was created for them. Yet only by examining the conditions that deny reality to others can our reality have meaning. When communication knows its limits, we may be able to end language's ability to silence—to hear along with tongues no longer tied tongues never tied at all.

NOTES

1. For a comprehensive overview of the debate surrounding the PBS screening, see Gary Rivlin and Sara Catania, "A Tongue Untied," *East Bay Express* 16, no. 31 (May 15, 1992): 10–14, 18–21.

2. It is suggestive that Buchanan's footage from the movie showed white homosexuals rather than the African Americans more central in Riggs' account. For an example of the process by which Riggs' film passes out of liberal discourse, see Eve Kosofsky Sedgwick, "Socratic Raptures, Socratic Ruptures: Notes Toward Queer Performativity," in *English Inside and Out: The Places of Literary Criticism*, ed. Susan Gubar and Jonathan Kamholtz (New York: Routledge, 1993), pp. 122–36. Here Sedgwick's participation in the "protest-*function*" following one station's refusal to screen the video affords her the occasion to muse about AIDS, chemotherapy, queer performance, and (white) theory without ever attending to the work itself.

3. By so placing Riggs *in* a context, I do not wish to reduce him *to* a context—to make him a "symptom" of (not to say "credit to") his cultural position. For a sensitive account of the limitations of the "comparativist" approach and especially of the problematic relation between individual talent and popular assessment, see Wahneema Lubiano, "But Compared to What?: Reading Realism, Representation, and Essentialism in *School Daze, Do the Right Thing*, and the Spike Lee Discourse," *Black American Literature Forum* 25, no. 2 (Summer 1991): 253–82.

4. See, for example, Riggs, "Black Macho Revisited: Reflections of a Snap Queen," *Black American Literature Forum* 25, no. 2 (Summer 1991): 389–94. For similar readings by other directors and critics, see Michelle Parkerson, "Birth of a Notion: Towards Black Gay and Lesbian Imagery in Film and Video," in *Queer Looks: Perspectives on Lesbian and Gay Film and Video*, ed. Martha Gever, Pratibha Parmar, and John Greyson (New York: Routledge, 1993), pp. 234–37; and Lubiano, "But Compared to What?"

5. For an excellent overview of the use of race by white gay and lesbian filmmakers, see B. Ruby Rich, "When Difference Is (More Than) Skin Deep," in *Queer Looks*, pp. 318–39.

6. Even after Riggs, white filmmakers remain oblivious to their racism. As an account of the sexual revolution in San Francisco, Armistead Maupin's *Tales of the City* books (1978–89) show their age. Yet when in 1994 PBS aired a film version of the first volume, it not only included no people of color, gay or straight; it unashamedly "featured" Dorothea, Maupin's black lesbian character who turns out to be a WASP in blackface.

7. Gus Van Sant's subsequent, more commercial films dealing with similar material—*Drugstore Cowboy* (1989) and *My Own Private Idaho* (1991)—have been even less explicit on the racial dimensions of street culture. The films of Rainer Werner Fassbinder, and especially his filmic use of his real-life lover the Moroccan actor El Hedi Ben Salem, offer a more complicated though not fully satisfactory account of the intersection between sexuality and race. In *Fox and His Friends* (1975), Salem plays an African hired to service Fassbinder's Fox, a working-class homosexual being taught the

privileges of the German tourist by his upper-middle-class boyfriend. In *Ali—Fear Eats the Soul* (1974), Salem is part of a working-class, interracial heterosexual relationship, but his body is fetishized for the camera in a way that might be characterized as homosexual spectatorship. On Van Sant and Fassbinder, see Rich, "When Difference Is (More Than) Skin Deep," in *Queer Looks*, pp. 423–25; Judith Mayne, "Fassbinder and Spectatorship," *New German Critique* 12 (1977): 61–74; and Kaja Silverman, *Male Subjectivity at the Margins* (New York: Routledge, 1992), pp. 125–56, 214–96. For more general considerations of the place of race within white film, see Richard Dyer, "White," *Screen* (1988); rpt. in his *The Matter of Images: Essays on Representations* (New York: Routledge, 1993), pp. 141–63; and Judith Mayne, *Cinema and Spectatorship* (New York: Routledge, 1993), pp. 142–72.

8. James Baldwin comments indirectly on Laurents' conflation of race and sexuality in his reading of the film in *The Devil Finds Work* (New York: Dell, 1976), pp., 81–82. The problem of sexual substitution informs much of Laurents' work. In his play *The Time of the Cuckoo* (filmed as *Summertime*) a female spinster on vacation stands in for the gay man cruising Venice. Such conglomerate identities come to a head (comically) in Laurents' script for *West Side Story*, in which homoeroticized chorus boys, arbitrarily divided into Polish and Puerto Rican, sing and dance a mix of ballet and Broadway, all under the sign of updated Shakespeare. For a general (generous) reading of *Home*, see Donald Bogle, *Toms, Coons, Mulattoes, Mammies, and Bucks: An Interpretive History of Blacks in Amer-ican Films*, new expanded edition (New York: Continuum, 1990), pp. 144–47. For skep-tical accounts, see Thomas Cripps, *Making Movies Black: The Hollywood Message Movie from World War II to the Civil Rights Era* (New York: Oxford University Press, 1993), pp. 221–26; and Michele Wallace, "Race, Gender, and Psychoanalysis in Forties Film: *Lost Boundaries, Home of the Brave*, and *The Quiet One*," in *Black American Cinema*, ed. Manthia Diawara (New York: Routledge, 1992), pp. 257–71. For a more general discussion of gay male appropriations of minority identity, see my *The Queening of America: Gay Culture in Straight Society* (New York: Routledge, 1995).

9. For complementary reactions to white lesbian representations of African Ameri-cans, see Parkerson, "Birth of a Notion," and Rich, "When Difference Is (More Than) Skin Deep," in *Queer Looks*, pp. 237, 318–39. For a debate on these issues in terms of the pivotal work of Sheila McLaughlin, see the discussion following Teresa de Lauretis, "Film and the Visible," in *How Do I Look?: Queer Film and Video*, ed. Bad Object-Choices (Seattle: Bay Press, 1991), pp. 264–76. For McLaughlin's own evaluation of her use of race, see Alison Butler, "*She Must Be Seeing Things*: An Interview with Sheila McLaughlin," in *Queer Looks*, pp. 368–76. More ambiguous in its implications is the way in which some narratives, like Nella Larsen's novel *Passing* (1929) and Julie Dash's film *Illusions* (1982), seem to figure racial passing as "like" homosexuality.

10. Much recent theory explores the fictionality of nonfiction film. See, for example, Bill Nichols, *Representing Reality: Issues and Concepts in Documentary* (Bloomington: Indiana University Press, 1991), pp. 32–75, 165–98; and Michael Renov, ed., *Theorizing Documentary* (New York: Routledge, 1993).

11. Minority film criticism has repeatedly problematized the role of "realness" in delineating difference. See, for example, Lubiano, "But Compared to What?"; Kobena Mer-cer, "Diaspora Culture and the Dialogic Imagination: The Aesthetics of Black Independent Film in Britain," in *BLACKFRAMES: Critical Perspectives on Black Independent Cinema*, ed. Mbye B. Cham and Claire Andrade-Watkins (Cambridge, Mass.: MIT Press, 1988), pp. 50–61; Trinh T. Minh-ha, "The Totalizing Quest of Meaning," in *When the Moon Waxes Red: Representation, Gender and Cultural Politics* (New York: Routledge, 1991), pp. 29–50; Valerie Smith, "The Documentary Impulse in Contemporary U.S. African-American Film," in *Black Popular Culture: A Project by Michele Wallace*, ed. Gina Dent (Seattle: Bay Press, 1992), pp. 56–64; and Ana M. López, "(Not) Looking for Origins: Postmodernity, Documentary, and *America*," in *Theorizing Documentary*, pp. 151–63.

12. For a more optimistic reading of Powell's objection, see Isaac Julien and Kobena Mercer, "Introduction—De Margin and De Centre," in *The Last 'Special' Issue on Race?*, ed. Isaac Julien and Kobena Mercer, *Screen* 29, no. 4 (Autumn 1988): 2–10.

13. For the conventionality of *Notions*, see Bill Nichols, "'Getting to Know You. . .': Knowledge, Power, and the Body," in *Theorizing Documentary*, pp. 186–88; and Riggs' own evaluation in Rivlin and Catania, "A Tongue Untied," p. 18.

14. In discussing Paul Robeson's popularity with both white and black audiences, Richard Dyer argues that however much they may seem to value the same things, "black discourses see [these virtues] as contributions to the development of society, white as enviable qualities that only blacks have." In light of this difference, Levine's explanation that blackface liberated whites to adopt purported black freedoms may not only be accurate, but repeat the error by internalizing white envy for the uniquely black. See Dyer, *Heavenly Bodies: Film Stars and Society* (New York: St. Martins Press, 1986), p. 79.

15. Kobena Mercer, "Black Art and the Burden of Representation," *Third Text* 10 (Spring 1990): 61–78.

16. Ron Simmons, *"Tongues Untied:* An Interview with Marlon Riggs," in *Brother to Brother: New Writings by Black Gay Men*, ed. Essex Hemphill, conceived by Joseph Fairchild Beam (Boston: Alyson, 1991), pp. 191–92, 193. Kobena Mercer cites an even more telling description by Riggs: "What films like *Tongues Untied* do, especially for people who have had no images of themselves out there to see, is give them a visible and visual representation of their lives." Kobena Mercer, "Dark and Lovely Too: Black Gay Men in Independent Film," in *Queer Looks*, p. 244.

17. The pressures exerted by white editors is a repeated theme in the scholarship of the slave narrative. See, for example, William L. Andrews, *To Tell a Free Story: The First Century of Afro-American Autobiography, 1760–1865* (Urbana: University of Illinois Press, 1986), pp. 19–22; and James Olney, "'I Was Born': Slave Narratives, Their Status as Autobiography and Literature," in *The Slave's Narrative*, ed. Charles T. Davis and Henry Louis Gates Jr. (New York: Oxford University Press, 1985), pp. 148–75. On the epistemological paradoxes of the slave narrative, see my "Reading Slavery: The Anxiety of Ethnicity in Douglass's *Narrative*," in *Frederick Douglass: New Literary and Historical Essays*, ed. Eric J. Sundquiust (New York: Cambridge University Press, 1990), pp. 118–40.

18. Kobena Mercer has dealt widely with the limitations of authenticity as a measure of documentary realism. See his "Diaspora Culture and the Dialogic Imagin-ation," in *BLACKFRAMES*, pp. 50–61; and on *Tongues* itself, "Dark and Lovely Too: Black Gay Men in Independent Film," in *Queer Looks*, pp. 238–56. For a critique of the use of a "narrative informant" to understand another culture, see James Clifford, *The Predicament of Culture: Twentieth-Century Ethnography, Literature, and Art* (Cam-bridge, Mass.: Harvard University Press, 1988), especially pp. 21–54.

19. On the importance of this "interactive mode" of documentary discourse, with passing reference to *Notions*, see Bill Nichols, *Representing Reality*, pp. 44–56.

20. The boundary between truth and literature becomes even less distinct when Riggs publishes his "autobiographical" poetic fragments under the title "Tongues Untied" in *Brother to Brother: New Writings by Black Gay Men*. Conceived by the late Joseph Beam and edited by Essex Hemphill, this volume is obviously in symbiotic relation to the film, from whose opening chant it draws its own title. The interpenetration of the two works—and their continuity with Beam's earlier volume *In the Life: A Black Gay Anthology* (Boston: Alyson, 1986) and with Isaac Julien's film *Looking for Langston* (1989)—suggests the extent to which the project, however differently realized by Beam, Hemphill, Julien, and Riggs, is in some very real sense a communal one.

21. See "Brother to Brother: Words from the Heart," in *In the Life*, pp. 230–42. Like Riggs' poem "Tongues Untied," Beam's essay joins together various ideas originally published separately. The incendiary sentence appears several times in the last three pages of the essay; the qualifying phrases are from p. 242. Riggs himself explicates the line in a similarly abstract way: "Many people do interpret 'black men loving black men' solely in terms of a sexual, romantic affinity, and love. But what I meant was love in the sense of friendship, community, family, and fraternity, which was far more important, in nurturing me as a black gay man, than the love of a particular lover who is white"; Simmons' interview, *"Tongues Untied,"* in *Brother to Brother*, p. 194. Riggs agrees with

Simmons' sense that "a love relationship, it's not a political act per se" (p. 194). For a balanced overview of the debate in both the black and white gay presses, see Rich, "When Difference Is (More Than) Skin Deep," in *Queer Looks*, pp. 331–39.

22. A similar misreading has informed criticism of Isaac Julien's *Looking for Langston*. Released shortly before *Tongues*, Julien's film employs not documentary analysis but the objectivizing conventions of the high art film to explore black gay culture. Nevertheless critics as different as Mercer and Gates insist on relocating Julien within a personalizing tradition. Each concludes, in virtually identical formulations, that though "we look for Langston, we find Isaac." Though offered as praise, the formulation nevertheless attests to the force of autobiography as minority authentication even in a work whose mode is objective and historicist. See Mercer, "Dark and Lovely Too," p. 250; and Henry Louis Gates Jr., "The Black Man's Burden," in *Black Popular Culture: A Project by Michele Wallace*, ed. Gina Dent (Seattle: Bay Press, 1992), p. 77. On Julien's film more generally, see as well Manthia Diawara, "The Absent One: The Avant-Garde and the Black Imaginary in *Looking for Langston*," *Wide Angle*, 13, nos. 3/4 (July–October 1991): 96–106; and Henry Louis Gates Jr., "Looking for Modernism," in *Black American Cinema*, ed. Manthia Diawara (New York: Routledge, 1992), pp. 200–207. The general critical preference for high art over documentary realism hurts Julien himself when, in his subsequent film *Young Soul Rebels* (1991), he experiments with popular narrative forms closer to those of *Tongues*. See Isaac Julien's claim that in the concept of "black popular culture" the first adjective overshadows the second: "Black Is, Black Ain't: Notes on De-Essentializing Black Identities" [with discussion], in *Black Popular Culture: A Project by Michele Wallace*, pp. 255–75.

23. For models of alternative spectatorship in minority film, see Manthia Diawara, "Black Spectatorship: Problems of Identification and Resistance," in *The Last 'Special' Issue on Race?*, ed. Isaac Julien and Kobena Mercer, *Screen* 29, no. 4 (Autumn 1988): 66–76; rpt. in *Black American Cinema*, ed. Manthia Diawara (New York: Routledge, 1992), pp. 211–20; and Teresa de Lauretis, "Film and the Visible," in *How Do I Look? Queer Film and Video*, pp. 225–76.

24. For an excellent discussion of Riggs' deconstructive use of snap and vogueing, see Marcos Becquer, "Snap!thology and Other Discursive Practices in *Tongues Untied*," *Wide Angle* 13, no. 2 (April 1991): 6–17. For a general consideration of the representation of vogueing in white film, with some reference to Riggs, see bell hooks, *Black Looks: Race and Representation* (Boston: South End Press, 1992), pp. 145–64.

25. For a general discussion of how avant-garde forms function within black gay film, see Manthia Diawara, "The Absent One: The Avant-Garde and the Black Imaginary in *Looking for Langston*," *Wide Angle*, 13, nos. 3/4 (July–October 1991): 96–106.

26. On the general problems of representing AIDS, see the articles of Douglas Crimp, especially "Portraits of People with AIDS," in *Cultural Studies*, ed. Lawrence Grossberg, Cary Nelson, and Paula Treichler (New York: Routledge, 1992), pp. 117–33. On the relation of the African American community to such representations, see Phillip Brian Harper, "Eloquence and Epitaph: Black Nationalism and the Homophobic Impulse in Responses to the Death of Max Robinson," *Social Text 28* 9, no. 3 (1991): 68–86.

27. The haunting posthumous *Black Is . . . Black Ain't* (1995) is Riggs' most extended attempt to reconcile sexuality and race. The film claims that identity categories only limit African Americans, and it offers homosexuality as a central example of the kind of thing excluded from traditional definitions of blackness. It is difficult, however, to be more specific about the film's reconciliation of the two identities, for Riggs did not of course have total control over the final form of the film, completed after his death in 1994.

28. Positioning is the explicit topic of the first celebrated film by an American lesbian of color, *Ten Cents a Dance (Parallax)* (1985), by the Japanese Canadian director Midi Onodera. In a controversial formalist innovation, Onodera symbolizes the ostracization of the lesbian of color through a narrative boxed into three sets of paired

stationary images, only one of the six including an "actual" lesbian, played by the director. For analyses of this groundbreaking work, a masterpiece of modern feminist filmmaking and implicit touchstone for subsequent work by African American lesbians, see Judith Mayne, *The Woman at the Keyhole: Feminism and Women's Cinema* (Bloomington: Indiana University Press, 1990), pp. 225–27; and idem, "A Parallax View of Lesbian Authorship," in *Inside/Out: Lesbian Theories, Gay Theories* (New York: Routledge, 1991), pp. 173–84.

Haile Gerima and the Political Economy of Cinematic Resistance

Although Haile Gerima's filmmaking career didn't begin until 1970, the foundation for his cinematic sensibilities was forged much earlier. Born in Gondar, near Lake Tana in northwest Ethiopia, Gerima was, early on, exposed to the concept of art as a political tool by his father, who oversaw an itinerant theater troupe. Describing him as "an orthodox priest, a teacher, a historian and a playwright," Gerima recalls his father's "plays of resistance" that he used "to mobilize people during the Italian invasion of Ethiopia." Yet, even as his father was largely responsible for bringing to Gerima the theatrical sensibilities that would serve him later in life, it was his mother and grandmother who taught him the equally important storytelling traditions of Ethiopia. As Gerima tells it, "both my mother and . . . grandmother were wonderful storytellers and as kids we used to spend many evenings, gathered around a fire listening to the legends and tales of the Ethiopian oral tradition" (Pfaff, 137). For Gerima, the place of storytelling in his own art is central since

> a filmmaker is a story teller, nothing more, nothing less; one who provides information, one who creates and explores the vital elements and innovatively synthesizes social relationships; one who plays a role in linking not only the historical but global human experience. (Gerima, *Filmfaust*, 46)

Here we can see how the contributions of his father and mother during Gerima's upbringing come together seamlessly in his description of a filmmaker. Gerima points to a politicized vision that "synthesizes social relationships" and theorizes both "historical" and "global" conditions, but always within the paradigm of the storyteller—"nothing more, nothing less." Françoise Pfaff, in *Twenty-Five Black African Directors*, notes that Gerima's job at a local movie theater was equally formative to his cinematic vision, bringing him in contact with Western filmic traditions and heroes. But unlike the influence of those close to him, the Western cinema, filled with images and narratives of colonization and genocide, represented, for Gerima, a "politically and psychologically damaging exploitation of [his] very being" (Gerima, qtd. in Pfaff, 138).

Even as Gerima received his early formation from family and Ethiopian tradition, it was only after traveling across the Atlantic and witnessing, firsthand, the brand of racism particular to the United States that he began to develop the global perspective necessary for his development as a filmmaker. After trying his hand at acting at the Goodman School of Drama in Chicago, Gerima began to realize that the effects of being a Third World person situated within a Western aesthetic didn't leave many possibilities for artistic development. But his planned escape to UCLA's drama school only offered more colonized and subordinate roles. In 1970, Gerima began to pursue a career in filmmaking at UCLA's film school, where he met fellow-filmmakers Charles Burnett and Ben Caldwell, both of whom worked with Gerima on *Bush Mama* (1976). Again, Gerima's early grounding in Ethiopian cultural and aesthetic traditions nourished his vision since, rather than produce introspective and subject-laden films in the traditions set out by Hollywood, Gerima began to conceive of the cinema "as a collective and communal experience" (*Filmfaust,* 54). Just as his father had attempted to politicize Ethiopians through plays of resistance, Gerima began to see cinema as "a rallying point for the advancement of consciousness." For Gerima, the cinema duplicates, in many ways, the centrality of the fireplace, of the hearth as a place of "gathering, warming, sharing" in many African societies and, hence,

> The fireplace tradition created time and space for observation and critical analysis, benefiting the entire social network, including artists. It is entirely appropriate to perceive the cinema as being symbolic of the fire—the central point of life, earth and energy. (Gerima, "Fireplace Cinema," 54)

Although the context from which he began to write, produce, and direct his films arose from the political and economic terrain specific to blacks in the United States, Gerima has remained grounded in the traditions of Ethiopian culture and artistic practices of his childhood.

With this "double-consciousness" Gerima has explored notions of struggle against oppression, community, and personal transformation consistently throughout his career. Gerima describes this "constant and very insistent theme" in his work as focusing on "transformation, change, realization" (Pfaff, 146). Beginning his film career in 1971 with a short (13 minutes), experimental film, *Hourglass,* Gerima began to explore these concepts. In it he follows a young black man who has grown up as a foster child in a white family. The main character leaves the predominantly white university and his spot on its basketball team when, as Gerima puts it, he "realizes that he's the new modern gladiator" and, instead, moves into a black community. Gerima's second film and first in 16mm (*Hourglass* was shot in Super 8), *Child of Resistance* (1972), works out, much more ambitiously than did *Hourglass,* notions of struggle and transformation as Gerima chronicles the surreal dreams and nightmares of a prisoner of the state being held for her political beliefs. Using a combination of black-and-white footage to depict the main character's experience and color sequences of the "world outside," Gerima examines the ways in which, ironically, "her imprisonment is her enlightenment" (Gerima, qtd. in Howard, 29). But where *Hourglass* may have been symbolic of certain realities, Gerima makes much more specific connections between the events that take place in *Child of Resistance* and the contemporary social and political world since the main character of the film, played by Barbara O. Jones, is clearly meant to find inspiration and parallels in Angela Davis's imprisonment. His third film, *Bush Mama,* though it was released at the same time as *Harvest: 3,000 Years,* was made a year earlier as his master thesis at UCLA. Though it did not receive the critical attention of *Harvest* and was seen, by many reviewers, as too angry or too technically rough, my focus on this particular film stems both from its deep examination of oppression and resistance within the welfare state as well as from its complex representational strategies.

Harvest: 3,000 Years represents both Gerima's physical return to Ethiopia as well as his tribute to the work and influence of his father and the Ethiopian countryside where he grew up. This film—partially a document of the struggles of Ethiopian peasants and partially a fictive account of one particular family's struggles—produced on a $20,000 budget with a cast of primarily nonprofessional actors, was produced in Ahmaric, the primary language of Ethiopia. Though it was meant for Ethiopian movie houses, it has, to this day, never been shown there. However, *Harvest* did bring Gerima to critical attention, winning the 1976 Oscar Micheaux Award for Best Feature Film from the Black Filmmakers Hall of Fame, the Grand Prix at the Locarno International Film Festival, the George Sadoul Prize from the French Critics Association, the Grand Prize at the Festival International de Cinema, Figueira da Foz, Portugal, and the Outstanding Film Award at the London Film Festival.

After *Harvest,* Gerima, becoming a faculty member at Howard University, began shooting *Wilmington 10—U.S.A. 10,000,* his first documentary, which chronicles the fight of the Wilmington Ten, who were accused of firebombing a grocery store in Wilmington, North Carolina. Returning to the color/black-and-white combination of *Child of Resistance, Wilmington* (16mm) runs two hours and features an original sound track written and performed by Sweet Honey in the Rock. While the intrigue of the case was certainly worth documenting, it was the "consciousness, instead of the conventional drama that intrigued [him]" (Gerima, qtd. in Howard, 39). As he has done throughout his career, rather than romanticize some essential notion of struggle against oppression, Gerima sought to contextualize this story within a long tradition of movement culture and the ways in which the Wilmington Ten "perceived the system."

The Wilmington Ten project was followed by two very different films, *Ashes and Embers* and *After Winter: Sterling Brown. Ashes* takes up familiar themes of transformation and resistance to structures of oppression as it follows the events in the life of a young black man as he returns home from the Vietnam War. *After Winter*, which runs sixty minutes, grew out of a class project by some of Gerima's students at Howard and seeks to tell the story of the black poet, critic, and essayist of the Harlem Renaissance. Certainly Gerima's film credits demonstrate a true range of talents, from the smaller productions to those of sweeping scope and focus, from black and white to color, in different languages, and various genres. Yet through this varied body of work, the central thread of "a collective and communal experience" binds these various pieces in a coherence that speaks of Gerima's commitment to cinematic activism—one that

> emerges as an effective catalyst bringing about dialogue between people, making a smooth transition as it assumes the (gathering, warming, sharing) "fireplace" concept found in most African societies. . . . It is entirely appropriate to perceive cinema as being symbolic of the fire—the central point of life, earth and energy. . . . I am advocating a cinema of electricity that affirms our great civilization, our history of resistance; a cinema with profound realistic passion for humanity, a cinema of boundless human vision. (*Filmfaust*, 54)[1]

The Political Economy of *Bush Mama*

In critiquing *Bush Mama*, many scholars have commented on a "documentary impulse"[2] that, such critics argue, seems to pervade the film. A common strategy in the relatively small body of critical work on *Bush Mama* is to focus on the opening footage of the film, in which we see the arrest of two black men by the LAPD. This opening scene, according to critics including Clyde Taylor (in *Jump Cut*) and James A. Snead (in *BLACKFRAMES: Critical Perspectives on Black Independent Cinema*), is of singular importance because it was not staged but is footage of members of Gerima's shooting crew for *Bush Mama* being harassed by the police. By Taylor's estimation, these shots bring a "realness dimension" to the film through which the audience is "more easily convinced that the daily actions of the black community's inhabitants are constantly policed" (*Jump Cut*, 168). Though I would not think of disputing the fact that an examination of the "real" has a central place in any discussion of *Bush Mama*, I am opposed to the critical tendency to reduce this film to a hybrid of cinema verité documentation. For all its praise, Taylor's comment seems to assume that Gerima's audience needs to be convinced of the fact that the "daily actions of the black community's inhabitants are constantly policed." If we, however, take into consideration Gerima's statements on the function of film as a community-building tool, then it seems, at the very least, presumptuous to imagine that Gerima intended *Bush Mama* to be directed primarily toward a nonblack audience. Further (and my criticism extends well beyond Taylor's comment) many critics have confined their discussions of *Bush Mama* to the anecdotal information about the film's opening "documentary" sequence, ignoring the fact that Gerima gives no markers that would indicate that these shots are anything but fictive in the literal sense.

Such critical assessments of *Bush Mama* (which remain all too common) belie the complexity of Gerima's film and do not begin to interrogate the several levels and sites at which the narrative functions. On the surface, *Bush Mama* tells the story of Dorothy, a "welfare sister" living as part of Watts' permanently submerged class. Her husband has been killed in the Vietnam War,[3] leaving her and her daughter, Luann, dependent on a "welfare job" to support themselves. Early in the movie, Dorothy meets T.C., a Vietnam vet, and the two begin living together in her apartment. But rather than find a job to alleviate the couple's impoverished situation, T.C. is accused and convicted of a crime he didn't commit and spends the remainder of the movie in prison, only communicating to Dorothy through his letters to her. Meanwhile, Dorothy finds out that she is pregnant and, faced with threats by a social worker that her AFDC aid will be cut off unless she terminates her pregnancy, Dorothy begins to consider abortion. What follows can be understood as a kind of battle for Dorothy's soul, as various friends attempt to make her see things the way that they do. From T.C.'s militantly politicized position, to Molly's "bullshittin', backbitin', and killin' each other" refrain, to Simmi's idea of community, Dorothy tries to sort through these various narratives as a means toward understanding the oppressive functions of the state in her own life. Yet only after police interrogators beat Dorothy, causing her to miscarry, and her daughter is raped by another police officer does Dorothy come to full consciousness, declaring to T.C. in a letter, "It's not easy to win over people like me. There's a lot of people like me. We have many things to fight for just to live. But the idea is to win over more of our people."

Even a short summary of the plot makes it clear that *Bush Mama* operates on several levels, deals with several narrative positions, and cannot be reduced to a simple tale of tough living in the "ghetto." In the remainder of this essay I would like to discuss, briefly, four levels of critical interrogation necessary to understand the complex narrative Gerima constructs for the audience in the film. First, Gerima's film depicts the structural crisis of the "crisis state" within the city by focusing on the ways in which state terrorism and state control shape and determine the lives of those who live in impoverished urban centers. Second, as Dorothy searches for an adequate explanation for the crisis-induced contradictions in her everyday life, she works out possibilities for and practice of resistance to the state's regime of terrorism and control. Third, Gerima's film points out the necessity to generate *multiple* narratives that all address different yet equally important aspects of the crisis as a precondition for sustained resistance and for the creation of *communities* of struggle. Fourth, Gerima's refusal to accept the dominant narratives concerning urban crisis (news media, political leaders, state apparatuses, etc.) leads to what I consider to be resistant representational practices that overturn these dominant narratives in both content and form.

As I mentioned earlier, Gerima shows the inescapable presence of state-sponsored terrorist activity, in the form of policing, as one of the central and defining features of crisis in Los Angeles. Without wasting time, Gerima begins his film with evidence of state terrorism with the police harassment scenes as, in the voice-over, a social worker reads off questions used to determine welfare eligibility.[4] From the outset Gerima establishes a police presence that continually returns to haunt Dorothy—first, as the police shoot the man with the ax outside the welfare office and, later, with the poster of "the brother . . . the pigs shot and killed" that Angie hangs up in Dorothy's apartment. This police presence comes up again, almost invisibly, with T.C.'s arrest and conviction that we only find out about later, in Dorothy's letter to T.C. It surfaces toward the end of the film with the police execution of the unarmed and nonthreatening man on the street just below Dorothy's window. And, most disturbingly, it returns in the police rape of Dorothy's daughter, Luann. In Gerima's version of Los Angeles, Dorothy cannot escape the LAPD terrorist activity or the inevitable surveillance that accompanies it.

But the LAPD's version of state-sponsored terrorism tells only half of Dorothy's story since, as is generally the case, no state terrorism exists without an equally coercive state control apparatus. Francis Fox Piven and Richard A. Cloward, who document the rise of the welfare state in the United States in *Regulating the Poor: The Functions of Public Welfare,* characterize the expansion of relief as a means of controlling the poor during periods of massive unemployment. For Piven and Cloward the workings of AFDC and other relief programs should not at all be viewed as the state's benevolent response to economic crises but as performing two main functions: maintaining civil order in periods of unusually high unrest and, after that has been accomplished, conditioning and reconditioning the labor force. As if in support of Piven and Cloward's point, Gerima makes it clear to the audience that the welfare office is a highly contradictory site for the poor. Though characters such as Dorothy, Molly, and the drunk man rely on assistance to support themselves and, in that sense, seem to benefit from the system, the audience also witnesses the killing of a black man with an ax who has come to the office precisely because he could not receive welfare. Gerima also hints at just how unhelpful the welfare office can be through the conversation between the two women sitting in the waiting room with Dorothy as the one woman tells the other, "You ain't gonna get no money."

The relatively high incidence of civil unrest in the second half of the 1960s and the large number of urban uprisings between 1964 and 1969 in urban centers across the country provided the impetus for the expansion of the relief rolls and not, as others such as Daniel P. Moynihan have suggested, a growing dependency of the urban poor on the state. In support of this interpretation, Piven and Cloward note the fact that the rise in AFDC recipients in 1964 came about not because the number of families in need increased but, instead, constituted a "political response to political disorder" (198). Far from reducing *Bush Mama* to a political "docu-drama" about the oppressive nature of the state, I want to argue that as Gerima traces Dorothy's contact with the welfare state, he means the audience to see how AFDC is used as a regulatory apparatus that fosters and maintains a dependency on the benevolent state. If the film begins with scenes of the regulatory and coercive functions of the welfare system, then it does not stop there. With the social worker's visit to Dorothy's apartment Gerima provides more evidence of state coercion as the social worker threatens to discontinue Dorothy's AFDC if she does not have an abortion. Even as the welfare system provides assistance as a way to maintain a large surplus army of black labor, so it controls that population through forced abortion. And, as if to underline Simmi's assertion that the "we have to have more black people . . . more black bodies," in the montage sequence in which Dorothy goes to a clinic and imagines having an abortion. Gerima cuts between Dorothy's body on an examination table and the poster of the man who's been shot by the police. At this point Gerima makes an active filmic connection between state-sponsored terrorism (i.e., man killed by the police) and the social control inherent in the welfare system.

Because Gerima's film (shot in 1976) takes place during fierce labor conditioning and the inevitable contraction of the welfare state in the 1970s, *Bush Mama* depicts the structural crisis of the crisis state and the centrality of crisis as a shaping force in the characters' lives.[5] As Stuart Hall has noted, these crises, insofar as they disrupt the regular workings of the state and hence, disturb the smooth reproduction of the relations of production, must be contained and managed with a combination of policing and control.[6] Gerima's understanding of crisis, similar to Hall's, goes beyond conventional wisdom of the inner-city populations as a "problem." In *Bush Mama* we see how the problem of policing blacks overlaps with the problem of policing the poor, *and* of policing the unemployed (Hall, 332), as well as how these multiple intersections result in the state's attempt to deal with the situation by combining what Hall calls "social problem" and "social control" approaches—the social problem approach to the criminalized black masses in the cities, matched by social control of the poor and unemployed—and with this combination, a "synchronization of the race and class aspects of the crisis" (333).

Gerima begins to explore the complexities of this race and class synchronization of policing and control in the film's opening sequence. As the camera zooms in on the film title, *Bush Mama,* painted on a brick wall, we hear the voice-over of a social worker asking questions used to determine AFDC eligibility ("Have you ever received noncash gifts in the form of free rent or free housing, free food, free room and board, free utilities, or other household expenses paid for by a person not a member of your household?"). But when we cut to the first sequence of the film— police frisking and arresting two black men—the voice of the social worker merges into that of a police radio dispatcher and the entire sound track is overlaid with the sound of a helicopter flying overhead. As the arrest scene continues and several other voices join the first welfare worker and the radio dispatch operator, the entire voice-over becomes a dissonant and seemingly inescapable chorus of the state's presence in these characters' lives. As if to point out the role that the state plays not only in Dorothy's life but in the lives of everyone who lives in "the neighborhood," Gerima cuts away from the arrest scene to a montage of black people on the street while he sustains the voice-over. Within this circular logic "black areas" in the city become the site for intense and unrelenting policing and control precisely because they are black areas; regulation and control of the poor are held synonymous with policing black areas because all black areas show the scars of unemployment and capitalist de-development. It is precisely the illogic of a combination of police surveillance/terrorism and social welfare that Gerima means the audience to understand as constitutive of the workings of the state. In this sequence the social control approach of the welfare state melts into the more antagonistic tactics of social problem, all against the backdrop of an inescapable police presence.[7]

By opening the film in this way, I would argue that Gerima locates and contextualizes Dorothy's story within what Antonio Negri has called the "crisis of the 'crisis state,'" in its "transition from the 'welfare state' to the 'warfare State.'"[8] As the film progresses, it becomes increasingly hard for the viewer to differentiate state-sponsored terrorism and state control where remedies for social problems become indistinguishable from the controlling and policing of the crisis. From the execution of the man with the ax, LAPD style, through to the end of the film, all distinctions between policing and regulation gradually disappear. At the film's climax, an interrogator tells Dorothy that

> Silence isn't gonna help you. You may think you're okay but things are changing. People are changing their attitude. And when they get ready to burn you I'm gonna have your head shaved for it.

But at this point the audience has no idea why Dorothy is being interrogated. We might assume that it has something to do with her refusal to have an abortion since only a few scenes earlier Dorothy leaves the clinic without going through with the surgery. But only after the sequence in which Dorothy is beaten can the audience begin to piece together the chain of events that lead to the interrogation. At that point the audience has seen Luann being picked up by a police officer and just after the extreme close-ups of Dorothy being slapped repeatedly, a voice on the sound track, presumably an interrogator, says to Dorothy, "Came to arrest you and all the crap you been doin' and for takin' really rotten care of your little whore daughter." Though Gerima may sacrifice some clarity by presenting the narrative in nonlinear fashion, he manages to truly blur the distinctions between policing and control since we have no idea who is interrogating Dorothy or why she is being held. And though we can piece together the sequence of events and explain each scene in the film's ending, Gerima never clarifies this point further. Though the "they" in Dorothy's letter to T.C. most likely refers to the police, it could just as easily be workers from the welfare office who, we have to believe, would not be disappointed to find that Dorothy had her baby "beat out of [her]." Time and again, Gerima, through the use of quick cuts and the juxtaposition of images of policing, control, and terrorism, manages to trace out the forces of oppression that perpetuate the kinds of structural inequality that the dominant social problem and social control approaches conveniently obscure.

Even as Gerima narratively and visually identifies the range of state coercion in its many forms by connecting its policing and regulatory functions, he also deepens our understanding of coercion by emphasizing the centrality of worklessness and wagelessness as the means for constituting and maintaining control over the reserve army of labor. The fact that T.C. is unemployed occupies the audience through the first quarter of the film. We find out that T.C. volunteered for a second tour in Vietnam not because of any love for the army or belief in the war but simply because he could not find a job. T.C. imagines that relief from the trauma that he experiences as a result of his service in Vietnam will come when he finds a job. Instead, his search leads him into the penal system. Though, as is the case with the film's ending, the narrative movement through this section may seem confusing, since we never see T.C. being arrested, charged, or given a trial for a crime that he never committed, these absences are consistent with Gerima's depiction of the logic of the state's control of poor blacks. As Gerima notes,

> in *Bush Mama,* I cut from a man leaving for a job interview to a scene with him in prison. Now, one of the experiences of being black in America is not going where you want to go, being stopped. . . . It is a truthful representation to cut from him leaving for the job interview to a prison scene without justifying how he got in jail. . . . That one cut in *Bush Mama* satisfies a truthfulness to a black experience. (qtd. in Safford and Triplett, 62)

For Gerima, then, the omission of these scenes should not be thought of as absences in the narrative but, instead, as a more logical representation of the cycle of worklessness and "not going where you want to go" that Gerima wants to convey.[9] Rather than sacrifice the clear connection between worklessness and the criminalization of black males by the state in order to satisfy dominant codes of narrative clarity, Gerima chooses to make this connection explicit and material. Dorothy watches T.C. leave for a job interview and, in the next scene, T.C. is being escorted to a prison cell as the song on the sound track tells the audience,

> Another walk down these prison halls
> I see that look on my brother's face
> A look that cannot be erased
> So I say to myself
> You know it happened to me.

Just as the "truthfulness to a black experience" of immobility demands that T.C. move from a job interview to the penal system, so, as the sound track points out, young black men are constantly being swept up in a cycle beginning with worklessness and ending in criminalization and incarceration by the state.[10]

But just as the sound track moves from T.C.'s song about criminalization to Dorothy's about the problems of being a "welfare sister," so Gerima parallels T.C.'s demise with Dorothy's status as a dependent on the state. Far from being lazy or parasitic, Dorothy spends her days walking the streets and waiting in lines simply to remain on welfare, while the lack of paying jobs keeps her dependent on the "first and fifteenth kind of check" just to support herself and Luann. The insidiousness of welfare as a form of social control becomes more obvious when we find out that, in order to receive AFDC, Dorothy must get an abortion and perhaps even be subjected to forced sterilization. Dorothy's song tells us,

> That if you want that first and fifteenth kind of check
> Here's what you better do.

Take this number, write it down and don't delay.
Abort that baby, tie your tubes and stay that way.

So, if structural unemployment has relegated Dorothy to the position of "dependent of the state," then the state also begins to exert its control over her, as part of the reserve army of labor, by regulating her reproductive rights as a condition of gaining state-funded subsistence.[11] Gerima makes the structural relation between male criminalization and female impoverishment concrete first by paralleling T.C.'s walk down the "prison halls" with Dorothy's constant walking and then by cutting between T.C. behind prison bars and Dorothy behind the bars that imprison her in her apartment. It is only after several seconds of the extreme close-up shot of Dorothy, as a curtain blows into the frame, that we realize that Dorothy is not, literally, behind prison bars but looks out her apartment window. By then Gerima has made his point—the bars of worklessness and welfare have been forged to lock in Dorothy, just as surely as those that imprison T.C., by a system of "money lovers" (T.C.'s second letter).

I want to turn to Dorothy's character and her search for an adequate set of explanations for the way in which she experiences crisis since not only does Gerima trace out lines of causality for Dorothy's impoverishment, but he also shows the ways in which she resists state coercion. Within this framework, the film can be read in terms of Dorothy's search for narratives of the crisis that can adequately communicate her own sense of dislocation, oppression, and devaluation, but that can also provide the threads of resistance, not unlike Ralph Ellison's narrator in *Invisible Man*. Throughout the film Dorothy encounters a number of state apparatuses and their inability to sufficiently narrate her experience of crisis. The inadequacy of these dominant narratives, and by extension, the entire social problem approach to narrate the crisis lies in their overwhelming tendency to blame the victim. The first instance of this problem comes in the rap session, where several participants accuse Dorothy of being an alcoholic, "pitiful," and suffering from "brain damage."[12] One male participant tells Dorothy that "the man" is "just adding [her] to the list" and there seems to be a general agreement within the group that Dorothy's problems stem from being wedded to a "bum." But if this narrative of Dorothy's situation seems rather unformed and disconnected from the state apparatus, we need only compare it to a later scene in which a social worker comes to counsel Dorothy about her welfare eligibility. Here, Dorothy confronts the same "blame the victim" narrative when the social worker assumes that a bottle of alcohol left by Molly is Dorothy's and goes on to trace out an explanation for Dorothy's dependence on the state. In the social worker's estimation, the combination of Dorothy's supposed alcoholism and the fact that "There's no man in this house and [Dorothy's] pregnant" are all the information that the social worker needs to explain Dorothy's predicament. In order to analyze the situation the social worker mobilizes dominant gender and racial narratives that include notions of what constitutes a stable household and the nuclear family in tandem with a refusal to consider the determinism involved in Dorothy's socioeconomic position. By accepting dominant narratives she falls into the kind of "pathologizing" prevalent in public/political discourse surrounding the African American family, the best example of which is the infamous Moynihan report.[13] If Dorothy's problem lies in her inability to adhere to dominant codes of proper behavior, then the solution (Moynihan's case for "national action") lies in abortion and taking away Luann—solutions that only represent a further fragmenting of the family. Yet not only can Dorothy see the inadequacy of such narratives; she actively resists them. As the social worker repeats her instructions, Dorothy hears the sound of prison doors slamming shut and imagines herself hitting the social worker over the head with a bottle. While at this point in the film Dorothy may only be able to imagine resistance, this scene, nevertheless, prepares us for the transformation to come.

Another set of narratives, what I call coping narratives, come from Molly and the drunk man. According to Molly, "It's the niggers that's gone crazy. Bullshittin', backbitin', killin' each other. Ain't no white folks harassin' me. 'Cept maybe the police." And, for Molly, T.C.'s letters represent the kind of "militant trash" that denies the reality that "white people are gonna go on!" With Molly we get the dominant discourses concerning blacks as problem and the poor as problem filtered through a Gramscian version of common sense. Molly's explanation of the crisis has reference to reality—violence, crime, white dominance—yet at the very same time it is shot through with contradiction. Even as Molly locates racial oppression ("white people are gonna go on") she places its cause solely on the black community and in doing so simply reproduces dominant "blame the victim" narratives of the crisis. Though we may feel sympathy for Molly—especially when she tells Dorothy about her own marriage—and the depth of her despair, Gerima clearly intends the audience to see that such cynicism, though it may provide a coping mechanism for the individual, is counterproductive to the needs of sustained resistance.

Gerima immediately moves from this conversation between Dorothy and Molly to the bar where the drunk man copes with the fact that "I didn't even qualify for no job in their society" by continually asserting, "They ain't never messed with me."[14] Though he wants Dorothy and Molly to hear a story in which, despite being buffeted by poverty, worklessness, the penal system, and the military, he can claim a sort of autonomy and self-reliance, it doesn't take more than a few minutes to see the narrative that lies just below the surface of the story he intends to tell:

> You know, I was born next to a plantation in Florida and they growed me up good. I robbed, I stole, and they put me in prison. But they ain't

never messed with me. I didn't have no time for schoolin myself, but I growed up good.

After his dishonorable discharge from the army he tells Dorothy and Molly, "Gotta do something. And I did like the rest of the colored folks. I got me a welfare job." Here, we have a sad distortion of the Horatio Alger story ("I growed up good") that remains overshadowed by a plantation/slave narrative as well as its inner-city correlative—worklessness, alcohol, and hopelessness. Gerima further emphasizes the unreality of the drunk man's narrative construction of himself and the helplessness that lies just below its surface by cutting to the poster picture of the man shot by the police, while in the voice-over, we continue to hear the drunk man repeat, "But ain't nobody gonna mess with me. Ain't never mess with me." By inserting Molly and the drunk man's stories into the film, Gerima shows the kind of hopelessness and despair that lie just beneath dependency in what Haki R. Madhubuti calls "the culture of short lives and low expectations."[15]

Narrating the Crisis

Even as Gerima gives us a bleak and seemingly hopeless world, one Dorothy feels powerless to escape, we see other characters providing alternative narratives that offer the possibility of agency as well as that of resistance. The first of these characters, Angie, places Dorothy's situation within the context of the larger struggles of Blacks across the globe. While, ostensibly, she comes to Dorothy's apartment to "teach history" to Luann, her lessons have much more far-reaching effects. She begins by bringing the poster of the man gunned down by the police and, later, the picture of the African freedom fighter who has a gun slung over one arm and holds a baby in the other. When Luann asks who the woman in the picture is, Angie tells her that she is "the mother of all of us" who "fights the white people that come from Europe to steal our land." Though Angie's mother may call such posters "militant trash," Angie recodes political militancy as positive for Luann when in answer to Luann's question, "What's militant stuff?" Angie replies, "Militant stuff? Well I guess anything mama don't wanna know. . . . Like the truth." As Angie teaches Luann not only does she historicize and contextualize struggles of blacks in the United States within the larger scope of blacks across the globe, but she provides a model of community activism for Dorothy and Luann. Angie demonstrates the fact that resistance needs to be grounded in radical historical consciousness. Although she may question the fact that liberation is the result of a "long process," she nevertheless introduces the idea of strategized resistance when she talks about the possibilities for liberation lying in broad coalitions between various communities of color. Angie's character also opens up the possibility for community education and its connections to an oral tradition as opposed to the bourgeois model of education in which legitimate knowledge always comes through an educational system which, itself, is part of an oppressive state apparatus.

T.C., on the other hand, provides a reading of the contemporary crisis in terms of a critique of capitalism. According to T.C., it is the "profit lovers" and their ability to mobilize the state apparatuses (welfare, penal system, etc.) who have caused "all the wrong deeds and doings you see in the world today" and have "subjected" blacks "to slavery in all its many faces." With T.C. we see a kind of conversion experience as he goes, at the beginning of the film, from believing that a job might end his bad dreams, to incarceration, and finally, once inside the penal system where he "[puts] a lot of broken things in [his] past together," to politicization and a "concrete foundation" of resistance.[16] Combined with this critique, T.C. also explains how oppression has been reproduced historically in his discussion of the prison guard (letter number one) and, especially, in one of Dorothy's dream sequences in which the church preacher has been replaced by the militant T.C. who asks the congregation, "How can you grab your tools and liberate God yo'self?" In this sequence T.C. recounts a history of the police state in which "the rope was replaced by the electric chair, the electric chair by the gas chamber, and the gas chamber by the firing squads on the boulevards of America."

Yet for all its accuracy in describing the "warfare state," T.C.'s narrative cannot adequately speak of or to Dorothy's experiences or, by itself, provide sufficient tools for resistance. Whereas Angie's history lessons have an increasing influence on Dorothy through the film, T.C.'s preaching seems to have just the opposite effect. Though he may be speaking the "truth," T.C. gradually moves from speaking *to* Dorothy to speak *at* her. In each of his first two letters he expresses his affection for Dorothy and tells her that "everything starts at home, mama" (Letter #2). But by the third letter T.C.'s critique of the commodification of African American culture crowds out any intimacy. Gerima emphasizes the distance that T.C.'s increasingly politicized and impersonal tone puts between T.C. and Dorothy in his choice of camera angles. For the first letter, Gerima uses an eye-level headshot and then dollies down the prison hallway. By the second letter, Gerima has switched to a low-angle shot in which T.C., literally, talks down to Dorothy. Gerima's cut to straight-on close-ups of T.C. behind the bars of his cell twice in this sequence tends to disrupt T.C.'s authority. But Gerima's return to the low-angle shot and his cut to a close-up of the despondent Dorothy reassert her indifference to his preaching. And finally, as T.C. reads the third letter, Gerima chooses not to show him. Instead, his words float in on the sound track to Dorothy, who sits on the bed in a medium long-shot with her back to the camera. Gerima, then, layers T.C.'s voice onto shots of

Dorothy cleaning the apartment. This move, I believe, reflects the inadequacy of T.C.'s rap to explain and speak of what Kimberlé Crenshaw has described as "the place where African American women live, a political vacuum of erasure and contradiction maintained by the almost routine polarization of 'blacks and women.'"[17] While T.C. can speak of racial oppression in terms of the black male and state-sponsored terrorism, he does little or nothing to address the kind of oppression that confines Dorothy and, which Crenshaw asserts, "is a location whose very nature resists telling."

Though T.C.'s political and economic critiques may be inadequate to telling Dorothy's story and thus an insufficient foundation for resistance, Simmi provides yet another narrative for Dorothy. Yet, unlike T.C. who, though he might offer the critique necessary for resistance, cannot create the kind of sustenance that resistance needs to perpetuate itself, Simmi understands the struggle can only happen in the context of community. When Dorothy first goes to Simmi, asking her advice about the abortion, Simmi tells her that she has "this idea of togetherness" that extends beyond Dorothy and Simmi to include "the whole neighborhood." As Simmi puts it, "the only way we can make it better is to keep us together and to have more black people. We have got to have togetherness and we have to have more bodies." As if to show her willingness to accept Simmi's notion of togetherness, in the scene right after Dorothy goes to the clinic but decides not to have the abortion, we see her imagining hugging the young boy who stole her purse at the beginning of the film.

Right after this scene, Gerima cuts to the restaurant where Simmi, speaking to her son, gives an extraordinary analysis of political organization and activism. As she tries to calm her son down, she tells him that

> We had all the things you got. We had blackness. We had justices. We had rights and wrongs. We had niggerness. We had all them things. But the thing we didn't have was a plan. Calculation. Uh huh. And to have that you need togetherness. So what you need to do is get all your friends together and have calculation and togetherness.

Here Simmi details a plan not simply for resistance as critique but resistance as a practice grounded in the idea of *communities* of struggle. Simmi goes on to insert into this a critique of capitalism when she speaks of getting "a big hunk of Uncle Sam's pie," but again it is rooted in community action. For Simmi the identity politics of "blackness" and "niggerness" will not suffice to deal with the present crisis. Identity only becomes effective in combination with a group identification as well as a grounding in theory or "calculation." In this scene, Gerima underscores the effect that Simmi's narrative has on Dorothy as she is finally able to address Molly's cynicism with more than "T.C. says. . . ." Instead,

Gerima connects Simmi's speech to her son with Dorothy's reaction by using a rack focus as the camera zooms out to show Dorothy as she rejects Molly's position because, I would argue, Simmi's narrative more accurately describes the crisis as Dorothy experiences it and projects a path for agency and action.

Through the film, Gerima shows that no single narrative is sufficient to the task of narrating the crisis to Dorothy in such a way that she can begin to formulate her own resistance. It is, rather, through a combination of Angie's historical understanding of the connections between African liberation and the crisis of the crisis state, T.C.'s critique of capitalism, and Simmi's plan for the practice of resistance that Dorothy can fashion her own resistance. In presenting multiple narratives, insufficient in themselves yet powerful when assembled into a entire picture of resistance, Gerima resists the idea of a master narrative of opposition and liberation. Part of the community's strength lies in its ability to generate multiple narratives which all, in some particularity, address the crisis and provide the space, small as it may be, for a critique and resistance to dominant narratives.

Cinematic Resistance

> Mainstream cinema is now novocaine, helpless and dependent. I want the viewer to participate. We should believe in debate and find our errors and solutions there. In making a film I try equally to combat an aesthetic that is enslaving human beings by, for example, violating the codes of cinema, and, at the same time, creating a structure in which the spectator can become an active participant. What kind of structure equally combats the conventions, makes people grow, and makes Hollywood accountable to humans? All this is a part of independent filmmaking. (Gerima, qtd. in Safford and Triplett, 61)

To this point I've tried to show how, in Dorothy's search for narratives that will adequately explain, define, and describe crisis as she knows it, that she rejects a number of dominant narratives. But, to end a discussion of *Bush Mama* with a critical examination of its content would be to miss the representational resistance inherent in Gerima's brand of independent filmmaking. We can be sure that as Gerima speaks of the "aesthetic that is enslaving human beings" embodied in mainstream cinema, that he means, in part, to critique the "escapist world outlook" that seeks to impose an entire set of universal representations "invented only to benefit in all aspects the Eurocentric world order" (Gerima, 71). However, I do not want to jump too hastily to the conclusion that Gerima provides the viewer with truer representations than those characteristic of Hollywood cinema because notions of truth tend to overdetermine realist representational practices. While it may be true that resistant filmmaking, insofar as it sets before itself the gargantuan task of destabilizing and delegitimizing whole bodies of social knowledge, must seek to recode and redefine those realities set forth within domain narratives, we cannot assume that this dictate entails simply providing a closer approximation to some reality "out there." To do so would mean (at the very least) to risk the all-too-common situation in cinema in which representation slides into representativeness—and, certainly, in a semiotic field full of monolithic constructions of subordinated peoples, such representativeness only plays back into such dominant codes.

But for all his desire to fundamentally change the terrain on which we debate black presence within urban space, Gerima never falls into this realist trap. Though he may speak of a brand of reality central to his own representational practices, it is always a "symbolic reality" that is meant not to impose narrative closure on a set of explanations for what it means to be, in this instance, poor, black, unemployed, and female but to interrogate the point at which, "when a black human functions how . . . he or she fit[s] into the context of symbols" (Gerima, in Safford and Triplett, 62). In *Bush Mama*, Gerima disrupts realist illusions of narrative transparency and closure by calling attention to the labor necessary in the construction of a narrative.[18] While I've already discussed what I take to be the most prominent of these moments in *Bush Mama*, the point at which T.C. goes from a job interview to prison, there are several others, including the non-narrative sequences showing Dorothy walking, the two shots of a group of people standing on a street that frame the scene in which Luann is raped by the LAPD officer, and Gerima's use of photographic evidence throughout *Bush Mama.*

Though I do not have the space to discuss all the disruptive moments in the film, I'd like to focus on the two posters that Angie gives Dorothy: one of the man murdered by the LAPD and the other of the African liberation fighter. Recalling that Angie brings the poster to Dorothy's apartment from a neighborhood demonstration, we can see how the first poster provides both visual evidence of state-sponsored terrorism as well as a symbolic focus for protest. As the story progresses, however, it becomes apparent that the photograph functions on a number of other levels as well. Gerima repeatedly uses it to undercut various characters' assertions of autonomy. Though the drunk man insists repeatedly that "the white man never mess with me," and the "Prince of Dahomey" tells of his royal feast, the poster contextualizes their remarks and, even as it undercuts these characters' statements, provides a description of the policing that produces such delusional fantasies. The poster also acts as a symbolic conjunction with Gerima's syntax. Rather than rely on more traditional diegetic elements to draw parallels between police murders, and, for instance, Dorothy's impending abortion, Gerima uses parallel shot sequences to establish this connection. Between shots of Dorothy lying on an examination table in the abortion clinic, Gerima cuts to slow pans of the corpse's bloated belly. And the juxtaposition of the poster with, presumably, the photo of Dorothy's husband in a military uniform certainly serves to draw a connection between the police murder and her husband's death in the Vietnam War.

The photographic evidence that Gerima utilizes in *Bush Mama* is interesting not only because of its status and functions within the narrative but also because of how it moves in opposition to more traditional functions of photographic evidence (documentary photography) in discourses surrounding the poor. In the United States, photographic documentation of the poor finds its most immediate roots in the New Deal era and, more specifically, in the photographic production of the Farm Security Administration (FSA). The pervasiveness of such images extends to the point that the Great Depression and the huge dislocations of U.S. agrarian populations are, now, largely understood as a series of images of barren land, breadlines, and forced migration. But, as John Tagg has noted, these representations, meant to make the massive restructuring of the U.S. agrarian economy visually concrete, far from constituting the actions of a benevolent government, actually sought to legitimize the state apparatus and the particular forms of social control entailed in the welfare state. In Tagg's view,

> Central to [the welfare state], therefore, was an emergent formation of institutions, practices and representations which furnished means for training and surveilling bodies in great numbers, while seeking to instill in them a self-regulating discipline and to position them as dependent in relation to supervisory apparatuses through which the interventions of the state appeared both benevolent and disinterested. (9)

Certainly, this passage echoes Piven and Cloward's identification of the labor-regulating functions of the welfare state and meshes, as well, with the social problem/social control approaches to dealing with the poor. Against this discursive legacy of representing the poor Gerima uses photographic evidence to deny the legitimacy of the state apparatus's poli-cing and controlling activities. The poster of the dead black man completely subverts the notion of a benevolent state as well as turns the practice of surveillance against those who use it.

The poster of the African freedom fighter functions quite differently. Whereas the first poster provides a critique and a focus for protest to state-sponsored terrorism, the second gives Dorothy a means of visually constituting her own resistance. Just as T.C.'s narrative stands in relation to Simmi's, so the two posters provide photographic evidence crucial to Dorothy's transformation. Unlike the poster of the man murdered by the police, which simply delegitimizes any notion of a welfare state, the poster of the African woman works toward a recoding of what black bodies mean within representational politics. Rather than being a site of deprivation, pain, despair, and victimization, this image embodies a very material form of political and social insurgency. In the conversation between Angie and Luann when Angie first brings the poster to the apartment, she calls the woman in the photograph "the mother of all of us." Luann responds.

> LUANN: She ain't my mama. My mama don't look like that.
>
> ANGIE: Girl, she's your mother mother. The original mother of all of us.
>
> LUANN: She got a baby. She got a gun. She must be stronger than my mama.

Clearly, here, we can see the transformation of the twin signs of black and female in Luann's mind, yet this scene only anticipates Dorothy's eventual transformation. Though Molly may attempt to insert the photograph of the African woman back into her own narrative of "niggers goin' crazy," Gerima follows this scene with that of Dorothy assessing the photograph and what it might mean for her. Finally, by the end of the film, when the transformation has been complete and "the wig is off [her] head" we see how Dorothy herself becomes the photographic evidence of resistance embodied in the poster. As he pulls from the poster to Dorothy in a rack focus and then freezes the frame, Gerima creates, from Dorothy and her story, a further image of resistance.

In both uses of photographic evidence, Gerima takes a form much more closely associated with the documentary mode of filmmaking and inserts it into a fictional narrative. By doing this, I do not believe that Gerima simply attempts to bring the facticity and realism associated with documentary to his fictional account; rather he disrupts the audience's tendency to assume the functioning of dominant cinematic codes of representation. Wedged into the gap between documentary and fiction, *Bush Mama* questions the validity of the construction of a monolithic reality. Gerima neither attempts to explain and present an unmediated reality that has an indexical relation to the historical world nor to represent and approximate that world within fictive cinematic space. Instead, Gerima positions his film in a separate space which, though it may occasionally approach or borrow from those two supposed poles of filmic representation, tries to tell Dorothy's story within a cultural context other than that inherited from dominant traditions. The audience can never be certain whether the photographs are real or if they have been staged and shot simply for the film. And insofar as the audience cannot be sure of the status of these photographic images, so these images suspend questions of authenticity and reality, which, otherwise, become central to cultural productions and representations of subordinated peoples. Gerima focuses doggedly on transformation and so even as we examine and interrogate Dorothy's transformation within the context of an oppressive political economy complete with state-sponsored terrorism and control, we witness Gerima's transformation of the filmic medium from a tool of political and social legitimation and hegemonic maintenance to one of cultural resistance.

NOTES

1. For a detailed biographical and critical overview of Gerima's work, see Pfaff in *Twenty-Five Black African Directors.*

2. In "The Documentary Impulse in African-American Film" Valerie Smith uses this phrase to describe a "strong documentary impulse [that] is evident in much contemporary black filmmaking" (Smith, *Black Popular Culture,* 57).

3. Gerima first hints at this when, in one of the shots of the poster of the man killed by the police, the camera pans to a photo of another man in combat fatigues. Then, when Dorothy is being "questioned" at the end of the film, the interrogator mentions her husband: "Good kid. Fought in Vietnam. Won a medal of honor.—Lays his life on the line for you and your little whores." The fact that Dorothy's husband has been killed in Vietnam is important because of the way that it frames her "dependence" on the state and because it disproves the rap group members' claim, at the beginning of the movie, that she married a bum.

4. I plan to come back to this scene later for a longer discussion.

5. Antonio Negri, in "Crisis of the Crisis-State," speaks of crisis as a form that capitalism uses to guarantee control of subordinate classes through a combination of policing and control techniques as the Keynesian state-planner form gives way to more explicitly authoritarian forms in which "development is now planned in terms of ideologies of scarcity and austerity" (181).

6. Stuart Hall et al., *Policing the Crisis: Mugging, the State and Law and Order* (New York: Holmes and Meier, 1978), 339.

7. Gerima's addition of the helicopter to the sound track implies the kind of surveillance and containment common to policing of the urban poor.

8. According to Negri, in such a situation the "needs of the proletariat and the poor are now *rigidly* subordinated to the necessities of capitalist reproduction" (181–82, my emphasis) and "the state has an array of military and repressive means available (army, police, legal, etc.) to exclude from this arena all forces that do not offer unconditional obedience to its austerity-based material constitution and to the static reproduction of class relations that goes with it."

9. I plan to speak of the aesthetics that underlie this choice as well, later in the essay.

10. It is interesting to note that the sound track often functions as a narrative device within the film. The audience would not know what has happened to T.C. or to Dorothy without the two songs that explain T.C.'s imprisonment and Dorothy's pregnancy.

11. In case the contemporary relevance of this film is lost in the fact that *Bush Mama* was made almost twenty years ago, recall the push to make Norplant a condition for female recipients of AFDC.

12. Though we get none of the traditional markers for locating and contextualizing this scene (dialogue, establishing shots, etc.) I read it as a "therapy" session that recipients of AFDC are required to attend.

13. Daniel P. Moynihan, *The Negro Family: The Case for National Action* (Washington, D.C.: U.S. Department of Labor, 1965).

14. The drunk man exemplifies the kind of welfare dependence ("I got me a welfare job") the New Right and neoconservatives love to point to.

15. Haki R. Madhubuti, "Missing Movement, Missing Fathers: The Culture of Short Lives and Low Expectations," in *Why L.A. Happened,* ed. Haki R. Madhubuti (Chicago: Third World Press, 1992).

16. I think Gerima intends to pun on the fact that T.C. is in prison, but he also points to the very real potential for politicization through criminalization.

17. Kimberlé Crenshaw, "Whose Story Is It, Anyway? Feminist and Antiracist Appropriations of Anita Hill," in *Race-ing Justice, En-gendering Power: Essays on Anita Hill, Clarence Thomas, and the Construction of Social Reality,* ed. Toni Morrison (New York: Pantheon, 1992), 403.

18. I've borrowed, here, from Kobena Mercer in his discussion of the "'reality effect'" and recent developments in black British independent filmmaking ("Diaspora Culture," 53–54).

WORKS CITED

Bush Mama. Written and directed by Haile Gerima. With Barbara O. Jones, Johnny Weathers, Susan Williams, Cora Lee Day, Simmi Ella Nelson, Bettie J. Wilson, Bob Ogburn Jr., and Ben Collins. Haile Gerima, 1976.

Crenshaw, Kimberlé. "Whose Story Is It, Anyway? Feminist and Antiracist Appropriations of Anita Hill." In *Race-ing Justice, En-gendering Power: Essays on Anita Hill, Clarence Thomas, and the Construction of Social Reality.* Ed. Toni Morrison. New York: Pantheon, 1992.

Gerima, Haile. "'Fireplace-Cinema' (Gathering, Warming, Sharing)." *Filmfaust* May–June 1984: 44–54.

___. "Triangular Cinema, Breaking Toys, and Dinkesh versus Lucy." In *Questions of Third Cinema.* Ed. Jim Pines and Paul Willeman. London: The British Film Institute, 1989. 65–89.

Hall, Stuart, et al. *Policing the Crisis: Mugging, the State and Law and Order.* New York: Holmes and Meier, 1978.

Howard, Steve. "A Cinema of Transformation: The Films of Haile Gerima." *Cinéaste* 14, no. 1 (1985): 28–29, 39.

Mercer, Kobena. "Diaspora Culture and the Dialogic Imagination: The Aesthetics of Black Independent Film in Britain." In *BLACKFRAMES: Critical Perspectives in Black Independent Cinema.* Ed. Mybe B. Cham and Claire Andrade-Watkins. Cambridge, Mass.: MIT Press, 1988. 50–61.

Negri, Antonio. *Revolution Retrieved: Writings on Marx, Keynes, Capitalist Crisis and New Social Subjects (1967–1983).* London: Red Notes, 1988.

Pfaff, Françoise. *Twenty-Five Black African Filmmakers.* Westport, Conn.: Greenwood Press, 1988.

Piven, Francis Fox, and Richard A. Clower. *the Poor: The Functions of Public Welfare.* 1971. New York: Vintage, 1993.

Smith, Valerie. "The Documentary Impulse in Contemporary U.S. African-American Film." In *Black Popular Culture.* Ed. Gina Dent. Seattle: Bay Press, 1992. 56–64.

Stafford, Tony, and William Triplett. "Haile Gerima: Radical Departures to a New Black Cinema." *Journal of the University Film and Video Association* 35, no. 2 (1983): 59–65.

Tagg, John. *The Burden of Representation: Essays on Photographies and Histories.* Amherst: University of Massachusetts Press, 1988.

Taylor, Clyde. "Decolonizing the Image: New U.S. Black Cinema." In *Jump Cut.* Ed. Peter Steven. New York: Praeger, 1985.

Valerie Smith

Telling Family Secrets:
Narrative and Ideology in
Suzanne Suzanne

During the past twenty years or so, black feminist writers have turned their attention increasingly to the family, broadly defined, as a site at which black women and children suffer the varied and conjoined effects of racist and patriarchal exploitation. Nineteenth-century black feminist theorists such as Anna Julia Cooper and Ida B. Wells denounced the large-scale cultural racism and sexism that impeded black women's access to the franchise, education, and the professions, but said little about the ways in which misogyny and patriarchy shaped the domestic lives of black women. Early- to mid-twentieth-century black women writers of imaginative literature such as Jessie Fauset, Zora Neale Hurston, and Nella Larsen articulated some of the ways in which the institution of marriage limited the options available to black women. But as Deborah E. McDowell and Patricia Hill Collins, among others, have indicated, only in recent years have writers such as Toni Morrison, Audre Lorde, Alice Walker, Angela Davis, Gayl Jones, Ntozake Shange, Michele Wallace, bell hooks, and Pearl Cleage mounted more trenchant and explicit critiques of black women's vulnerability to domestic violence.[1] Increasingly, they have addressed as well what Shange calls the "conspiracy of silence" that constructs as disloyal or anti-male any black feminist attempt to name the vulnerability of black women to abuse at the hands of black men.[2] Although this kind of secrecy is at least partly an overcompensation for mainstream associations of black masculinity with immorality and violence, Hill Collins is right to equate this silence with "the bond of family secrecy that often pervades dysfunctional families," thereby enabling the abuses to continue.[3]

This group of black feminist writers thus replaces narratives of black consensus and unity, predicated on women's silence, with narratives

Originally appeared in *Multiple Voices in Feminist Film Criticism*, ed. Diane Carson, Linda Dittmar, and Janice Welsch (Minnesota: University of Minnesota Press, 1994). Used by permission of the author.

of disruption and dissent. They reconceptualize the idealized notion of a monolithic black community; as such they interrogate the family romance on which this notion of community relies.[4]

In her recent essay "Reading Family Matters," McDowell likewise situates within the context of a family romance the virulently misogynist response on the part of some black male critics to the work of some black feminist writers. Offering a detailed critique of certain reviews of the work of Wallace, Shange, Morrison, Jones, and Walker, McDowell shows that these writers have been excoriated since the mid-1970s for exposing male abuses within "the family," be it the nuclear family or the broader black community. McDowell suggests that to the extent that these writers belie the family romance—"the story of the black family cum black community headed by the black male who does battle with an oppressive white world"[5]—they are represented by certain male critics as traitors to the race who are overly influenced by the white feminist agenda. To the extent that within their texts they problematize the status of the nuclear or racialized family, they are constructed as errant daughters by some members of the black literary establishment.

Such criticism notwithstanding, it is of course crucial that black feminists continue to shatter the secrecy that surrounds the issue of domestic violence within black communities. As Judith Lewis Herman, Lorde, Linda Gordon, Wallace, hooks, Davis, and many others have argued, naming the prevalence of domestic violence with any racial group or economic class profoundly threatens public consciousness and patriarchal values.[6] Naming domestic violence constitutes a refusal to mask the ways in which ideologies of race, class, and gender conspire to subjugate women who are physically, economically, or psychologically vulnerable.

To borrow Kimberlé Williams Crenshaw's formulation, within the context of domestic violence, the intersectionality of racial and gendered hierarchies makes itself evident.[7] Precisely because of the complex culture and psychopathological forces that enable domestic violence to continue, it is an area sorely in need of feminist interventions. Black feminist interventions are especially critical in analyzing domestic violence within black communities, since they illuminate the specific impact of constructions of blackness on the abuse to which men submit women. By this light, black feminist analyses of the nexus of classism, misogyny, and racism might enable a discourse around black domestic violence that constructs black men simultaneously as victims of racism and perpetrators of physical abuse; that locates individual responsibility within the context of oppressive cultural circumstances and conditioning; that explores the sexualization of race and class oppression; that examines the subtle mechanism of black women's own internalized self-loathing; and that critiques constructions of masculinity and femininity more broadly. Continued silence, by contrast, perpetuates the circumstances that allow the abuses to continue and isolates victims and victimizers alike.

Many readers are familiar with black feminist theoretical and "literary" critiques of black women's victimization within heterosexual domestic configurations. Black feminist directors are no less concerned with breaking the silence around women's exploitation, but their work is less widely accessible than is that of their counterparts who work in the medium of print. *Suzanne, Suzanne,* independently produced and directed by Camille Billops and James V. Hatch, provides a compelling example of the nature of black feminist cinematic work that addresses the issue of domestic violence.[8] A 16mm black-and-white documentary shot in 1977 and released in 1982, the film places the narrative of physical and drug abuse in a specific family within the context of a more expansive critique of the nuclear family. The demystification both of this family and of the idea of the middle-class family is achieved within the context of a nonfiction film that repeatedly destabilizes the status of the truth. In this discussion of the film I examine how *Suzanne, Suzanne's* interrogation of the space between the "real" and the "fictional" functions within the film's critique of a specific family and the myth of the normative, nuclear family.

The extracinematic circumstances that led to the production of *Suzanne, Suzanne* remind us that no documentary is ever "true" or "objective"; the "truth" is inevitably constructed. Billops and Hatch undertook this film intending it to be the story of Billops' niece Suzanne Browning's battle against drug addiction. During the course of their interviews with Suzanne and other relatives, the story of Suzanne's and her mother's—Billops's sister Billie's—experiences of abuse emerged. The film that was to situate Suzanne as a recovered drug addict thus became additionally, if not instead, an exploration of the suffering to which women are vulnerable in the nuclear family. The filmmakers then constructed an implicit narrative forged from sequencing, crosscutting, and the interpolation of still photographs and footage from home movies that identifies domestic violence as a major factor in Suzanne's addiction.

The film begins with a still photograph of Brownie (the abusive husband and father) lying in repose in his coffin. First in a voice-over and then on camera, Suzanne reflects on her turbulent and ambivalent relationship with her father. In the opening sequence, Suzanne's comments are crosscut with her mothers' on-camera reflections about her own profoundly mixed feelings about her late husband. Throughout much of the film, in scenes shot in and around the family home in Los Angeles, Suzanne, Billie, Michael (their respective son and brother), and the grandparents answer Billops's questions about topics such as the importance of fashion and beauty to the women in the household; Suzanne's addiction and criminal behavior; and Brownie's abuse of his wife and daughter. The characters for the most part speak to Billops, the codirector and interviewer. However, in two powerful scenes that occur late in the film, Billie and Suzanne talk to each other in a highly stylized context. In these scenes, the two women appear to achieve some recognition of the relationship between their experiences of abuse.

The film is composed of at least three different representational modes: twenty-five still photographs; eight clips from Bell & Howell home movies taken by Walter ("Mr.") Dotson, Billie's and Billops's stepfather; and the frame of the film, which includes the interviews and the music and possesses the authority of sound.[9] By negotiating the relationship among these three modes through juxtaposition and crosscutting, the filmmakers produce their cinematic narrative as well as the critique that underlies that narrative.

In an interview with playwright-director George C. Wolfe, Billops says that she and Hatch "could not arrive at what the film was about until [she] told their editor . . . about Mr. Dotson's home movies." She continues: "These were the missing pieces that gave the film its focus. . . . [The home movies] gave the family a history."[10] The footage and photographs certainly function to place the characters within a generational, class, and regional context. They also produce much of the narrative tension in the film, by prompting questions about how the beaming young girl shown at age eight becomes the adult addict, how the seemingly stable family becomes fractured.

What is perhaps most striking about these interpolated images is their familiarity. Several of them fix moments that have become ritualized within the construction of the nuclear family: pictures of Brownie smiling, embracing his children; footage of the family off to church in their Sunday best; a photograph of the dead Brownie lying in repose in his open coffin; footage of Billie holding Camille's infant daughter, Christa—all establish the family in familiar middle-class respectability. These pieces of documentary evidence thus memorialize a picture-perfect family, one whose history might be reconstructed out of the photographic record of public events: holiday celebrations, deaths, births, and so on.

And yet it is precisely the familiarity of these images that the film contests. If viewers were to rely solely on spoken critiques of the family romance, we would perhaps be less likely to consider our own implication in what Annette Kuhn calls the "signification process."[11] However, the silent record of the still photographs and the home movies encodes a subtext of family stability and safety that viewers interpret and that Billops and Hatch's film challenges. The juxtaposition of

Suzanne's and Billie's stories with the images from the family history prompts viewers to question both the process by which we attribute meanings to images as well as the explanatory power of certain rituals. Perhaps more important, the use of these materials enables the film to address at once the psychopathology of this particular family as well as the nature of the oppressive cultural weight that the image of the nuclear family bears.

The inequitable distribution of power within the nuclear family that, taken to its outer limits, allows husbands to tyrannize their wives and children is here the most obvious cause of the family's circumstances and Suzanne's addiction. However, the internalized effects of the commodification of women's bodies within a gendered and racialized hierarchy are shown to have produced substantial psychological damage as well. The world of fashion and beauty culture as represented in the film clearly provided an opportunity for women to control their labor and express their creativity: Billie and her mother, Alma, share a gift for sewing and fashion design; both love the opportunity for self-display that performing in fashion shows allows. These activities are thus to some degree emancipatory; however, they contribute to a climate in which the value of women and children is located in their appearance and objectification.

Within the film, Michael, Suzanne's brother, is assigned value both because of his status as only son and eldest child, and also because he has inherited what the family considers his mother's good looks. He is introduced as Suzanne's "handsome brother," and he appears grooming his oversize moustache in the bathroom mirror three of the times he is evident in the film. Clearly delighted with his appearance, he grows and waxes a moustache that is a virtual parody of itself, and takes pride in the comments his mother wrote in his baby book. Suzanne, on the other hand, says that she grew up believing herself to be ugly. She inherited Browning, not Billops, features—what she calls "puffy eyes, sorta set back into the head." The still photographs suggest that her sense of being unattractive may bear a particular racial valence, for she has broader features, coarser hair, and darker skin than does her mother. While Michael can delight in the pride Billie took in his good looks, Suzanne recalls the humiliation of being considered less attractive than her mother.

In the scene, Billie applies makeup to Suzanne's face until the two of them discuss issues having to do with their respective appearances. Visually and discursively, this scene dramatizes the extent to which Suzanne may have felt betrayed by her mother. This scene recalls its earlier counterpart in which Billie applies makeup to her mother Alma's face while both are facing the camera. The two women are positioned in that earlier instance—Billie bending over Alma's shoulder to apply her blush—so that both may be introduced to the viewer. In the latter scene, however, which focuses explicitly on the issue of appearance, Suzanne's face is turned away, hidden, from the camera while her mother, facing the camera, applies her makeup. The staging of this scene allows greater access to Billie's confident subjectivity while concealing and thereby reinforcing Suzanne's expression of her self-loathing. Furthermore, it provides a visual counterpart for the story Billie and Suzanne recount during the scene.

The two women describe the reactions of Suzanne's friends upon meeting Billie:

> BILLIE: In the very beginning, I didn't really pay that much attention to it. But then, later on, I began to watch Suzanne's face when she would say to her friends, "I want you to meet my mother." And they'd say, "Oh, how do you do Mrs. Browning?" And then they'd turn and say, "Well, what the hell ever happened to you?" And that would just really get to me. I didn't like it, because they were making too much of a comparison. And I realized at that time that Suzanne did not like that at all.

> CAMILLE BILLOPS: Suzanne, did you believe that?

> SUZANNE: What they were saying? Sure. You know, I knew it. Because when I looked at my mom . . . you know my mother was beautiful . . . you know she's still a beautiful woman. You know, I got a really big complex from that. I thought I was extremely ugly.

By the standard of physical attractiveness, Suzanne always loses to her mother, her self-esteem always negated. Billie seems strikingly unaware of the destructive power of her investment in appearance. Her secondhand disapproval of Suzanne's friends' response to her exposes her insensitivity—she noticed that the comparison between her daughter's and her own looks was inappropriate only when she perceived Suzanne's pain, when she realized that "Suzanne did not like that at all." It is striking as well that on the heels of Suzanne's admission that she felt less attractive than her mother, Billie boasts about having entered the Mrs. America contest of 1979. The sequencing here—the makeup scene, Billie's displaying of her beauty pageant photograph, Michael's grooming of his moustache—exemplifies the nature of the causal links that the filmmaker sought to establish and suggests a closer connection between mother and son than that between mother and daughter. The staging and sequencing in these scenes exemplify the ways in which the filmmakers impose a specific interpretation on the experiences described.

Mr. Dotson's Bell & Howell home movies enact the commodification of women and children that Billops and Hatch's film critiques.

Virtually all the footage from these films centers on women and children, under the proprietary, controlling gaze of the male—the absent father—behind the camera. Displayed in Easter finery or in scenes of domestic delight, they are signs of the family's, particularly the father's, achievement.

Suzanne, Suzanne, however, is the product not of the father behind the camera but of a daughter with her partner/codirector and cinematographer. Here, women and children are not silent collaborators within a family romance. Rather, they speak in response to questions that Billops poses or that they pose themselves. Moreover, while cinematographer Dion Hatch, like Mr. Dotson, is not visible within this film, Billops, one of two producer-directors, is both audible and, more important, visible. Twice she appears standing side by side in the mirror with Michael. The image of a woman with braids and a faint but discernible moustache, standing beside a man waxing his moustache, also deconstructs conventional standards of beauty that the film problematizes elsewhere.[12]

Billops' appearance in the mirror reminds the viewer of the constructedness of the film and the cinematic process. It is also a figure for the black feminist intervention within the family romance. Simultaneously director and subject, relative and observer, insider and outsider, she occupies the position from which the multiple manipulations of parents, sons, and daughters are visible.

Camille Billops' liminal role as both subject and observer is evident at the juncture of cinematic and extracinematic discourse. Within the film, Billops appears in Bell & Howell footage as the young mother of an infant daughter, Christa. As these scenes appear, Camille and this same daughter, now an adult, sing the title song, which Christa composed. However, as Billops and Hatch's most recent film, *Finding Christa* (1991), recounts, the space between birth and duet is occupied by a narrative that is, in its own way, as disturbing as Suzanne's. Christa's father is absent from these scenes not because he is behind the camera, but because he has abandoned his family. In the years between birth and duet, Billops, a single mother, determined that she was unable to care for Christa adequately and gave her up for adoption when the child was four years old. The choices enacted in this extracinematic narrative further critique the images of motherhood and family enshrined within the Bell & Howell home movies; the narrative of this fragmented family anticipates the story told in *Finding Christa.*

Through juxtapositions and the multiple interrogations of its material, the story that *Suzanne Suzanne* tells problematizes the potentially destructive nature of the middle-class nuclear family; the film's discourses work to dismantle the image of the ideal family created by the photographs and home movies. Indeed, the inclusion of these materials in the film interrogates their very status as evidence. However much one might wish to read photographic images as denotative—signs of what really existed—they too are fictive constructs; like the techniques of cinematic or literary realism, they represent a body of conventions that privileges particular ideological positions. The shot of Alma and her granddaughters going off to church—the one in an elegant suit, the other in dresses with crinoline slips—memorializes an eminently readable image of family harmony, recalling the popular conception of the ostensibly religious nuclear family: the family that stays together because it prays together. Given the subtext of family violence, however, this Bell & Howell moment suggests the central role of performance and imitation in the ways that families, like individuals, construct their identities.

These considerations about the place of performance within real life, and about the artificiality of documentary evidence, shape the ways we interpret the two scenes between Billie and Suzanne that are set in a darkened room, with the two women, shot from midchest up, simultaneously facing the camera.[13] This darkened space provides an alternative to the domestic locations used for the rest of the film—rooms that recall the past history of family relations. In striking contrast to the scenes that are shot in and around Alma and Walter Dotson's Los Angeles home, these dark, stark, partially scripted scenes are constructed as pivotal and self-consciously dramatic. In this setting, the relationship between mother and daughter is altered dramatically.

Billops says that Hatch provided Suzanne with a list of questions to ask her mother in these scenes. One such question is the one with which Suzanne begins: "Do you love me?" By providing Suzanne with a list of questions, Hatch and Billops allow her to assume the role of interviewer. But at some point, Billops says, Suzanne began to ask her own questions, assuming the role of both interviewer and director. This recollection is confirmed by the transcript of unused footage from an interview in which Suzanne admits that she used this occasion to ask some of her own questions:

> BILLIE [BB]: I knew that in the very beginning it was going to stir up something, but I thought, well Suzanne and I, we have never really talked. . . . I didn't know what was going to happen. . . . Yesterday . . . the last thing I ever wanted to do was to cry. . . . I didn't know that she was going to ask me about did I know what it felt like to be on death row. . . .

> SUZANNE: . . . It wasn't Jim. . . . I told you Sunday, I have questions—of my own. You know, there's like a lot of things that come to my head. You know, and I wanted an answer. . . . I was there to ask some of those things.

Up until the exchange between Billie and Suzanne that we see in the film, the family members have, for the most part, answered the questions that are asked of them. But here Suzanne takes advantage of the context to address her own nagging concerns. And Billie uses the occasion to tell her own story. When Suzanne asks, for instance, if she'd like to know what it was like to wait on death row, Billie doesn't really respond to her, but rather explains both to herself and to her daughter why she would retreat into the shower whenever Brownie came home, answering the question she had posed indirectly earlier in the film.[14]

The staging of these scenes calls attention to their artificiality even as their sheer emotional power bestows on them a quality of authenticity. I am tempted to read these scenes as "real" at the moment when Suzanne asks if Billie's beatings were like being on death row. At this point, Billie's head shifts and her facial expression changes, apparently signaling a recognition of their shared circumstances. Not only were both victims of physical violence, but both also endured the psychological terror of imagining and awaiting each instance of Brownie's abuse. The sense of process evident here is coded as being more authentic than the communication that occurs in the rest of the film. But the very fact that the film exists within a frame that questions the "real" renders such a determination problematic. These scenes in the darkened space suggest minimally, however, that to the extent that domestic relations are captured (if not fabricated) in our interactions with private as well as public media, they might be reconstituted as well through the intervention of the artificial.

I have considered here ways in which the intersectionality of black feminist analysis inflects this narrative of domestic violence. *Suzanne, Suzanne* constitutes a cinematic discourse that interrogates a host of interconnections, those between cultural circumstances and individual responsibility, documents and ideology, truth and artificiality, and, indirectly, racism and misogyny. The film seeks to disrupt the facade of orderly respectability that depends on the conspiracy of silence within the family. Yet nowhere is the tension between the disruptive power of the cinematic process and the seductive power of the family romance more powerful than at the end of *Suzanne Suzanne,* where the film appears to satisfy viewers' desire for closure and healing.[15]

In the second of the "staged" scenes between Suzanne and Billie, Suzanne partially faces her mother and tells her about one particular beating when Brownie whipped her until she bled. This description is particularly harrowing, yet Billie seeks to recuperate Brownie's behavior by reassuring Suzanne that she was her father's favorite. Billie's explanation pales when contrasted with this vivid account; the juxtaposition reveals the price narrators and viewers alike pay for narrative closure and the sentimentalization of family.

NOTES

I wish to thank Marianne Hirsch, Clyde Taylor, Richard Yarborough, Linda Dittmar, Diane Carson, and Janice Welsch for their advice and help as I wrote and revised this essay. I am especially grateful to Camille Billops and James V. Hatch, without whose advice and encouragement I could never have undertaken this project.

1. Deborah E. McDowell, "Reading Family Matters," in *Changing Our Own Words: Essays on Criticism, Theory, and Writing by Black Women*, ed. Cheryl A. Wall (New Brunswick, N.J.: Rutgers University Press, 1989), 75–97; Patricia Hill Collins, *Black Feminist Thought: Knowledge, Consciousness, and the Politics of Empowerment* (Cambridge, Mass.: Unwin Hyman, 1991).

2. Interview with Claudia Tate quoted in Hill Collins, *Black Feminist Thought*, 187. A recent example of this kind of silencing occurred during the confirmation hearings of Supreme Court Justice Clarence Thomas. Various African American women and men believed that Professor Anita Hill was disloyal to the race for submitting Thomas to public scrutiny (and potential humiliation) by accusing him of sexual harassment. The misogyny of this response is evident in the presupposition that his embarrassment is considered inherently more damaging to African Americans than is the continued abuse Professor Hill allegedly underwent.

3. Ibid.

4. I draw here on Marianne Hirsch's version of Freud's definition of the family romance. Hirsch writes that "the family romance is the story we tell ourselves about the social and psychological reality of the family in which we find ourselves and about the patterns of desire that motivate the interaction among its members. . . . The notion of family romance can thus accommodate the discrepancies between *social reality* and *fantasy construction*, which are basic to the experience and the institution of family." See Marianne Hirsch, *The Mother/Daughter Plot: Narrative, Psychoanalysis, Feminism* (Bloomington: Indiana University Press, 1989), 9–10.

5. McDowell, "Reading Family Matters," 78.

6. Judith Lewis Herman, *Father–Daughter Incest* (Cambridge, Mass.: Harvard University Press, 1981); Audre Lorde, *Sister Outsider: Essays and Speeches* (Trumansburg, N.Y.: Crossing Press, 1984); Linda Gordon, *Heroes of Their Own Lives: The Politics and History of Family Violence* (New York: Penguin Books, 1988); Michele Wallace, *Black Macho and the Myth of the Superwoman* (New York: Dial, 1978); Wallace, *Invisibility Blues: From Pop to Theory* (New York: Verso, 1990); bell hooks, *Thinking Feminist, Thinking Black* (Boston, Mass.: South End Press, 1989); idem, *Yearning: Race, Gender, and Cultural Politics* (Boston, Mass.: South End Press, 1990); Angela Davis, *Women, Race, and Class* (New York: Vintage Books, 1993); Davis, *Women, Culture, and Politics* (New York: Random House, 1989).

7. Kimberlé Williams Crenshaw, "Demarginalizing the Intersection of Race and Sex: A Black Feminist Critique of Antidiscrimination Doctrine, Feminist Theory and Anti-racist Politics," *The University of Chicago Legal Forum* (1989): 139–67.

8. Another example is *Secret Sounds Screaming: The Sexual Abuse of Children* (1985 by Ayoka Chenzira.

9. Theresa L. Johnson produces this numerical breakdown in her unpublished essay "*Suzanne, Suzanne*: Oral History in a Visual Frame."

10. George C. Wolfe, "Camille Billops," *A Journal for the Artist* 6 (Spring 1986): 27.

11. Annette Kuhn, "Textual Politics," in *Issues in Feminist Film Criticism*, ed. Patricia Erens (Bloomington: Indiana University Press, 1990), 250.

12. I am grateful to Elizabeth Gregory for calling this detail to my attention.

13. Leo Spitzer first and then other viewers have remarked to me that the artificiality of this scene is heightened by the fact that the positioning of Billie and Suzanne within the frame recalls a similar scene with Ingmar Bergman's *Persona*.

14. Earlier in the film Billie says, "No matter what time it was, . . . the minute I heard [Brownie's] car door slam, I knew that he was drunk. So immediately, I'd get up and go get in the shower and cut the water on. I don't know what the water was doing for me, but I think it gave me time to compose my thoughts so I would have an answer for him, because I didn't know what he was going to say."

15. I thank Patricia Schechter for this observation.

Annotated Bibliography

Bambara, Toni Cade. 1993. "Reading the Signs, Empowering the Eye: *Daughters of the Dust* and the Black Independent Cinema Movement," in Manthia Diawara, ed., *Black American Cinema.* New York: Routledge, pp. 118–44. This nuanced essay positions the style, diasporic consciousness, feminism, and use of history in Julie Dash's film in relation to other work by LA rebellion filmmakers.

Bogle, Donald. 1973; rpt. 1989. *Toms, Coons, Mulattoes, Mammies, and Bucks.* New York: Continuum. Classic survey of images of African Americans in Hollywood pictures from *Birth of a Nation* through the late 1980s. Argues that despite superficial changes, many strategies of representation remain constant.

Chrisman, Robert. 1989. "What Is the Right Thing? Notes on the Deconstruction of Black Ideology," *The Black Scholar* 21:2, 53–57. Close reading of Lee's Do the Right Thing that focuses on its ideological ambivalence

Cripps, Thomas. 1977; rpt. 1993. *Slow Fade to Black: The Negro in American Film, 1900–1942.* New York: Oxford University Press. A social history of blacks on both sides of the camera until the early 1940s. Usefully positions race movies in relation to Hollywood representations of African Americans.

___. 1978. *Black Film as Genre.* Bloomington: Indiana University Press. Offers readings of six black genre films from *The Scar of Shame* through *Sweet Sweetback's Baadasssss Song.*

___. 1993. *Making Movies Black: The Hollywood Message Movie from World War II to the Civil Rights Era.* New York: Oxford University Press. The second of two volumes that explore the way in which changing ideas about race in U.S. culture inform the politics and strategies of representing blacks on screen.

Diawara, Manthia. 1988. "Black Spectatorship: Problems of Identification and Resistance," *Screen* 29:4, 66–81. Drawing on psychoanalytic and feminist film theories of spectatorship, this article examines the positionality of the black, resistant spectator through readings of several Hollywood movies. Includes an especially suggestive discussion of *Birth of a Nation.*

___. 1993. "*Noir* by *Noirs:* Toward a New Realism in Black Cinema," *African American Review* 27:4, 525–38. Through a richly textured, extended reading of Bill Duke's *A Rage in Harlem,* demonstrates how contemporary black-directed films influenced by film noir discourse revise the genre and the conventions by which it has historically represented and coded blackness.

George, Nelson. 1994. *Blackface: Reflections on African-Americans and the Movies.* New York: HarperCollins. An account of the author's development from viewer to producer. A well-known music critic, George offers compelling reflections on the relationship between the music industry and African Americans in films. Includes a movie time line featuring major African American cinematic ventures from the mid-1960s through the 1990s as well as provocative if brief commentary on the achievements of Sidney Poitier, Richard Pryor, and Spike Lee.

Gray, Herman. 1994. "Black Masculinity and Visual Culture," in Thelma Golden, ed., *Black Male: Representations of Masculinity in Contemporary American Art.* New York: Whitney Museum of American Art, pp. 175–80. Suggestive discussion of politics of black male self-representation in visual media as response to hegemonic constructions of black masculinity. Incorporates figures of black jazz men, hip hop artists, criminals, neo-nationalists, and heterosexual members of the middle class.

___. 1995. *Watching Race: Television and the Struggle for "Blackness."* Minneapolis, University of Minnesota Press. Informed by the theoretical assumptions of cultural studies, this book examines how ideas about blackness are constructed, reproduced, and critiqued in television. Focuses especially on selected 1980s sitcoms and offers insightful discussion of the interplay between these shows and media coverage of African American life.

Guerrero, Ed. 1991. "Negotiations of Ideology, Manhood, and the Family in Billy Woodberry's *Bless Their Little Hearts*," *Black American Literature Forum* 25:2, 315–22. A rich analysis of changes in the class and gender ideological positioning of Woodberry's protagonist. Explores how the craft of the film undergirds its content and assumptions.

___. 1993. *Framing Blackness: The African American Image in Film.* Philadelphia: Temple University press. Examines the shifting representations of African Americans in Hollywood films from *Birth of a Nation* through the early 1990s. Offers subtle readings of a broad array of films and offers valuable discussions of the power of the motion picture industry to shape representational practices.

Harper, Philip Brian. 1994. "Walk-on Parts and Speaking Subjects: Screen Representations of Black Gay Men," in Thelma Golden, ed., *Black Male: Representations of Masculinity in Contemporary American Art.* New York: Whitney Museum of American Art, pp. 141–48. Discussion of representations of African American gay men from the late 1960s until the present. Explores how these constructions, in both mainstream Hollywood and black-directed independent films, respond to hegemonic notions of race, sexuality, and gender identity.

Hartman, S. V., and Farah Jasmine Griffin. 1991 . "Are You as Colored as That Negro?: The Politics of Being Seen in Julie Dash's *Illusions*," *Black American Literature Forum* 25:2, 361–73. Through an insightful close reading of Dash's film, raises complex and provocative questions about the dynamics of black spectatorship and problematizes the idea of a black woman subject. Examines some of the contradictory positions and assumptions contained in the film.

hooks, bell. 1990. "Counter-hegemonic Art: *Do the Right Thing*," in *Yearning: Race, Gender and Cultural Politics.* Boston: South End Press, pp. 173–84. Problematizes the racial, gender, and sexual politics of the film. Analyzes the range of representations of black masculinity and considers the implications of Lee's strategies of characterization.

___. 1991. "Micheaux: Celebrating Blackness," *Black American Literature Forum* 25:2, 351–60. Argues that Oscar Micheaux made transgressive use of melodrama in his film *Ten Minutes to Live*.

___. 1992. "The Oppositional Gaze: Black Female Spectators," in *Black Looks: Race and Representation*. Boston: South End Press, pp. 115–31. Historicizes and theorizes the idea of a black female gaze within a cinematic context that largely excludes black women from the realm of the visible.

James, David. 1989. "Cinema and Black Liberation," in *Allegories of Cinema*. Princeton, N.J.: Princeton University Press, pp. 177–94. An examination of black-themed and black-directed cinema from the early 1960s through the mid-1970s blaxploitation era. Situates liberal integrationist films such as Shirley Clarke's *The Cool World* and Michael Roemer and Robert Young's *Nothing But a Man*, radical separatist projects such as the Oakland Black Panther Party films *Black Panther, Mayday,* and *Interview with Bobby Seale,* as well as blaxploitation pictures (especially Melvin Van Peebles's *Sweet Sweetback's Baadasssss Song)* in the context of changing racial and political conditions. Argues that ultimately the period lacked a truly re-visionary black cinema tied to the goals of progressive movement politics.

Jones, Jacquie. 1991. "The New Ghetto Aesthetic," *Wide Angle* 13:3–4, 32–43. Argues that the new jack movies of the late 1980s and early 1990s reinscribe the ideological assumptions of Hollywood formula pictures, eclipse alternative African American cinematic perspectives, and rely on misogynist representations of women.

___. 1993. "The Black South in Contemporary Film," *African American Review* 27:1, 19–24. Analyzes the construction of the South in Dash's *Daughters of the Dust* and Burnett's *To Sleep with Anger.*

Masilela, Ntongela. 1993. "The Los Angeles School of Black Filmmakers," in Manthia Diawara, ed., *Black American Cinema.* New York: Routledge, pp. 107–17. A social and intellectual history of the influential group of largely UCLA-based filmmakers in the early 1970s that included Haile Gerima, Charles Burnett, Ben Caldwell, Billy Woodberry, Julie Dash, and Alile Sharon Larkin.

Mercer, Kobena. 1994. "Monster Metaphors: Notes on Michael Jackson's *Thriller,*" in *Welcome to the Jungle: New Positions in Black Cultural Studies.* New York: Routledge, pp. 33–52. Resonant analysis of the music video *Thriller* that explores the construction of Jackson's racial and sexual indeterminacy.

Mitchell, W. J. T. 1990. "The Violence of Public Art: *Do the Right Thing,*" *Critical Inquiry* 16:4, 880–94. Considers the violence and controversy surrounding public art in the late 1980s. Insightful discussion of Lee's film as a work about art in the public sphere.

Musser, Charles, and Adam Knee. "William Greaves, Documentary Film-making, and the African American Experience," *Film Quarterly* 45:3, 13–25. Comprehensive analysis of the work and influence of one of the premier directors of documentary film.

Omi, Michael. 1989. "In Living Color: Race and American Culture," in Ian Angus and Sut Jhally, eds., *Cultural Politics in Contemporary America.*

New York: Routledge, pp. 111–22. An overview of strategies by which stereotypes of diverse racial and ethnic groups are circulated and maintained in popular media. The essay contrasts representations of people of color while identifying and analyzing patterns and themes common to constructions of diverse groups.

Rogers, Richard A. 1993. "Pleasure, Power and Consent: The Interplay of Race and Gender in *New Jack City*," *Women's Studies in Communication* 16:2, 62–86.

Smith, Valerie. 1992. "The Documentary Impulse in Contemporary African American Film," in Gina Dent, ed., *Black Popular Culture.* Seattle: Bay Press, pp. 56–64. Contrasts the ways in which new jack pictures and black-directed experimental documentaries invoke and problematize constructions of the "real."

———. 1994. "Black Masculinity, Labor, and Social Change," in Thelma Golden, ed., *Black Male: Representations of Masculinity in Contemporary Art.* New York: Whitney Museum of American Art, pp. 119–26. Discusses the effect of labor on the construction of gender roles in Michael Roemer's *Nothing But a Man* (1964), Charles Burnett's *Killer of Sheep* (1977), and Billy Woodberry's *Bless Their Little Hearts* (1984). Argues that men in each film are shown to experience poverty and unemployment more profoundly than do women.

Snead, James A. 1988. "Images of Blacks in Black Independent Films: A Brief Survey," in eds., Mbye B. Cham and Claire Andrade-Watkins, *BLACKFRAMES: Critical Perspectives on Black Independent Cinema.* Cambridge, Mass.: MIT Press, pp. 16–25. Brief yet valuable overview of black independent filmmaking through the mid-1980s. Usefully problematizes the category of "independent filmmaking" even as it offers insightful discussions of the various periods of African Americans working in film outside the context of Hollywood.

———. 1994. *White Screens/Black Images.* New York: Routledge. Published posthumously, this book offers a semiotically informed reading of the practices by which racial difference has been coded in Hollywood movies from *Birth of a Nation* through the mid-1980s.

Taylor, Clyde. 1985. "Decolonizing the Image: New U.S. Black Cinema," *Jump Cut* (1985), 166–78. Characterizes the work of African American filmmakers in the late 1960s. Traces their ideological commitments and aesthetic innovations.

Wallace, Michele. 1992. "*Boyz N the Hood* and *Jungle Fever*," in Gina Dent, ed., *Black Popular Culture.* Seattle: Bay Press, pp. 123–31. Analysis of the sexual and racial economy of the two films. Argues that black women and black women's sexuality are demonized in the films in the service of the construction and recuperation of black male identity.

Contributors

DONALD BOGLE is the author of landmark studies of blacks in Hollywood film, including *Toms, Coons, Mulattoes, Mammies, and Bucks: An Interpretive History of Blacks in American Films, Brown Sugar: Eighty Years of America's Black Female Superstars,* and *Blacks in American Films and Television: An Illustrated Encyclopedia.*

THOMAS CRIPPS is retired University Distinguished Professor at Morgan State University. His numerous studies of race and film include *Slow Fade to Black: The Negro in American Film, 1900–1942, Black Film as Genre,* and *Making Movies Black: The Hollywood Message Movie from World War II to the Civil Rights Era.*

JANE GAINES is associate professor of literature and English and director of the Program in Film and Video at Duke University. She has published *Contested Culture: The Image, the Voice, and the Law* and is currently working on a book entitled *Other/Race/Desire: Early Cinema and Nationhood* as well as co-editing a collection to be published by Smithsonian Institution Press, *Oscar Micheaux and His Circle: The Silent Years.*

NATHAN GRANT is assistant professor of African American Studies at the State University of New York at Buffalo. He has written several articles on African American literature, art, and film. His forthcoming book is entitled *Jean Toomer and Zora Neale Hurston: Black Men and Modernism.*

STUART HALL is professor of sociology at Open University, Milton Keynes, England, and a central figure in the development of cultural studies as a discipline. His books include *Resistance Through Ritual: Youth Subcultures in Post-War Britain,* with Tony Jefferson, *Minimal Selves,* and *The Hard Road to Renewal: Thatcherism and the Crisis of the Left,* with Martin Jacques. David Morley and Kuan-Hsing Chen have edited a collection of writings by and about Hall entitled *Stuart Hall: Critical Dialogues in Cultural Studies.*

TOMMY LEE LOTT is professor of philosophy at the University of Missouri, St. Louis. He has published essays on modern philosophy and African American social philosophy. Co-editor, with John Pittman, of the *Blackwell Companion to African American Philosophy,* he is author of a forthcoming book on Alain Locke's theory of African American culture entitled *Like Rum in the Punch.*

WAHNEEMA LUBIANO is associate professor in the Duke University program in literature. The author of numerous articles on African American literature and culture, she is the editor of a forthcoming collection of essays entitled *The House That Race Built: Black Americans, U.S. Terrain.*

MIKE MURASHIGE is assistant professor of literature at the University of California, San Diego, but his home is Los Angeles. He is currently working on a book about transformations in capitalism, labor, and racial representations in contemporary Los Angeles.

VALERIE SMITH, professor of English at the University of California, Los Angeles, is the author of *Self-Discovery and Authority in Afro-American Narrative* and a forthcoming study of black feminism and contemporary culture. The author of articles of African American literature, film, and black feminist theory, she is also the editor of *New Essays on Song of Solomon* and *African American Writers.*

JAMES SNEAD was assistant professor of English at the University of Pittsburgh at the time of his death in 1989. He wrote *Figures of Division: Faulkner's Major Novels,* the posthumously published *White Screens, Black Images: Hollywood from the Dark Side,* and numerous articles on literature and film.

DAVID VAN LEER, professor of English at the University of California, Davis, has published widely in American literature from the seventeenth to the twentieth centuries. The author of *Emerson's Epistemology: The Argument of the Essays* and *The Queening of America: Gay Culture in Straight Society,* he is currently editing a collection of essays called *Looking Over,* on the intersections between race and sexuality in gay and lesbian films.

Index